S

Jenny Uglow grew up in Cumbria. A former ~~~~~ & Windus, she is the author of prize-winning biographies and ~~ al histories, from *The Lunar Men: The Friends Who Made the Future* (2002) to *In These Times: Living In Britain through Napoleon's Wars, 1793–1815* (2014). Her interest in text and image is explored in *Words & Pictures: Writers, Artists and a Peculiarly British Tradition* (2008), and in biographies of William Hogarth, Thomas Bewick, Walter Crane and most recently in *Mr Lear: A Life of Art and Nonsense*, winner of the Hawthornden Prize in 2018. She was given an OBE in 2008, and was Chair of the Royal Society of Literature 2014–16. She lives in Canterbury and Borrowdale, Cumbria.

'Outstanding . . . The intensely visual prose . . . makes the reader feel like they are flicking through a colourful sketchbook . . . Characters come charmingly to life.' Lucy Davies, *Daily Telegraph*

'Few historians write better about pictures than Uglow, and her commentaries make you look and look again at bright colour plates that deliver little shocks.' Norma Clarke, *Literary Review*

'[Andrews' and Power's] relationship has been dissected in scintillating, sympathetic detail by Jenny Uglow in *Sybil & Cyril*. An experienced biographer, Uglow delivers a gripping, mysterious love story which also sheds light on British culture between the wars . . . It would make a terrific movie.' Rachel Spence, *Financial Times*

'Excellent, vividly illustrated . . . [Uglow] demonstrates her skill at conjuring up lives in time and her light touch in assembling images and ideas from contemporary culture.' Charlotte Hobson, *The Spectator*

SYBIL
&
CYRIL

CUTTING
THROUGH
TIME

JENNY
UGLOW

faber

First published in 2021
by Faber & Faber Limited
Bloomsbury House
74–77 Great Russell Street
London WC1B 3DA
This paperback edition first published in 2022

Typeset by Faber & Faber Limited
Printed and bound by CPI Group (UK) Ltd, Croydon, CR0 4YY

A CIP record for this book
is available from the British Library

ISBN 978-0-571-35416-0

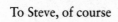
To Steve, of course

RHYTHM – is the pulsating arrangement of
lines, spaces, masses, colours, emphasis . . . which
carries the design and makes it live.

Cyril Power

Movement is a continuous line or curve.
Find that curve and feel the leap.

Sybil Andrews

CONTENTS

IV. MOVING

V. PARTING

PLATES

All are linocuts unless otherwise stated.

1

1 Cyril Power, *Air Raid*, 1935
2 Sybil Andrews, *The Star Inn from the back*, watercolour, 1920
3 Cyril Power, *The Star Inn from the back*, watercolour, 1920
4 Sybil Andrews, *Greyfriars*, watercolour, 1921
5 Sybil Andrews, 'The Martyrdom of St Edmund', tapestry, 1930–75
6 Sybil Andrews, *Market Day*, 1936
7 Sybil Andrews, *Sledgehammers*, 1933

2

8 Cyril Power, 'Westminster, shadow pattern, 1 April 1926', drawing
9 Cyril Power, *Westminster Cathedral, Evening*, 1928
10 Cyril Power, *The Crypt*, 1928
11 Sybil Andrews, *Concert Hall*, 1929
12 Sybil Andrews, *Theatre*, 1929
13 Sybil Andrews, *Oranges*, 1929
14 Sybil Andrews, *Straphangers*, 1929
15 Sybil Andrews, *Rush Hour*, 1930
16 Sybil Andrews, *The Winch*, 1930
17 Sybil Andrews, *The Giant Cable*, 1931
18 Cyril Power, *The Tube Staircase*, 1929
19 Cyril Power, 'Notting Hill Underground', drawing, 1923
20 Cyril Power, *The Escalator*, 1929

BEGINNINGS

On the evening of Thursday 4 July 1929, women in cloche hats and chiffon dresses, men in chalk-striped suits, or blazers and cravats, clattered up the steps to the Redfern Gallery in Old Bond Street. Inside they found a glowing array of prints, ochre and scarlet, sky blue and sea green, wild geometric patterns alongside boldly cut scenes of buses and escalators, horses and machines – the first exhibition of British linocuts. Some people laughed, others were entranced. This was a democratic art, claimed the organiser Claude Flight, and everyone could try it. Lino was cheap, he said, the best cutting tool was an old umbrella spoke and the easiest way to get a good impression was to rub the paper with the back of a toothbrush. Was this a joke, a child's art class posing in a London gallery? Or was it, as Flight proposed, a new form, perfect for the modern world? It seemed that he was right. Linocuts, a small yet significant corner of avant-garde art between the wars, became a craze, their clear lines and bright colours shining out against the darkness of the Depression. Over the coming decade, the Redfern's artists would see their work shown around the world, in exhibitions across Britain and Europe, in the USA and China, Canada and Australia.

Linocuts were cheap, two or three guineas, good for presents – and that is how my own interest began. As a student, my father rowed in the college boat, 'the eight'. When he married my mother, his best man, who had rowed in the same boat, gave him two linocuts on tissue paper. These were *The Eight* by Cyril Power and *Bringing In the Boat* by Sybil Andrews. I have known them all my life – in my father's study, then my mother's hall, blasted by sunshine, and finally on the stairs in my own home, and though I loved them I walked past them without a thought for years, hardly even reading the signatures. Recently, however, I began to wonder about the artists and their lives. When I found out more, I wanted to tell their story and look more closely at their work.

In 1922, when Cyril was nearly fifty, he abandoned his twenty-year career as an architect, left his wife and four children, and set off to London to join Sybil, a twenty-four-year-old art student. At the end of her long life, far away in Canada, Sybil roundly denied that they were lovers – and who can deny her the right to possess the facts of her own life? There are many kinds of couples. If this story is, in the end, a love story, it may not be the kind we expect. To their friends they were certainly a unit, 'Cyril and Sybil'. For twenty years they worked together until they went their own ways in 1943. At that point, or later, a great clearing-out occurred: all the letters that they wrote to each other over the years have disappeared, burnt, destroyed, lost. I have a vision of smoke rising from braziers in back gardens, scorched pages fluttering and curling, handwriting vanishing into air.

They left scraps and fragments, Power scores of sketchbooks, Andrews scribbled appointment diaries and scrapbooks stuffed with cuttings and photos, music and cards – a ragged collage of two lives. We can, however, follow their journey as artists, from oddly matched watercolourists in a country town to innovatory print-makers at the heart of the London scene, from 'Sybil and Cyril' to 'Andrews and Power'. Their prints summed up the dizzying mood and unease of the late 1920s and early 1930s, while at the same time they looked back, to a dream of a pre-industrial life. These contradictions, too, were part of their world. Their work, in all its variety, is the heart of the story, the core of this book.

I: MEETING

Cyril Power, *The Runners*, 1930

1: WAR

When Sybil Andrews came home to Bury St Edmunds in late 1918 the town was not quite the same. But then neither was she. Bury felt small after Bristol, where she had been welding aircraft parts. The smell of malt and hops still wafted over the streets from the Greene King brewery. She could still look up at the ironmongers, Andrews and Plumpton, in Guildhall Street, and see the window of the room where she was born, walk down to 117 Northgate Street where she had lived since she was seven and past the cathedral and the abbey ruins, to the rivers Linnet and Lark, meeting and flowing on to join the Ouse, running through the wetlands to the Wash and the grey North Sea. Yet though much was familiar, Bury had been marked by the war.

The Suffolk Regiment served in all major battles on the Western Front, and in Macedonia and at Gallipoli. Sybil's elder brother Geoffrey, a twenty-year-old engineer in 1914, fought in France and Belgium until a hunt for men with experience of motors led to a transfer to the Royal Flying Corps in 1916. He came home, wounded, after the Armistice, swathed in bandages and causing a stir in St Mary's Church. But many boys never returned. Others were maimed, gassed or shocked. 'It can seem very personal,' Sybil said, 'one's friends going away, coming back mutilated or not coming back at all.' She kept some relics all her life, like the sheet music marked 'sent from the trenches, from Billy Harvey', a setting for 'A Perfect Day' ('Le Jour Divin') with its poignant ending:

> *Quand le crépuscule touche à sa fin,*
> *Et l'ami rend son dernier baiser!*

———

War had always seemed near, yet unreal. At two Sybil had seen her uncle Henry Gardener Andrews in his Suffolk Yeomanry uniform with its bright yellow frogging, when he came to say goodbye to her mother before setting off to fight in the Boer War. (Henry stayed in South Africa, married and had children.) At six, in 1904 in the Butter Market, she watched the unveiling of the statue to the fallen in that war. In September 1912, when she was fourteen, a huge training exercise took place around Thetford, twelve miles away over the Norfolk border, drawing observers from across the world, from Germany to Argentina and Siam. Local papers reported that ten thousand people turned out to see the planes.

That was entertainment. Real war was not. Yet it felt exciting, in the baking summer of 1914. Boys Sybil knew were billeted in tents among the lakes and ponds, oaks and beeches of Hardwick on the edge of the town. They came to the Andrews' house for meals or a bath and it amazed her that 'here were all these men with aeroplanes and the latest equipment practicing manoeuvres on the Buttes, the place where they practiced with bows and arrows in earliest times'. Her bedroom window looked over stable yards, and she could hear the cavalry coming, 'the clip of the horses hooves and the sharp commands of the officers – going off to the Station and to war.' Sybil organised dances at the Angel Hotel with a schoolfriend, Dorothy Jarman, daughter of the town photographer, who 'met and married a young man right off' – not Sybil's style . 'How sad dance music has sounded ever since the war began,' as Rebecca West wrote.

Townsfolk grew used to soldiers in the streets, coming in from nearby training camps: the Argyll and Sutherland Highlanders in their kilts, and men on their bikes from the local Cyclist Corps. In 1916, on the great Elveden estate in the heaths and forests of the Brecklands, north of Bury, men were trained to use the first tanks, to be shipped to the Somme that September. The noise of mock battles boomed across country, yet the Elveden Explosives Area became known as 'the most secret place on earth'. Meanwhile, streams of wounded were sent back from the front. Four doors from Sybil's home a house at 113 Northgate Street became a Red Cross hospital, and many women volunteered. Sybil had a photo of her mother Beatrice, serious in her nurse's uniform, hands in the pockets of her starched skirt, her narrow waist cinched by a belt, hair tucked beneath cap, watch pinned to chest.

On the night of 29 April 1915, a Zeppelin crossed the East Anglian coast, pounding Yarmouth and Ipswich before heading for Bury. First a looming shadow appeared against bright moonlight, then booms and thuds, the clatter of roof tiles and roar of flames. All the street lights were on, despite the Lighting Act, and more light flooded out as people opened windows to see what was happening. One incendiary narrowly missed the Andrews' ironmongers, which escaped burning only because the east wind blew the flames away. A year later, on 31 March 1916, a second Zeppelin attack killed seven people, including a young mother and two of her four children. The horse-drawn funeral procession weaved past pavements packed with soldiers, small boys in caps and women pushing prams. When the War Memorial was put up in 1921, it bore the names of 427 Bury men who died overseas, and the seven who perished at home.

———

Sybil was quick and clever. When she left Thetford Grammar School in the summer of 1915, aged seventeen, she worked for five months for a land agent in Daventry in Northamptonshire, leaving with a glowing testimonial to her typing and shorthand and keeping of rentals and wage-books. But then, as she said, she was 'pitchforked into war'.

In Bury, the garage of Thomas Nice & Co. in Abbeygate Street became a small munitions factory where women made shells, and the engineering firm of Robert Boby was subcontracted to Vickers, to make armaments. In July 1915 Boby's appealed to the Women's Social and Political Union (who turned from suffrage to a nationalistic war effort) for women who could work lathes and drills. Sybil could work a lathe: she had spent her childhood running in and out of the family ironmongers, and in 1916 she enrolled in the Women's Welding School at Notting Hill. The first of its kind, the school was run by Miss E. C. Woodward, 'a metal worker of long standing', squat and smiling in her overalls and leather apron. The first thing Sybil learned was how to use the low-pressure acetylene torch, her eyes protected by black goggles, her hair under her cap, aiming at 'metal so welded you feel it is impossible it ever could have been two pieces'. From London Sybil went to the Standard Motor Works in Coventry, welding parts for biplanes like the Sopwith Camel, clocking in at six thirty in the morning and off at eight at night. The next stop was Bristol, working on the first all-metal planes. The legendary 'Bristol Fighter', the F2B with its Rolls-Royce engine, made its maiden flight in September 1916: within eighteen months the factories at Brislington and Filton, where Sybil worked, were producing over two thousand aircraft a year. The atmosphere was intense: the flashing sparks, the foot-long yellow flame flaring from the nozzle of the blowpipe, the smell of oil and hot metal, the shouts and quips and songs. She could always work furiously under pressure and she joked about the dangers in a poem, 'Ten Little Welder Girls':

> Ten little welder girls sitting in a line.
> One blew up her safety valve,
> Then there were nine.

She remained inspired by the power and dynamism of industry and labour. In her linocut *Sledgehammers* (1933; PLATE 7), men swing hammers at a central forge, its glow lighting their arms and faces. She based this on a scene remembered from the war. At Coventry the women welders only used the smaller blowpipes, but one day there was a call from the blacksmith's shop to bring a large blowpipe to tackle something awkward that they couldn't deal with in the furnaces. As all the men were busy, she was sent, forced to handle a huge blowpipe that she had never used before. 'It frightened the life out of me,' she said, adding briskly, 'most exciting':

> There were five men waiting in the Blacksmiths Shop with sledgehammers – the dark shop – just the glow from the furnace. They were stripped to the waist and heavily tattooed and made a wonderful picture and together with the rhythm of the sledge strikes, for me, unforgettable. 1 Stroke 2 Stroke 3 Stroke 4 Stroke 5 Stroke Crash-Crash – and the sparks flying and the glow from the red-hot metal – it was like something out of time, old time.

When the Armistice was declared on 11 November 1918, the Filton factory closed for three days' holiday. Two weeks later the Ministry of Munitions ended all contracts for Bristol Fighters. Like hundreds of others, Sybil went home.

She kept a photograph taken in Bristol, in a serious pose, wearing pearls and black muslin sleeves, her thick brown hair swept to one side. This was not the Sybil her friends knew. In other pictures she is slim and gangly and slightly awkward, with a chopped-off fringe, broad face and grin. But the photo held a certain truth, for her war work also showed her serious side. When she fell ill with pneumonia in Coventry, a friend took her to a Christian Scientist healer, a connection she returned to later. And if physical sickness could be healed, emotional pain could be thrust down too. 'I'm so sorry, old thing, that years back you had trouble,' wrote one of Sybil's friends, 'G', who had been jilted. 'Why didn't you tell me about it & let me try to help when you were in Cov.? Still you evidently are braver than I . . . However, my dear, you are happy again now & I am awfully glad. You always were wonderfully cheery.'

True, Sybil was cheery, glad to be back with her family. But she was also restless. After an independent life it was hard to settle back.

———

Some of the planes that Sybil Andrews worked on were sent to the airfields on the Kent coast, like the one at Lympne, high on an escarpment looking down over the town of Hythe, where Second Lieutenant Cyril Edward Power – CEP as he often signed himself – was in charge of aircraft repair. A few miles away, in Folkestone, thousands of refugees had arrived from Belgium in 1914, and the small resort soon became the main embarkation point for France. During the war over ten million soldiers sailed back and forth – going out, coming home on leave and returning to the front.

When war began Cyril, an architect and historian of medieval buildings, had been married to his wife Dorothy ('Dolly') for ten years and had two sons and a daughter. He was forty-two, too old to fight, but in 1916 he volunteered for a commission in the Royal Flying Corps and trained as an equipment officer and administrator. Practical and enthusiastic with a dry sense of humour, he was good at getting on with people, organising the ground crew, sending out planes, arranging repairs and modifications in response to urgent suggestions from pilots. Ships and aircraft had always fascinated him. A comic sketch from 1909 showed 'An architect's flying machine, not remarkable for gaining great altitude', with the airman in his goggles sitting in front of a gas canister labelled 'reserve of ideas' and absurd captions for different parts. In London, Cyril had watched the balloon and aeroplane races round the capital with his small children: at nine or ten the eldest, Toby, became obsessed with flying, subscribing to the weekly magazine *Flight*, which, he said, 'enabled me to confound young pilots that I met at my father's aerodrome'. Many of those young pilots would die in the air, their planes crashing into the mud of the trenches or plunging into the

Sybil in Bristol, 1918 – Cyril in Bristol, 1916

sea. At the start of the war, aircraft were fragile biplanes, unarmed and used only for reconnaissance, 'eyes in the sky'. The pilots took guns with them and grenades in their pockets to ward off attacks, and soon machine guns were added, to make primitive fighter planes, and bomb racks so that bombs did not have to be dropped by hand – but they still had no navigational aids except unreliable compasses and basic maps.

Lympne started life in November 1915 as an airfield for the Machine Gun School at Hythe, but in March 1916 work began on a new site, an emergency landing field for the Royal Flying Corps. When Cyril arrived the team were making do with tents and temporary wood and canvas hangars, but by October 1916 they had six brick sheds for repairs. Lympne became the 'No 8. Aircraft Acceptance Park', a hub for aircraft going to France or being sent back for repair. Rapid design improvements and increasingly powerful engines brought waves of new planes, each more sophisticated, a marvel to those who flew them. Much later, in 1930, combining two of his passions, Power wrote:

No sooner do we evolve and perfect something than by the laws of progress it is superseded and scrapped in favour of something which proves better and more efficient. If you want a historic example of this, take the evolution of medieval building structure as manifested in the scientific experimental development in French cathedrals. Or, if you prefer a modern example, the rapid progress of Aircraft design during the Great War.

While ultra-modern planes absorbed his mind, Cyril loved Lympne as a place 'steeped in history', Sybil remembered – the ancient Portus Lemanis, a shore fort at the end of the Roman 'Stone Street'. Time present and time past flowed together.

Ancient history and modern wizardry meant little to others on the coast. When the wind was in the east they could hear the guns booming from France. On the Somme there were over a million casualties between 1 July and 18 November, with the deaths of 125,000 British troops – each a separate tragedy to those who mourned the 'undone years', in Wilfred Owen's words. The horror filled the poetry of Owen and his peers, making the trenches nightmarishly present. In Britain the price of food doubled. Thousands of men and horses had been sent to the front, reducing production; the wheat harvest was poor, the potato harvest failed, and German U-boats attacked supply ships. While hunger grew, the home front faced a new threat. On 25 May 1917, twenty-three Gotha G.IV bombers launched a daylight raid on London – the first air raid by planes rather than airships – and when dense cloud forced them to turn back, they attacked the Channel ports and army camps. It was early evening, around six o'clock. In Folkestone, people squinted skywards as the planes approached, saying later that they looked like a swarm of insects with the evening sun glinting on their wings. It was Whitsun Bank Holiday: children were playing in the streets and women were queuing outside a grocery shop, where a new load of potatoes had been delivered. The bomb that landed on the queue killed forty-four people instantly and seventeen more died later.

No British planes could climb high enough to stop the German aircraft: at Lympne they dropped nineteen bombs on the airfield. Power's 1917 sketchbook shows a litter of wrecked aircraft. He was appalled by the destruction and loss of life, yet captivated by the power of the machines themselves, a dual response expressed in his vertiginous linocut *Air Raid* (PLATE 1) of the mid-1930s. Memories of war stayed with him, imparting a darkness to his work. At Lympne the grimness was amplified by the bizarre doings almost next door, where the flamboyant Sir Philip Sassoon, who had succeeded his father as MP for Hythe and was aide to Field Marshal Haig, commander-in-chief of the British forces, was building a house, splashing out the Sassoon inheritance and the Rothschild fortune from his mother. His house, Belcaire, looked out across Romney Marsh to the sea, and when the war ended the designer Philip Tilden was hired to make it 'the epitome of all things conducive to luxurious relaxation after the strenuousness of war. It was to be a challenge to the world, showing people that a new culture had risen from the sick-bed of the old, with new aspirations, eyes upon a new aspect, mind turned to a new burst of imagination.' Sybil Andrews and Cyril Power would also see their art as part of an innovative post-war culture, 'a challenge to the world', with new imaginative visions. But theirs was not Sassoon's world, with its Rex Whistler murals and Italian gardens.

In April 1918, when the RFC and the Royal Naval Air Service merged to become the RAF, Lympne gained full status as a First Class Landing Ground, the base for 120 Squadron. After the Armistice squadrons coming home waited here to be disbanded, but soon the RAF left and the base was closed. Cyril, like so many others, had to start civilian life again. He went back, not to London, but to his wife's home town, Bury St Edmunds. On leave he had visited his family here while they lived with Dolly's parents, George and Alice Nunn, in Berril House, set in its long garden running down to the River Lark, with pear trees trained against the wall. For Dolly's father, bedridden after a stroke, Cyril made an illuminated chart showing where the five Nunn sons were serving – the eldest, George, had emigrated to Australia and was a lieutenant with the ANZAC forces; Gerald, who had gone to Canada, fought with the Canadian infantry like Sybil's brother Geoffrey, and died at Amiens in September 1918; the third, Sidney, was with the Suffolk Regiment at Ypres and in the Balkans; and the youngest two, Hugh and Ernest, were also with the Suffolks in the trenches. This was just one Bury family, looking at the maps, following the war overseas.

The losses of the war were unbearable – over seven hundred thousand men had died and a million and a half were injured – and up to 230,000 men, women and children died in the flu epidemic of

1918–19. Lloyd George had promised 'a country fit for heroes' but a short post-war boom was followed by a slump and unemployment rose as state-run industries like shipbuilding or aircraft manufacture were handed back to their owners. There were protests and marches and fears of unrest in the wake of revolution in Russia – 120,000 troops were sent to Glasgow to deal with the riots in 'red Clydeside' – and blotches were appearing on the pink map of Empire, with trouble in India and the protectorates of the Middle East. Idealists pinned their hopes for world peace to the League of Nations, founded in January 1920 after the Paris Peace Conference. But in Bury St Edmunds, where Cyril Power and Sybil Andrews were facing a peacetime life, the townsfolk's main concern was to re-establish their old commercial and social patterns – to make the world, not new, but as close as they could to what had gone before.

2: SYBIL

Sybil Andrews was an artist of the machine age but she was also a girl from a Suffolk town, formed by its life and traditions. 'From my earliest recollections', she wrote, 'Bury St Edmunds has been the centre of my life.' She saw her linocut *Market Day* (1936; PLATE 6) as typifying 'the whole life of an agricultural town like Bury St Edmunds', since without the market 'there would be no reason for its existence'.

> Market day was very important to the whole community. There came the fresh fruits, vegetables and meats, the farm wives in their best clothes came into town for their day off, and, afterwards, the men came and swept up the cabbage leaves from the vegetable stalls. And what would the country be if, all over, there were not similar communities who grew up, as we did, around the Abbey?

Others in this abbey community found it tight-knit and dull, with tension between labourers, pushy tradesmen and smart gentry. In an earlier generation the novelist Ouida (Maria Louise Ramé), who was born in Bury, wrote the town off, disguised as Cantitborough, as an old maid dressed for a party, 'the slowest and dreariest of boroughs', where 'the inhabitants are driven to ring their own door-bells lest they rust from disuse'. But the Andrews family had no need to ring door-bells. Sybil's grandfather Frederick Charles bought the ironmonger's business in Guildhall Street in 1862, two years after Ouida's sneer, advertising it as 'a furnishing ironmonger, bell-hanging, whitesmith and iron-foundry, and stockists of plough shares, knife machines, iron bedsteads' and 'maggot and sheep-dipping lotions'. The business flourished and in 1884 Frederick became Mayor of Bury, re-elected

Sybil, Joyce, Margaret and Geoff Andrews, c.1903

three years later. When his son Charles married Beatrice Martha Trigg in 1893, they moved into the rooms above the shop: Sybil was born here, on 19 April 1898. She was the third child, after Geoffrey, born in 1894 and Joyce ('Joy') in 1895. In photographs the family grows around her: Sybil as a baby in Beatrice's arms; a two-year-old on the arm of her mother's chair, with Joyce and Geoffrey behind; aged four, in a frilled dress, the group now including Margaret ('Mike'), born in 1902; aged five, with neat fringe and lurking smile, a year before the youngest child, Henry ('Hal'), was born.

Charles Andrews was a gentle man, much loved by his younger sisters, a naturalist and artist, producing memorable studies of plants and birds, the odd one out among the mechanical, practical Andrews men. The Andrews looked forward, selling modern tools: Beatrice's family, the Triggs, looked back. Beatrice's father Henry (who changed his name to Trigg from Prigg, a name already changed, understandably, from Prick) lived on the edge of town at Babwell Friary by the River Lark, in a sixteenth-century house with a smart Georgian front, built among the ruined walls and fishponds of a Franciscan friary. A keen antiquarian, Henry resigned from the National Provincial Bank to be curator of the Museum of Antiquities for the Suffolk Archaeological Society, becoming known as 'one of the leading lights of the Suffolk Institute, more truly an archaeologist in the modern sense than others of his generation'. His pride was his dig around the village of Icklingham, nine miles away, where he proved the existence of a Roman villa and cemetery. Beatrice helped him, and after he died in 1894 she and her sisters gave some of his finds to the Bury Athenaeum, the town's main library; these formed the core of the collection when Moyse's Hall, a twelfth-century merchant's house, became the town museum in 1899. Two years later Beatrice published her father's findings, with manorial documents and wills, in the *Icklingham Papers*.

That year, when Sybil was three, the family moved from the shop to the sixteenth-century 'Greyfriars' at 60 Whiting Street, five minutes away: this was the house that she called 'my childhood home'. Beatrice was friends with the leading local historians, one of whom, the pioneering archivist Lilian Burroughs, remembered Sybil as a small girl 'shepherding Margaret in a white pinafore, while Henry was a baby, tucked under one of his mother's arms, so that she could practise scales with the other hand'. Music was always important to them, and Sybil remembered her mother 'rippling up and down the piano'.

The children played in the walled garden with its walnut tree, bowling green and croquet lawn, and in the abbey ruins with its great bed of fennel, whose smell Sybil hated. To begin with they had a governess, and Sybil went weekly to dancing at 'Miss Tinkler's class' in the Angel Hotel. Each Christmas, when her Andrews grandparents Fred and Carrie gave a party at their home, Ivy Lodge, a solid red-brick villa with shrubbery, Fred sent a sedan chair to carry the children. She loved her grandfather's shop, with its 'smell of Parafin, oil and tools. I think of going into the old original A & P and wanting scissors or pocket knife and the beautiful items one was offered to choose from.' Her aunt Agnes did the book-keeping in old-fashioned copperplate, 'all stiff and starched, just like old Aunt Agnes'. Agnes was one of a bevy of aunts – her father had four sisters.

Childhood, she said, was full of happy memories. But a family rift grew after 1901, when Frederick took his nephew Robert Plumpton as partner alongside Charles: in 1905 Charles left the business, citing 'illness'. To economise, the family took a smaller house, 117 Northgate Street, still within the medieval grid of streets. At nine, Sybil went to the Langton School in nearby Hatter Street, and that July she was the youngest participant in the great Bury Pageant in the abbey gardens. Historical pageants, evolving from the Arts and Crafts interest in folk culture at the end of the previous century, became newly popular after the impresario Louis Napoleon Parker staged a hugely successful one in Sherborne, Dorset, in 1905. The Bury show (directed by Parker himself, as Master of Ceremonies)

Beatrice and Sybil dressed for the pageant

lasted a whole afternoon, and was staged eleven times, only once being drowned by summer rain, when the actor playing the Abbot of Beaufort bravely wore a mackintosh over his costume. Over 1,800 people were involved, acting, building sets, making costumes, playing in the orchestra.

Like most pageants Bury's was stubbornly local. Its seven episodes ran from a white-clad Boudicca shouting her resistance to the Romans (neatly, Bury's mayor was the arrogant Roman leader), past the oath of the barons that preceded the Magna Carta, to end with the visit of Elizabeth I. Inevitably, the central scene was the martyrdom of St Edmund, King of the East Angles, killed by the Danes in 869 for refusing to renounce his faith: tied to a tree, shot with arrows and then beheaded (PLATE 5). His head, thrown into the woods, was miraculously guarded by a wolf. Sybil thought Edmund 'a man of real courage – chin-up to that gang of murderous Danes', but her favourite scene was the procession of the Benedictine monks evicted at the dissolution, a swaying row of men, heads bowed beneath their hoods, their cloaks black against the bright costumes of the crowd.

A pioneering cinematographer, Ronald Bates, made a vivid half-hour film of the pageant, full of twirling court dances and energetic fights, boisterous Morris men and lines of heralds and pages. Women chatter, children push and giggle, men stride past, their sideways glances suggesting a determined keeping-up with the Joneses. Although pageants claimed to involve the whole community all leading roles went to local dignitaries. As one correspondent to the *Bury Post* complained: 'Bury has paraded in fine clothes, and reproduced many noble acts in pageant, but what has she learned to do in deed, or was the lesson all in vain? What is she going to do for her unemployed this winter, and the families who are in cold and want?'

The Andrews family all paraded in those fine clothes, and the drama and colourful patterns of movement would have been exciting for an artistic child, yet Sybil's memories mix nostalgia and coercion.

She had to join in, she said, as all her family had a role. She loved dressing up but on the back of a photo of her mother and herself in Tudor costume she scribbled:

Sybil *would* laugh & was forbidden to laugh or smile – the more she was forbidden, the more she laughed & could not stop, till the photographer got angry & Mother became angry & after dire threats Sybil somehow gripped her jaws together & the picture was taken.

I remember it as though it was yesterday.

In those days no one was allowed to smile or laugh when a photograph was taken. Why? Why not laugh? What else would a child do? & how unnatural not to laugh on a memorable occasion.

She was hard to hold still, prone to laughter, always on the move. This had its perils. Twice a week cattle were led to and from the butcher's shambles through the narrow Looms Lane, across the road from her home. If caught between the high walls as the cattle came down, there was no escape: 'So I would have to flee at the top of my speed to get myself round the corner out of the way, if I saw cows coming.' Once a bull followed her when she took shelter in a yard, 'so I was not much better off, because I got inside and we were both inside, to my terror.'

There were other terrors, harder to describe. In May 1910, when relations with his father had become strained to breaking point, Charles Andrews set off for Canada, leaving Beatrice and their five children. His reasons, and Beatrice's reaction, are unknown. Spurred by the row with his father, he may have seen a chance to prove himself in a new world and planned to bring the family out after him. Whatever the cause, that spring he offered to escort his cousin Maud and her four children, who were sailing to meet her husband John Edwards, already in Saskatchewan. Sybil was twelve when Charles left. She missed him badly.

Her father's departure haunted her. When she was nearly sixty she asked his sister, her elderly aunt Mabel, what had happened, telling her that Charles never heard from his own father again. 'What disclosures we seem to be making!' replied Mabel. She herself had always stayed in close touch with Charles, and was horrified to hear that he never had a single letter from Frederick. 'That certainly surprises me because in every other way the latter was *such* a real Christian . . . Where was his conscience and balance of conduct?' On the morning that Charles and Maud set out, taking the 8.40 train to Liverpool, he left a distraught family at his parents' home, Ivy Lodge. Mabel and her sister Agnes had rushed from the breakfast table to see them off at the station. Coming home, they found their elder sister Edith red-eyed, the maids distressed and the dining room in disarray. At family prayers, when they were all kneeling, Frederick Andrews had suddenly burst into tears, pushed the Bible aside 'and bowed his head, unable to utter another word'.

Mabel remembered her elder brother with deep affection – the way Charles called her 'Little May', how he gave her 'a beautifully made doll's swing, ready to suspend', how he made prints from leaves with Indian ink. 'Did he ever show you these works of art, & the way he did them, & the useful gifts he gave?'

He was a rare one for drawing birds in minute detail. Poor old Charlie – he was such a dear fellow, but all through his life he missed parental affection and attention and was to my mind deprived of sympathy and recognition, encouragement as to his talents. He was a lone and affectionate member of the family, but always, as it were, shelved. His was a most sad life, if only you knew. It was in him to love his home and especially his children, but odds were always against him.

In Liverpool, with Maud and her children, Charles boarded the SS *Victorian*. On his docket his previous job was given as 'none', and future 'farming'. From Halifax in Nova Scotia he took the long, slow train, travelling over 2,700 miles to Delmas, a hamlet in western Saskatchewan. A year later he was in the small town of Battleford nearby with Maud and her family. Over the next twelve years he moved around, working in hotels, on the railways, in the fields. When war broke out in 1914, Sybil's brother Geoffrey, perhaps thinking that this was a last chance, sailed to Canada and met Charles before joining the Canadian forces. Sybil too kept in touch, and in July 1917, when she told him how much she enjoyed her welding work, he wrote easily, their manual labour a bond: 'I suppose it is aluminium work that you are on now. That must require very careful handling, as it is awkward stuff to weld. Don't you find it very hot work this weather?' Was she having to work as hard as she had in London? Did the factory work on Sundays? Did she wear a uniform or just overalls over her clothes? He told her of his garden, full of vegetables: 'if I should be here another year', he said, he would get chickens. He was there another year and more, writing home affectionately to Mabel and to Beatrice, his 'dear Bee', and to his children.

———

So far as Sybil knew there were no artists in her family – apart from her father, with his studies of birds – but painting was always part of her life:

> We children all had paintboxes from our cradle, not with the idea that we were going to be wonderful artists but to keep us quiet & amused on bad days. I loved my paintbox & well remember the birthday which brought me my first proper paintbox with little china pans of colour . . . I remember the smell of it now. It was my best loved possession.

At school there was drawing and painting every week and later, she wrote, 'I was in & out of the local School of Art at times, evenings copying plaster casts & such like dull things, not much fun.' She had one local role model in the artist Rose Mead, who had trained in London and Paris, becoming a friend of Augustus John, and had exhibited at the Royal Academy until she came back to nurse her sick mother in 1897, the year before Sybil was born. She made her living largely from portraits, including one of Sybil's grandfather, and was the costume designer for the pageant in 1907. A striking figure, Rose was a firm feminist, keen for women to have a career, and Sybil remembered her fondly. She did remarkable work for those days, she thought, and was 'very kind and helpful to myself in my early Art struggles'.

During the war drawing was an escape from welding work, and in 1918 Sybil enrolled in John Hassall's Correspondence School, studying after work and at weekends. Hassall (father of the wood engraver Joan Hassall) had worked in advertising and was famous for posters like 'The Jolly Fisherman' jumping across the sands announcing 'Skegness Is So Bracing', and the 'Kodak Girl' brandishing her camera. One can sense the legacy of his flat colours and thick black lines, his economy of reference and skill at movement – and his humour – behind Andrews' linocuts. His London art school closed at the start of the war and in 1917 he launched his extremely successful correspondence course (many soldiers were encouraged to draw as relaxation). His advertisement has the same ring as Sybil's own writings – forward-looking, ditching convention, convinced of the importance of the artist's role: 'Don't be content with doing mere conventional Art work or sketching just to amuse yourself. Break away and be yourself. Be greater than yourself. Put passion into your work. Impose the power of your talent on others. It is the hand of the Creative Artist that fashions the world.' 'Art is Life,' wrote Hassall. Sybil agreed.

Hassall gave his students clear guidance, like crisp instructions about combining colours in a print, and sent painstaking personal comments on their work. His course-book cover showed a woman perched on a high stool, peering at an easel announcing 'The John Hassall Way', above a scrawled *'Tempus Fugit'*. Time did fly for Sybil. After the war, she became an assistant teacher at the Portland House School in Guildhall Street, a square Georgian house with pedimented door. It was run by the two Misses Underwood, Polly and Edith Mary, whom John Hallily (later the actor John Le Mesurier), a pupil there at the time, remembered smelling 'of hot milk, petit-beurres biscuits and ever so slightly damp mackintoshes'. Edith was in charge, and since she signed her name with her initials, was always known as EMU. Sybil taught literature, history, natural history and geography – everything except maths – and her pupils missed her when she left. 'Drawing and painting were never the same again', wrote one:

and I don't know what happened to Eng Lit. The Ancient Mariner has been part of my life. I think you gave us a competition to draw & paint the beasts out of the sea also the Forsaken Merman, Robert Bruce and his spider and the Lady of Shalott. I am still at home in the text of Henry V. You chose all the right bits to learn.

While she taught, Sybil kept up her correspondence course, 'getting all I could from it. Getting up at 5 am & doing my Life Drawing studies from myself & a long mirror. It was sometimes jolly cold at that hour of day.' Life classes for women artists were still disapproved of, and it was hard to find models, but Sybil was tenacious: even with frost on the windows and fingers stiff with cold, she could be her own model. She knew what she wanted to do. She was busy at the school, but her true career, she hoped, would be her art, and that demanded sacrifice and effort. 'I was one of five, and no father. There was no money. I had to work for what I had – but the work was the exciting part.' Later, in a book for her students, she wrote adamantly, adopting the masculine pronoun:

The refrain of this book is
'work, work, work'
But to the artist – 'work'
Does not mean some horrible, boring chore,
But his Life-blood
And when he is not working,
Then for him, it is wasted time,
Wasted life.

In 1919 she rented a studio and two years later she appeared in the town directory as 'Sybil Andrews – artist'.

3: CYRIL

In 1920 Cyril too was restless. But while Sybil was just starting out, he already had a full life behind him.

Bury St Edmunds seemed a sensible place to start again after the war, but it was very much Dolly's home town, not his, full of her family's history and connections. The Nunns and the Debenhams, her mother's family, came from generations of Suffolk farmers and although their fortunes had suffered from grain imports from the United States and Canada, she had grown up in a moated farmhouse at Beyton, seven miles from Bury. By now her father George had retired from farming to become a corn agent, but the hall of their house in Bury was still full of guns and carefully polished riding boots. Until his stroke George set out twice a week to the market, 'renewing old friendships, stick in hand and walking with his fist punched into his back'. His wife Alice was more austere. Her grandson Toby thought her cruel, but he also remembered her teaching him bezique and cribbage, and 'snoozing by the fireside in a large cane chair with the *East Anglian Daily Times* draped over her head'.

Cyril's background was different. His grandfather, Edward William Power, told him that the Powers were traders and sea captains from Waterford in south-east Ireland. 'They were Catholics & I understand half of them became Protestants & it caused a break in the family & my great grandfather (or possibly it was his father) Captain John Power left Ireland with the other Protestant members of the family & settled at Bristol.' Captain Power sailed from Bristol to the West Indies, and, possibly in the triangular trade, to Africa: 'Shipped slaves to the West Indies? And brought sugar cargo back to Bristol?' This was mere surmise, but uncomfortable nonetheless.

By contrast, his aunt Alice assured him that one relative had been Mayor of Cork, and another the Bishop of Newfoundland (Michael Power, 1804–47, actually the first Catholic Bishop of Toronto). 'She also told me, as did my grandfather that his father (or grandfather, I am not sure which) went out to fight for the Poles, under Kosciusko & was known as Kosciusko Power.' This ancestor served in the late eighteenth century under Tadeusz Kosciusko, who fought in America in the Revolutionary War, becoming a friend of Thomas Jefferson, and then gained fame as a national hero in Poland's struggles against Russia and Prussia. 'I have not done any researches into this,' Cyril scribbled, abandoning his scattered notes of emigrants, sea captains and adventurers, soldiers and bishops.

Despite ups and downs of fortune – 'My grandfather came into money (inherited from his father presumably) but I believe he spent it all' – the household into which Cyril Power was born, in Chelsea, on 17 December 1872, was well off and stoutly respectable. On both sides his parents' families had, literally, played a part in building Victorian Britain. His paternal grandfather and his father were architects. His mother's father, Zephaniah Deacon Berry, who began as an ironmonger, like Sybil's grandfather, was an engineer with his own iron foundry. Based in Pimlico, Z. D. Berry & Co. installed gaslights all over London and when Cyril was five, a fair-haired boy in frogged coat and Eton collar, they cast the iron benches for the Victoria Gardens on the newly built Embankment. That year, after decades of delay, workmen finally hoisted up the huge obelisk of Cleopatra's Needle, and the nearby seats had monumental Egyptian-style armrests of kneeling camels and busty sphinxes: they stood (and still stand) on raised platforms so that strollers could watch the barges on the Thames. The main designer was George Vulliamy but the detailed working plans were apparently drawn up by Berry's son-in-law Edward William Power, Cyril's father.

Cyril, the eldest child, grew up with his brother Ralph and two sisters, Edna and Yevonde, in a high-Victorian world of plush furniture,

Cyril Power, 'Papa, Edna and Yevonde at Dover', 1887

aspidistras and dinner gongs, with the clear expectation that he would follow his father as an architect. Encouraged to draw from childhood, in quick sketches he caught his family life: his bearded grandfather peering over his spectacles; his father, with obligatory whiskers, tweed jacket and tight waistcoat; 'Mamma at dinner', on a chair with her bustle behind her and a potted palm on the table; his brother practising cricket strokes; his sisters in sailor dresses and tam o' shanters, holding their father's hands on Dover quay as fishermen unload their baskets.

The drawings are full of detail and wit. On a stray page he writes a quick diary for July 1887: visiting his father's office, watching a cricket match and sketching at Hampton Court and Sunbury Lock, where he drew an atmospheric crush of boats deep in the lock, with the tall gates ahead and the water slowly pouring in. By seventeen he could evoke a sailboat swinging into the wind in a few bold strokes, but he could also render the fine detail of Hertford's timbered buildings and the 'Norman work, arches capitals etc at St Margaret's Church at Cliffe', and produce delicate drawings of his cello and violin. In one atmospheric ink and wash sketch, stretching across two pages, he drew a lane in Southgate, near his grandparents' home, the backs of houses floating beyond a shadowed fence, an effect both precise and haunting.

Cyril's mother Amelia died in 1891 and when Edward married Ada Barnes two years later Cyril acted as a witness, signing his name with a flourish. In his father's office in Queen Victoria Street, his professional start was unconventional, but successful. His designs appeared in the magazine *The Builder*, ranging from plans for Arts and Crafts-style houses in Walton-on-Thames to an elaborate drawing of proposed alterations to the neo-Gothic interior of St Cuthbert's church in Kensington in 1896. St Cuthbert's would become the centre of high Anglo-Catholic worship, and its design had a pre-Reformation feel. In the 1890s, emulating medieval craftsmen, artists, architects and craft workers often organised themselves into 'guilds' and Cyril – a lover of early church architecture – was asked to design objects at St Cuthbert's for 'the Guild of St Oswald'. But his ambitious plans went further, including a grand new organ and reredos, and caused heated disputes with rival designers. Although he insisted that his designs had been approved by the vicar and parish, the reredos commission was given instead to the clergyman Ernest Geldart.

In 1900 he won the Royal Institute of British Architects' Soane Medallion, awarded 'to an architect under 30 who submits best design for specified subject', with a design for an art school. With the medallion came a £100 studentship for continental travel. This suited Cyril, who loved France: in 1898 he had supervised the building of a hotel on the promenade at Dieppe on his father's behalf. (In 1942 his son Kit, a naval lieutenant taking part in the raid on Dieppe, was given orders to blow up the same hotel.) By his thirtieth birthday in 1902, he was well on his way, and was elected an Associate Member of RIBA.

The study of British churches was also related to his faith: as the century turned, he converted to Roman Catholicism. He recorded no agonies over his conversion, no sense of wrenching himself away from his Anglican upbringing. Like the brilliant apologist Ronald Knox, who would convert in 1917, he had already drifted into the Anglo-Catholic 'ritualist' side of Anglicanism, feeling that an accident of history, the Reformation, had severed the English church from its true roots. His Catholicism was an affirmation of continuity, of being at one with old traditions of belief, sharing the community of pre-Reformation worshippers and builders. Sybil later said that his Catholicism was born more of a love of pageantry and ritual than a debate over doctrine, and this was partly true, but beneath his joviality and worldliness lay some profound inner need – a hunt for grace, a deep searching for a place to belong, a vision of sacrifice and redemption that transcended the rush of modern life. Although his profession was practical, he was driven by a dream.

On one of his trips, cycling across the country collecting material on old churches, he visited St Ethelbert's church in Hessett, near Bury – a typical Suffolk Perpendicular church, still with its fifteenth-century rood screen. The vicar here was a high church Anglican and, as Cyril's son Toby explained, he was 'attracted by a rural church where the aesthetics of ritualism could be found in pure and simple background'. The attraction was not, however, restricted to rood screens and ritual. Through this connection he met the vicar's niece Dorothy Nunn, ten years his junior.

It was a long engagement. Dolly, who waited patiently while Cyril tried to get himself established, followed him into his new faith, received into the Roman Catholic church in Bury, in July 1903. They were married on 27 August 1904 in the Catholic church of St Edmund in Bury, and moved into a flat in Kenilworth Court, Putney. Here their first son, Edward Raymond Roper Power – always called Toby – was born in November 1905. By then Cyril had an office in Lamb's Conduit Street in Holborn, and soon a job with the Ministry of Works, where he helped with the design for the King Edward Building, the imposing new General Post Office in the City of London. He was doing well, and the Powers' next home was 'a bijou rough-cast villa' downriver in Sheen, with dinner guests in formal clothes. They seemed set for an unspectacular suburban middle-class life. Then, suddenly, after some unexplained financial crisis, they were off to a flat above a police station in a poor area of Catford in south-east London: their second son, Cyril Arthur, was born here in 1908. By now Cyril's parents had died, and the only relatives of the older generation were his unmarried uncle Charles Berry, secretary to the Berry engineering company, and his aunt Ellen, who shared a gloomy, over-furnished house in Belgravia, 'redolent of the Forsytes'. But although the family silver came from this respectable pair – worthy of Galsworthy's Forsyte novels – hard cash was not forthcoming.

Nonetheless, Cyril's fortunes brightened again. The Powers moved further into the city, to Greenwich, to a street next door to the Naval

College. Greenwich was a busy, lively place, loved by all the family. They made good friends in the dockyard and the naval museum, and Cyril took the children along the river and up on the hill behind. In winter they went skating on the pond at the top of the hill, to the tunes of the organ-grinder, among stalls selling roast chestnuts and oranges. From the Observatory they looked down over the elegant buildings of the Queen's House to the sweeping curve of the Thames, bending round from St Paul's in the west to the marshes in the east. Across the river, busy with shipping, lay the great West India, Royal Victoria and Albert docks, linking London to the world beyond. In their own house, so close to the river, 'there was much excitement', Cyril's son Toby remembered, from the dock fires nearby, including one night when all the family had to turn out in their dressing gowns, 'my father clutching his violin!' – his most precious possession.

In all this time, Dolly seemed to take everything with equanimity. She was a quiet, unflappable, affectionate woman who let trouble flow over her, happy to walk through the streets of Greenwich with six-year-old Toby rattling his stick against the railings of the museum as she trundled his small brother in a pushchair, 'seated on a box containing a pair of live lobsters that we were taking to the fishmonger for boiling.' To add to their income, Cyril gave classes on medieval architecture at Goldsmith's College in South London. From 1906 he was also 'Instructor in Design' at Birkbeck College, and taught at University College London. A natural teacher, engrossed and ebullient, he was happier in this role than in his struggles as an architect. Writing notes for his students, he explored ideas of architecture as organic, developing cell from cell, and elsewhere he mused on the different emotional impact of vertical and horizontal lines. Sometimes he was writing for them – or for himself – as artists, almost forgetting their architectural aims: 'Make the most of the materials at hand,' he urged. 'It is wonderful what there is to be got out of what are at first sight unpromising materials. Bee can extract sweetness from the humblest flower.' On a page headed 'ON ELIMINATION', he stressed the need to refine a subject to its essentials. Opposite a sketch made on a rainy morning, 'Tone heavy and grey relieved with highlight. Overcast. Leaden sky', he noted that this might seem uninviting, but,

> on half closing the eyes one saw immediately how to compress the subject & eliminate all the secondary detail. Looking at it thus, the foreground of the station platform with their reflected lights stood up strongly & the signals beyond silhouetted themselves against the background. All the minor uninteresting & distracting detail disappeared, while the principal masses & details stood out clearly & the background simplified itself & became subordinate.

Sybil Andrews would later echo his words, stressing the importance of drawing, of abstracting 'in order to learn what is vital, what is basic . . . Simplicity is Knowledge.' The urge to simplify and the finding of beauty in unexpected places would be guiding principles.

Cyril loved music, theatre and film – he had a friend who was a projectionist in one of the new cinemas, and took the boys up to town to see the films. He was in London when Roger Fry's exhibitions of Manet and other post-Impressionists caused upset and ecstasy in equal measure in 1910 and 1912. He was there too for the dynamic Futurist shows of 1912, when the group's leader, Filippo Tommaso Marinetti, proclaimed excitedly that 'London itself is a Futurist city!', praising its flashing, coloured electric lights, 'enormous glaring posters' and 'brilliant hued motor buses'. But Cyril, at this point, looked to the past more than the future: he was a historian, a recorder of churches rather than railway stations. Based on years of weekends travelling and researching, cycling to distant towns, looking and drawing, his lively, scholarly three-volume *History of English Medieval Architecture* was published in 1912. A pioneering work – admired as such by Nikolaus Pevsner – it was full of appreciations of the structural and decorative genius of medieval builders. Struck by the windows and traceries of the late thirteenth-century choir at Gloucester, Power wrote:

> It was a daring conception, revolutionary in character, and as audaciously carried out. Step by step as the windows had widened since the mid XIIIth century, so had the glass painter followed hard behind the mason, greedily seizing on and jewelling the traceried panels with all their glory and radiance of scintillating colour attainable by stained glass alone.

He never lost that ingenuous excitement. Almost every page is illustrated, sometimes with delicate drawings of bosses or carvings, sometimes with cross-sections of individual features such as mouldings, showing how these varied and developed. However distant their subjects, these accurate diagrammatic drawings, with their right angles folding into curves and swellings, and their fluid lines reduced to near-abstraction, also foreshadowed his future style.

Soon the Powers moved again, to the suburb of Hither Green a little to the south, and then again, back to Catford. 'Though my mother must have found my father difficult owing to his failure to be an adequate Provider, and his somewhat "Gauguinesque" behaviour, I never became aware of marital quarrels,' wrote Toby, adding that 'doubtless this was due to her long suffering patience and practical good sense.' Six moves in ten years suggest that Cyril could never settle, never quite earn enough to keep the family secure, but it also shows a pattern typical of the times, renting rather than buying, and moving on when the lease ran out to somewhere more attractive, or, more often, just to somewhere cheaper. Catford seemed a safe haven, a place to stay: Cyril rented an allotment and filled the house with seed catalogues, and painted a banner for Empire Day celebrations at ten-year-old Toby's school, with the school motto, 'Perseverance Conquers'. His small sons (the priest called them 'Bubble and

Gloucester choir, from Cyril Power, *English Medieval Architecture*, 1912

Squeak') became altar boys at the local Catholic church. In July 1914, their third child, Joan ('Peggie'), was born. Then came the war, with the Zeppelin raids, searchlights piercing the night sky and the sound of exploding bombs. When Cyril volunteered in 1916, Dolly took the children to live with her parents in Bury. The family's London life ended.

———

After he was demobbed, Cyril tried to pick up the threads of his architect's career in Bury. He took a house at 4 Crown Street, Chequer Square, in the shadow of the Norman Tower, right in the town's historic centre. In front was the busy square and behind lay the churchyard gardens and the west front of the ruined abbey where the swifts whirled and shrieked in the long summer evenings.

But – there was always a but – Dolly and the boys sighed over Power's lack of business sense. When he was demobbed he received a gratuity of £500, a huge sum, enough to buy lasting security. Instead, in a burst of exuberance, he bought top-of-the-range bicycles for Dolly and himself and blew the rest on an HMV gramophone and a pile of records, remembered by Toby as 'a lot of opera, the whole of Carmen and Tannhauser, several songs by Galli-Curci, Liza Lehmann, the Shropshire Lad, Borodin, Stravinski, Debussy, Ravel, Peter Dawson, Rachmanninoff, Wagner and many more. Over a hundred in all.' The house was full of music. Cyril played the piano, viola, fiddle and organ, and belonged to an octet which practised in their house, with Dolly providing coffee and plates of coconut pyramids. (Toby also remembered 'the angry throwing up of the window of a house opposite in the square loudly protesting about my father's piano playing about midnight'.)

The Theatre Royal was only a couple of hundred yards away, and every year a repertory company put on two weeks of opera – *Carmen*, *Aida*, *La traviata* and *Il trovatore*, Gounod's *Faust*, *Pagliacci* and *Cavalleria rusticana*. Another company provided an annual fortnight of Shakespeare, and still others put on pantomimes, musical comedies and revues, or variety shows like 'The Conrad Troupe of Crazy Coppers'. As soon as a new show arrived, Cyril immediately befriended the actors, who stayed in theatrical lodgings the other side of Chequer Square. The Powers were also involved with the Amateur Operatic and Dramatic Societies, with the boys acting as prompters or stagehands or taking small roles, like Kit's walk-on part, blacked up as a boy in *Othello*. Nearby, they could see the latest films at the cinema, from Charlie Chaplin to *Tarzan of the Apes*.

Meanwhile, having blown his demob money, Cyril had to make a living: his teenage sons felt very conscious of their 'slenderness of means', wincing at the lack of new clothes. Briefly, the family fortunes were saved when he was given a commission to work on alterations to Chadacre Hall near Long Melford in Suffolk. The Irish brewer and philanthropist Edward Cecil Guinness – created first Earl of Iveagh in 1919, and owner of the huge estate at Elveden – had bought the grand Regency house, with its parkland, terraces, lake and walled garden, from the Halifax banking family, planning to make it the first agricultural institute in England, providing 'free agricultural education for the sons of farm labourers, small-holders and small farmers'. At Chadacre, which would open in September 1921, Power designed the new buildings and the conversion of the maze of rooms.

It seemed that he had found the perfect patron. He had smaller commissions too, like designs for the cricket pavilion and club house at Clacton, where they sometimes went on holidays, and for work in the village of Mistley, forty miles away near Manningtree in Essex, where his younger sisters – of whom he was very fond – farmed next to each other. Edna and Yevonde Power had married brothers, Tom and Leonard Champness, who had both turned to farming in their twenties after beginning professional careers. (Cyril's brother Ralph, a stockbroker, married their sister Maud, but this ended in divorce in 1918, to all-round shock and distress.) The Champness brothers' move to the country – an unusual choice for their class – was driven by romantic views of the countryside rather than realistic calculation. At Mistley, Edna and Tom ran the Church Farm, while Yevonde and Leonard had the Dairy Farm, with byres, bull shed and a long cool dairy full of metal churns and wooden butter-making machines. This was not toiling in the fields but gentry farming, with tennis parties, houses full of books, and gardens with long herbaceous borders where the sisters 'trailed around in long Liberty fabric dresses'. At the Dairy Farm, beyond the kitchen, which was always full of people coming and going, Cyril embellished the hall fireplace with painted decorations, 'heraldic, floral and calligraphic'.

Mistley would always be a refuge. But in the early post-war years, although he was not earning much, Cyril appeared blithely satisfied with life at Crown Street, always sure, in Micawberish fashion, that something would turn up. And something did, though not in professional terms. In 1919, three minutes' walk away from his house, past the cathedral and the Athenaeum and the imposing Abbey Gate, across the wide open space of Angel Hill, Sybil Andrews was renting her studio.

4: ANGEL HILL

Sybil's studio was in Crescent House, curving round a corner at 28 Angel Hill. From her wide, airy room the old town was spread out before her. 'My window faced directly onto Angel Hill . . . and the whole expanse of the Abbey gate . . . together with St James's cathedral, the Athenaeum, the Norman Tower (ten bells) St Mary's church (8 bells), eighteen bells if I remember rightly and what a glorious sound.' Cyril showed this view in a watercolour, *The Athenaeum and Angel Hill*, in 1921. By then they were working together.

How did they meet? Sybil's recollection was that they simply met on the street – she was struggling to draw a house and he stopped to offer her advice, and then began to teach her perspective. But it would have been strange, anyway, if they hadn't met eventually. Dolly Power's family, the Nunns, were related three times to the Andrews family by marriage, and she went to Hatter Street school a few years before Sybil and her sisters. The families belonged to the same network of merchants, farmers and professionals – Dolly's relatives included a teacher, a solicitor and an auctioneer – that formed the core of Bury society. They all went to plays in the little Regency playhouse, the Theatre Royal, and to concerts and talks and dances at the Athenaeum, the girls dressing up in ball gowns, with kid gloves and dance cards. In this milieu, the Power family rubbed shoulders with the Andrews. Cyril became friendly with Sybil's mother, Beatrice, only three years his senior, through their shared interest in history and archaeology. He was already a Fellow of the Royal Historical Society and now threw himself into Bury history, joining the local archaeological society, helping with excavations at the abbey and giving lectures at the Athenaeum. He and Beatrice were both members of a group concerned with restoration of the cathedral, about which he felt passionately: his own drawings included an elaborate 'Restoration of the West Front' of the abbey, as it was around 1500. A second bond was music, and Beatrice sometimes accompanied him when he played his violin at informal concerts. Inevitably, he and Dolly met her children: Geoff, Joy and Sybil, now in their early twenties, and Margaret and Hal, aged sixteen and fourteen, not much older than the Power boys. In October 1920, when Cyril gave a talk on medieval church architecture, he thanked Sybil Andrews for making the slides and sketching the diagrams.

Sybil became Cyril's companion in his latest obsession. Over the months, Toby noted wryly, his father became noticeably less interested in the grind of work as an architect than in 'dashing off before breakfast to paint watercolours en plein air around the town setting up his camp stool and impeding the traffic'. He had begun painting at Lympne during the war. Now he bought the book of George Clausen's lectures to Royal Academy students, *Aims and Ideals in Art*, and made diligent notes on realism, Impressionism and colour, on freshness of touch and the importance of light. In 1919 and 1920, often surrounded by inquisitive onlookers, he and Sybil sketched the streets of the town together. If his drawing was more precise, hers was swifter, more atmospheric. Looking east up the central street of Abbeygate, she made a rapid, impressionist sketch of one side of the road, scribbling in the names of the shops, while Cyril, sitting next to her on his camp stool, drew the tall gabled houses on the other side, converging on Abbeygate's junction with Guildhall Street. At the far end of the street, his sketch showed Andrews and Plumpton, ironmongers, with a line pointing to a first-floor window, and the note 'Sybil was born'.

They worked together too on their watercolours: Sybil labelled a hazy wash view across fields to the spires of St John's church as number one, 'On the spot, 1919'. She painted the same scene,

Cyril Power, 'Abbeygate Street', with Andrews & Plumpton
in the background, and the note 'Sybil was born'.

glowing gold on a frosty morning, while Cyril made the shadows of the winter trees shine blue against the grass. Soon she was confident enough to paint alone. On the back of a scene of the lane she had rushed through as a child, dodging the cattle, she wrote, 'My first watercolour outdoors by myself. 7.00 am Looms Lane 1920'.

They shared paints and paper – one of her watercolours of Bury has his architectural drawing on the back. Gradually, they learned to use colour to dramatic effect. Sybil painted streets with sunlight bouncing off the walls, set off by blue door and window frames and dappled violet shadows: several paintings were of her childhood home, Greyfriars in Whiting Street (PLATE 4). Cyril's rendering was more detailed, the crisp lines of gables, the run of tiles on old roofs, windblown trees leaning over the wall. Following each other, they set up their easels in odd corners, like the yard behind the old Star Inn with its angled roofs and walls. Sybil's view was a symphony of dove-grey angles and shadows, while Cyril's, painted from a few yards further back, was warmer and looser, with scribbles of children playing (PLATES 2 AND 3). Sometimes, too, they took trips out of Bury, painting the old houses of Lavenham and other villages and towns of Suffolk.

One can understand the appeal they had for each other, the easy chemistry. With his booming laugh and his penchant for bad jokes Cyril was fun. More than that, he was emotional and erudite, widely read, curious about other cultures, other forms of art and faith. Toby remembered that as parents Cyril and Dolly were loving and kind, but 'did little to create an atmosphere of lively discussion and argument'. By contrast Sybil practically embodied lively argument, eager to learn, excited by all she saw. To the end of her life her eyes would light up at the sight of something new, at a trick of the light, the memory of something odd, and she would throw back her head and laugh. They could talk to each other, thrash out ideas – discuss poetry, music, literature and art.

Over the months, their relationship was continually strengthening. Cyril's brisk encouragement gave Sybil just the spur she needed:

Those to whom I am most indebted would be first of all CYRIL POWER an architect and artist. He used to sit me down (or stand) in front of the hardest buildings, & twisting, turning streets we could find & say 'Now get on with it' & leave me to struggle correcting me *after* I had done the best I could on my own.

She devoured all he could tell her: he was a born teacher, she said, 'for young or old. To me it was like a university course, Art Architecture History Archaeology Music.' She shared her mother's interest in local history and, she added, 'His book "Medieval Architecture" is standard . . . he was so full of enthusiasm & work. A splendid companion'. He gave her this book, inscribing it for her on 13 March 1920. In his memory, the Easter weekend three weeks later marked a special stage in their relationship – but he did not say why.

For Cyril, what had begun as a teacher–pupil relationship, kindness to the daughter of a friend, was becoming something different: he was falling in love. He was also caught in a dilemma. In the summer of 1920 or 1921 – he could not remember quite which – doodling and brooding on a train, he wrote a poem called 'Woman!' It reads as if he was turning his own feelings of guilt about Dolly, the mother of his children, and also about Sybil, the young, free woman, into an accusation against men in general:

> Behold me!
> For I am Woman, the Mother of Man!
> They shackled my feet
> And fettered my hands,
> But I have burst my bonds & am free.
> They made me a drudge of toil, their slave,
> Their plaything or their toy,
> & petted & spurned me.
> They bartered my maidenhood
> & degraded my maternity.

I – who brought forth man from the inmost
Shrine of my being.
I – the life bearer & sustainer of life
Thus did they reward the author of their being.
In their joys they forget me
But in their sorrow come to me for comfort
And in the storm for shelter.

In 1921 Cyril too rented a studio in Crescent House. Sybil's studio was at the front and his at the back, looking over the gardens, and that summer they decided to have a joint exhibition, to show their paintings and make a little money. Sybil needed funds and so did Cyril, especially as Dolly was pregnant again, and they worked hard building up a portfolio. Life was busy. Sybil was still teaching at Portland House School, and Cyril had his work and his involvement in the archaeological society, the theatre and music. At the start of December, a week before their exhibition was due to open, he was playing the viola in the orchestra for the Amateur Dramatic Society's production of *Tom Jones*. Then, on 11 December 1921, two days after the show opened, his son, Edmund Berry Power (known as Kit) was born. He now had three growing children and a baby to provide for.

Their show ran for a week from 9 December in Sybil's studio. Together they showed around ninety-five watercolours and fifty pastels. Although their approach sometimes differed, they had developed a shared style, simplifying outlines, emphasising gable ends or the horizontal lines of walls against the verticals of trees and posts, floating the streets with colour. The reviewer from the *Bury Post*, nervous about 'revolutionary and difficult' contemporary art, found their watercolours 'charming' but also distinctly modern, 'emphasising beauties of lighting and composition perhaps not generally realised by others in their daily life'. But not too modern – the pastels, studies of familiar buildings at dawn and dusk, or under surging storm clouds, reminded him of Whistler's 'Nocturnes' of the 1870s and 80s. And if their style seemed new in Bury, in essence their paintings were conservative, celebrating the permanence of place after the war. Their watercolours were a world away from the modernism of the Vorticists and Cubists of London and Paris, far from the fractured images of T. S. Eliot's *The Waste Land*, which would be published the following year.

The show bracketed them together as a unit, a partnership, with their studios back to back in Crescent House. Rumours began to spread (springing chiefly from Dolly, Sybil later said bitterly) that the closeness was personal as well as professional: that if they were not lovers now, they soon would be. No diaries survive from 1919 to 1921, but it is clear that from now on Cyril was more than a teacher. In the bitter cold of January 1922, with snow thick on the ground, Sybil scribbled brisk pencil entries in her small pocket diary, noting his doings more than her own: 'Cyril to Chadacre . . . C to Stanton', 'C to Sudbury by 7.26 . . . came back about 6 pm, felt better by 10 o'clock', and next day 'Cyril better'. After trips away on work, he came back to her at Crescent House, not to Dolly in Crown Street. She drew his portrait, one of many that would follow – 'did excellent "eyes" of Cyril'.

By the spring Cyril was writing his own notes in her diary, marking dates like his election on 26 April as a council member of the Suffolk Institute of Archaeology. They painted together, went to the theatre and to concerts together, worked on his designs for church decoration together. At the end of June, when a group of townspeople concerned to preserve the abbey ruins toured the grounds and pored over the excavations, he and Beatrice Andrews helped to give tea at the Abbey House, and then he gave a talk on the abbey's history. As a local reporter noted, 'splendidly executed diagrams, plans and drawings, the work of the lecturer and Miss Sybil Andrews were provided to illustrate the lecture. Pointing to one of these comprehensive drawings, Mr Power said, "Look at your Bury Abbey and be proud. See how it outclassed all the others."'

That evening Sybil crammed the day's events into her diary, ending exuberantly, 'most successful day, great feather in the cap of CEP'. His emotional investment in his adopted town was clear – Bury could become another Canterbury, he said, if all its fine points were displayed. It seemed impossible that both he and Sybil would turn their backs on the place within a year.

II: SETTING OUT

Sybil Andrews, *The Gale*, 1930

5: THE MOVE

Sybil was the first to move. She was young, it was a new age – unstable and uncertain but full of promise, bursting with energy – and she wanted to be part of it. She had cut a dash as a talented amateur in a provincial town, but she yearned to be a professional artist. She wanted to train properly, in London. In April 1922 her father Charles wrote from Canada for her birthday, sending his letter as his neighbours gathered after the first thaws and dances on the prairies went on until dawn. It seemed a world away. What was she going to do in London, he wondered? He never knew: soon he was ill and that August he died in hospital in Saskatoon. By then, Sybil was already on her way.

On the first weekend in May she wrote: 'Saw EMU and broke the fatal news.' Edith Underwood gave her a reference, describing her as 'bright and energetic' as a form teacher and helpful as a colleague. Above all, 'She has been particularly successful in her teaching of Drawing and Painting and has shown great insight in developing the individual powers of the children.' All that was now over. She left Portland House School at the end of the summer term, taking a photo of her class sitting on the steps, and enrolled in Heatherley School of Art, in London.

In pouring July rain, Sybil and her mother hunted for a flat – most of them were too small, too expensive, 'too piffling', but they finally found one a month later in Bernard Street, near Russell Square Underground, 'very excellent I think'. Like eager tourists they spent the Bank Holiday weekend going to the Zoo, meeting Sybil's brother Geoff and lunching at Lyons Corner House, walking along the Embankment and having tea in the park, wandering the streets until they were so tired that they collapsed in a Regent Street cinema. Back at Bury in the hot summer weeks Sybil sorted her things and cleared her studio. 'And then', she wrote, 'it was up to town and to Heatherleys and away we go!' On Thursday 14 September 1922, Sybil and her mother, who stayed with her while she settled in, took the train for London. The following Monday her new life began. 'Such an interesting day,' she wrote that night.

Ever since the spring, when Sybil had decided to leave, Cyril was determined to go too. It seems that he felt he could not go on without her, as if he needed her, with her floppy fringe and flashing blue-green eyes, her rapid walk and her fierce immersion in her art. She was twenty-four, while he was fifty: being with her allowed him to feel young again, to dream of breaking into a new world, opening doors onto a life of art. His infatuation was a post-war crisis as much as a mid-life crisis. Mass death in the trenches had made life seem so short that many men and women felt it was imperative – almost a duty – to live true to one's deep desires and talents, to escape the ruts. But Cyril's impulsive move meant tearing up precious ties with his family. And following Sybil meant having to keep up with a woman half his age. It was a recipe for insecurity.

That summer, he made arrangements for the future in headlong impatience, seemingly blind to his family's needs. Toby was about to study for a scholarship to Peterhouse, Cambridge, to read history, but instead, to bring in money, Cyril arranged for him to sit an examination for a job at the local Midland Bank. Dutifully, in May 1922 Toby turned up for his interview and got the job. Rather than wearing a student's mortar-board, he was doomed to scurry through the back streets in embarrassment, wearing a bowler hat, arriving at the bank at nine every morning for a salary of £40 a year. Bitterly hurt by his father's 'defection' and by his treatment of his mother, Toby began using her family name of Roper as part of his surname. Dolly herself gritted her teeth, and with her children at least, she was silent.

It took a few months for Cyril to settle everything. In early September, Sybil wrote in her diary, 'Had our anniversary feast – hors d'oeuvres, fruit salad & graves.' During her first three months in London he went down on Friday afternoons to meet her as she came out of Heatherleys, and at the weekends they went to concerts, plays and exhibitions. In January 1923 he finally left Dolly and his four children. In London he enrolled at Heatherleys, giving his addresses as his studio, Crescent House, Bury, and his rooms at 15–16 Newman Street, just down the road from the school. Before he left, Toby moved to a post away from Bury, in the Midland Bank's branch in St Albans in Hertfordshire, and Dolly and the other children moved there with him. For good Catholics divorce was out of the question, but apart from occasional visits, Cyril would not stay with the family for over fifteen years. If Sybil ever thought of any parallel with her own father, who had left when she was twelve, she never mentioned it. As far as she was concerned a choice was a choice, and that was that. The thing was to follow it through, to make it work.

Setting off for London, one after the other, Sybil and Cyril left a trail of gossip behind them. The Andrews family as a whole were significant figures in Bury. Charles Andrews' disappearance to Canada was the subject of speculation and Beatrice, with her absent husband and her scholarly archaeological interests, had been both a part of, and slightly out of step with, the town society. As for her children, they were long talked of there. 'All very plain', declared one woman who had known them in her childhood, 'and all eccentric.' Hal was the oddest, seen striding through the town in his deerstalker hat and green cloak. But Sybil was spoken of with bated breath, as having run off to live with a married man.

6: HEATHERLEYS

Heatherley School of Art, then at 75 Newman Street, in London's Fitzrovia, just north of Soho, advertised itself as 'a Paris studio in London'. The nod to the French atelier system, with its stress on drawing from life and on practical training, signified its freedom from the strict curriculum of schools like the Slade or Royal Academy Schools. A more liberal ethos had been part of the school since its foundation in 1845, when students chafing at the restrictions at the Government School of Design in Somerset House started a class of their own. In the late nineteenth century it was run for thirty years by Thomas Heatherley, who gave it his name (it is still affectionately known as Heatherleys), and the impressive list of former students, who often added classes here to formal art training elsewhere, ranged from Rossetti and Burne Jones to Greenaway and Sickert. When Sybil arrived, the mildly eccentric Henry Massey and his wife Gertrude, a talented miniaturist (and famous painter of royal dogs), had owned the school for the past fifteen years. Massey, now in his sixties, had trained in Paris, and knew Gauguin at the artists' colony at St Aven – a long while ago, but the connection still had a touch of glamour. Massey was a democrat, posting the motto 'Abandon swank all ye who enter here' on the studio door. His pupils could enrol for as long as they liked – a year, a quarter or a month – paying separately for the courses they chose to follow, portraiture, print-making, illustration and sculpture.

Not everyone was impressed. Evelyn Waugh, who enrolled two years after Sybil, was disdainful. Depressed after leaving Oxford without a degree, he went to Heatherleys because there he could draw from life straight away rather than spending months drawing

Massey at Heatherleys, 1920s.

from plaster casts of the antique, as the grander schools still demanded. But he sneered at the setting, full of pieces of armour and historical costumes, a hangover from old Heatherleys days, and at the students. The majority 'were respectable girls who, like myself, were believed at home to be "artistic" . . . No one seriously aspired to High Art.'

> The tuition was negligible. The proprietor had a white beard, a very red nose and a hand which trembled so grievously that the charcoal was invariably shattered when he attempted a demonstration. The studio merely provided an opportunity for drawing. We sat on 'donkeys' ranged round the platform on which a model stood in the traditional attitudes. In the mornings the pose was constant for a week. In the afternoons there was a succession of ten-minute poses which we sketched in pencil.

In his short story 'The Balance', and in his diaries, Waugh was even ruder. Most of the women were 'underbred houris . . . in gaudy overalls', while the men were 'bent upon making commercial careers for themselves by illustrating *Punch* or advertising things'.

Massey's hand may have trembled, yet Waugh admitted that as a result of the studio exercises, his own eye grew sharper and his hand more responsive, 'but I was totally lacking in that obsession with solid form, the zeal for probing the structure of anatomy and for relating to one another the recessions of planes which alone could make the long hours before the models exciting.' Sybil Andrews, by contrast, was ready for long hours and hard work, and burned with zeal for structure and form. Massey, she thought, 'was a wonderful man. So practical. You weren't just doing pretty pictures all the time. You were really learning to draw.' She particularly liked the afternoon classes with a time limit for each pose: 'Five minutes was good practice – you had to get the essentials. You didn't have time to be fussy.' Longer sessions came next, of ten or twenty minutes.

While Sybil was a full-time student at Heatherleys, Cyril signed up for only two days a week, filling his sketchbooks with life studies, and fitting the classes in with his architect's work. He was cooler, less admiring, while Sybil lapped everything up, flinging herself into the work and the spirit of the place. Sometimes Massey kept her after class, giving her private lessons and forcing her to concentrate. 'He used to say "If you want to do two years' work in one year, whatever you have been doing in class do it from memory on Saturday at home."' She found it extraordinary, after the week's hard study, how easily it came from memory, 'how much better than the work fought out *on the spot*'. That 'fought out' was an indicator of how furiously she attacked all aspects of her work. Once, when they had a model dressed in black and white, Massey asked her which was the brightest light. 'I didn't know. I hadn't thought.' He made her half-close her eyes and look at the tones – the brightest spot, it seemed, was the gleam of light in the model's eye, 'and that gleam cannot be just any old dab of white paint. The eye is a ball, set well back in its socket, and half hidden by eyelids. So that little touch of light in the eye must follow the curve of the eyeball and the direction of the light.'

At the weekly composition class, students were given abstract subjects ('such as "conflict"', wrote Waugh despairingly) and had to work from imagination – one of Sybil's first efforts was based on a book cover for *Treasure Island*. These classes, 'although they scared me cold at first', were the highlights of her week. Many students tried to sneak out, but Massey stood at the door barring their escape: 'We had five minutes to get our ideas down. Five minutes from his giving out of the Title.' He taught them about colour and the effect of juxtaposition, insisting that you could not really see a colour at all until you put it against another: 'Witness what happens if you put a cool, dull green against a much stronger red scarlet. How much brighter and greener it appears by contrast.' Deepening the tone did not necessarily add richness: this came from the use of complementary colours, hot and cold. He showed, too, how the variation of line brought mobility and depth, a third dimension, onto flat paper or canvas:

> He would lay a walking stick on the ground, and there it would lie, flat, two dimensional – doing nothing. He would pick it up and hold it upright like a walking stick and still it was up and down and doing nothing. It went nowhere, It was purely static.
>
> But then, he let go, and immediately things began to happen. Being no longer balanced and held, it began to fall at all angles . . .
>
> . . . If we want the magic to occur which gives us the impression of going miles and miles beyond that flat surface, all our lines must lead us inwards – must move. If you want action, your line must give that action. Lines and corners and angles and spaces all must follow the same law of movement.

Heatherleys was a sociable place, with a sketch club on Fridays and dances after school, and Sybil, ready to talk to everyone, became part of the school life. In 1923 she made a banner for Massey's show at the Brook Street Gallery – 'Mr Massey very pleased' – while Gertrude Massey took her under her wing, showing her their musical instruments and giving her a book on lettering. She liked Massey's humour, his insistence that one should relax, have a late breakfast, come to the studio and see the work afresh. Students should not worry if things go wrong; 'You can only learn by experiment, by experience.' They should be self-critical, which was easy to do if you pretended the work was not yours but someone else's: 'Imagine that it is mine if you like – that will make you very critical and also give you a chance of getting a little of your own back.' Most important of all, and this was something that Cyril Power also took to heart, Massey insisted that figurative work should not be pictorial, a mere record of what was seen: 'You do not see with your eyes, you see with your brain. Your eyes are only lenses. They have no more intelligence in themselves than a pair of opera glasses. You don't see with them you see through them. It is not what you see but what you feel which is important.' Years later, looking at Power's linocuts of Underground stations, his son Kit remembered, 'My father always said that he put down what he *felt* about a subject rather than what he saw.'

7: LONDON

At the start of 1923 there was a sense that life was finally beginning to return to normal although the immediate post-war grimness was still felt: prices were almost double those of pre-war days and wages had fallen; unemployment was still high and men were trudging from Glasgow to London on the first hunger march. But new things were happening. Paper boys shouted out headlines. In the last year wireless had arrived, the Prince of Wales made the first public broadcast and the BBC was formed; Lloyd George's government collapsed and the Conservatives under Bonar Law took office; across the Irish Sea, Northern Ireland voted to stay in the Union and in Dublin the Irish Free State was born; in Egypt, Howard Carter broke into Tutankhamun's tomb.

It was the beginning of the Jazz Age, the era of the Bright Young Things. Yet the shadow of the war lingered as military bands collected money and war memorials were unveiled. There were jokes about 'superfluous women' and it was rare to find a novel of the 1920s without a grieving woman at its heart. There was darkness of a different kind too, a sinister, baleful tone in the press, with its jokes about 'blackamoor' jazz bands and its rancorous anti-Semitism. In December 1922 Mussolini had arrived in London for discussions on German post-war reparations – dapper in spats, butterfly collar and top hat, complaining about the fog. At Victoria Station and Claridges black-shirted supporters sang the fascist marching song 'Giovinezza'. When he laid a wreath at the Cenotaph, British followers knelt and raised their arms in the fascist salute, a gesture that had to be explained to the newspaper-reading public. The British dignitaries and press found all this absurd and faintly amusing.

'To Chelsea hunting studios', Sybil wrote in early January 1923. To Londoners their city in the aftermath of the war seemed grey and sad, with little in the shops and disabled veterans begging on street corners. But for Sybil, from Bury St Edmunds, it was a move into freedom and colour. Cyril was a Londoner, used to the city, but for her, everything was new. She was one of many young, single women in the capital carving out an independent life after the war: the detective writer Dorothy Sayers was living in a poky flat in Bloomsbury, eking out the money she earned as an advertising copywriter, staring at the hole in her cheap rug and inventing her hero, Lord Peter Wimsey, who dined at the Ritz and could order an Aubusson carpet whenever he liked. If money was short, life was exciting (Sybil's favourite word), with new art, new music, new books. At Foyle's bookstore in Tottenham Court Road, one could buy new novels, from Agatha Christie's *The Secret Adversary* to Virginia Woolf's *Jacob's Room*; in October 1922, *The Waste Land* appeared in the *Criterion*, and earlier in the year, across the Channel, Sylvia Beach published Joyce's *Ulysses*. In the ramshackle Poetry Bookshop in Bloomsbury, run by Harold Monro since 1913, famous poets read by candlelight flickering off walls pasted with hand-coloured rhyme sheets.

In Bury there were only a few cars, but in London lorries and vans with flat black roofs surged into side streets, while alongside them dray horses still pulled the carts from the breweries. The trams, with their outside staircases curling up to the wooden seats on top, were now competing with buses, more luxurious, with upholstered seats. From 1922 dozens of 'pirate buses', run by independent companies, raced the London Transport buses, hurtling and swerving, as young Elizabeth Dalloway discovers in Virginia Woolf's novel:

Buses swooped, settled, were off – garish caravans, glistening with red and yellow varnish . . . The impetuous creature – a pirate – started forward, sprang away; she had to hold the rail to steady herself, for a pirate it was, reckless, unscrupulous, bearing down ruthlessly, circumventing dangerously, boldly snatching a passenger, or ignoring a passenger, squeezing eel-like and arrogant in between then rushing insolently, all sails spread, up Whitehall.

Pavements were thronged with office workers and shoppers, the men wearing bowlers, trilbys and flat caps, and most of the women in long coats and old wide-brimmed hats. But already there was a sprinkling of new fashions – dresses with hip-length tops and skirts just below the knee, tight cloche hats, buckled shoes.

Sybil made her own clothes but she too liked new styles, voguish hats, modern jewellery, something to stand out in the crowd. Cyril never bothered: he always looked the same, burly and tall, in crumpled tweed or linen suits. But being back in the city invigorated him, especially the new buildings and the growing London Underground network, its tunnels and escalators, platforms and crowds. Railway stations were being revamped and he sketched these too, and the docks and the river. When Sybil and Cyril looked east from London Bridge to Tower Bridge they saw cranes on both sides, coasters at the wharves, steam-tugs in the distance, barges tied up four or five at a time, laden with sacks, barrels and crates. Among them a red-sailed barge might glide downstream, like the horse-drawn carts amid the traffic – the Thames of Eliot's *Waste Land*:

> The river sweats
> Oil and tar
> The barges drift
> With the turning tide
> Red sails
> Wide
> To leeward, swing on the heavy spar.

Everything was on the move. A crowd of two hundred thousand swarmed to the newly built Wembley Stadium to see the Cup Final between West Ham and Bolton in 1923 and had to be driven from the pitch by mounted police. Lights flashed on the hoardings at Piccadilly Circus where new electronic billboards appeared, with whizzing wheels, a rushing motor, a bottle of port filling and refilling a glass, and an enormous sign for Bovril. Lights flickered too over Shaftesbury Avenue, where Fred and Adele Astaire were making their London debut in Gershwin's *Stop Flirting*, with hits like 'Oh Gee, Oh Gosh, Oh Golly, I Love You'. The West End was humming, with Somerset Maugham's satirical *Our Betters* and Tallulah Bankhead wowing fans in *The Dancers* with Gerald du Maurier. The following year would see Edith Evans in the premiere of Shaw's *Back to Methuselah*, and his *Saint Joan*, with a heart-stopping performance from Sybil Thorndike, a role written specially for her.

Sybil and Cyril saw Thorndike in Hammersmith, taking the lead in *Medea*. Often, they crossed the river to the Old Vic, where Lilian Baylis, who had taken over ten years before from her aunt, the reformer Emma Cons, managed to stage the whole of Shakespeare's folio, as well as medieval drama, such as *Everyman* ('splendid', thought Sybil) and the *Chester Nativity Play*. In June 1923, standing in the Old Vic gallery, they saw a feast of plays – *A Midsummer Night's Dream*, *Henry IV Part I* (twice), *Measure for Measure*, *Much Ado* and *Merry Wives of Windsor* – with Goldsmith's *She Stoops to Conquer* thrown in. 'I used to want to see all the Shakespeare I could,' Sybil remembered, 'in the standing room, near a nice warm radiator. The Old Vic cost fourpence, fourpence to travel there, fourpence for the show and fourpence to travel back. I would watch the dramatic positions of the actors and keep them in my mind till I got home and could draw them.' She wasn't always admiring: a *Hamlet* matinee was a 'ghastly failure' and *The Merchant of Venice* a 'great disappointment . . . Generally rotten. Good in patches!' The theatre addiction continued and in one festival week in 1926 Cyril jotted down their timetable, a play each day, plus matinees: *The Tempest*, *Macbeth*, *Julius Caesar*, *As You Like It*, with *The Rivals* as a break from Shakespeare.

As in Bury, Cyril became friends with the actors, and Sybil developed a lasting bond with Baliol Holloway ('Ba'), who starred as a variety of Shakespearean villains and heroes – Richard III and Shylock, Mark Antony and Othello, and a famous Falstaff in *Henry IV Part II*. Over the next few years Ba became a good friend to them both, writing to them jointly when he was away on tour, giving them tickets in the stalls, finding contacts to sell their prints. Sybil kept a scrapbook of Holloway's performances and modelled a plaster bust of him gazing boldly to the sky. In 1926 Cyril drew him with Edith Evans in Dekker's *The Shoemaker's Holiday*, where he played the master shoemaker Simon Eyre. The critics loved the play, although Holloway later told Sybil, 'I *hate* the d—n part, loathe and detest it bitterly.'

Theatre was a passion, but also a teacher. The theatre, Sybil would tell her students, 'is a school where you may learn the emotions and their effect on the body and character and learn to feel', excellent too for the 'study of lighting effects, pattern, colour and design'. This fed into their work, blending with more obvious forms of learning. They heard lectures at the Royal Academy, explored the British Museum, the National Gallery, the Victoria and Albert Museum in South Kensington and the Geffrye in Hoxton, with its domestic furniture and woodwork. Art was everywhere around them, in public spaces and galleries and intimate corners. Even carriages on the Underground, under the inspired direction of the Yorkshireman Frank Pick, became a gallery, blazing with the posters of the American Edward McKnight Kauffer, like the woolly mammoth against rays of sunlight and rainbow semicircles, coaxing people to visit the Natural History Museum. Yet they had missed so much, and had so much to catch up with.

Sybil had been a schoolgirl and Cyril had been preoccupied with gargoyles and Gothic spires when Fry's post-Impressionist exhibitions caused a storm in 1910 and 1912. Although ten years had passed, Fry's ideas were still followed avidly: his influence spread through his role as editor of the *Burlington Magazine* and his collected essays in *Vision and Design* in 1920, and although his Omega workshops had closed in 1919 their fabrics and furniture still filled smart interiors. After the gap of the war, interest in recent continental art revived. Matisse, in London to design Stravinsky's *Le Chant de rossignol* for Diaghilev in 1919, had a much-praised exhibition at the Leicester Galleries. By contrast, Picasso's 'Cubistic' show in 1921 was a commercial flop. Undaunted, the Leicester mounted more solo shows, beginning with *Van Gogh* in 1923 (the National Gallery bought *Sunflowers* the following year), and *Gauguin* and *Cézanne* in the next two years. Looking back from twenty years later in *Brideshead Revisited* and mocking the aspirations of his hero Charles Ryder, a new student at Oxford in 1923, Evelyn Waugh rolled all the fashionable clichés of the day into Ryder's rooms: 'On my first afternoon I proudly hung a reproduction of Van Gogh's *Sunflowers* over the fire, and set up a screen, painted by Roger Fry with a Provençal landscape, which I had bought inexpensively when the Omega workshops were sold up. I displayed also a poster by McKnight Kauffer and Rhyme Sheets from the Poetry Bookshop . . .' Ryder's 'meagre and commonplace' books included Fry's *Vision and Design*, the Medici Press edition of Housman's *A Shropshire Lad* and Lytton Strachey's *Eminent Victorians*.

Van Gogh and Cézanne were among the artists Sybil most admired, but she and Cyril were also curious about other artists and galleries. The Whitechapel Art Gallery in the East End showed 'Modern British Art' each spring and the London Group, heavily influenced by Fry, put on defiant shows of modern art at Heal's in Tottenham Court Road. Heal's was a key to the link between art and 'design' in a wider sense of furniture, decoration and ways of living. Ambrose Heal, a lover of new art and close friend of Frank Pick, opened his new Mansard Gallery in 1917, a symbol of the bright post-war world, linked to the floors below by Cecil Brewer's stunning spiral staircase. It was ready to provoke and inspire: the opening exhibition showed Underground posters; in 1919 Sacheverell Sitwell's exhibition of modern

French art included Picasso, Matisse and – for the first time in Britain – the 'shocking' work of Modigliani; in 1920 Wyndham Lewis held his 'Group X' show here. Moving to design, the gallery held the first display of modernist tubular-style furniture (later their 'Economy range', to suit the Depression of the 1930s, would include Mies van der Rohe's famous tubular chair, Gropius's elegant, reclining 'Long Chair', and furniture from other Bauhaus designers).

Revolutionary art filled the news but a welcoming of the modern was offset by nostalgia. Wyndham Lewis rejected his pre-war Vorticism for figurative painting; C. R. W. Nevinson, once a fervent admirer of Italian Futurism, painted and etched the Thames in ways that recalled Turner, Constable and Whistler; Paul and John Nash, painters of bleak wartime scenes, were beginning to evoke 'the spirit of the place' in evocative landscapes. Traditional and cutting-edge work both found space in new galleries. In 1923, the Beaux Arts Gallery opened in Bruton Street, while the Redfern in Old Bond Street was formed as an artists' co-operative, showing the student work of Henry Moore and Barbara Hepworth a year later. Around these and other galleries, new groups formed. 'There is a distemper prevalent amongst artists of today,' wrote John Nash in the *London Mercury*; 'I refer to the mania for group forming.' Groups, he concluded gloomily, invariably swung from enthusiasm to quarrels and divisions, baffling the public and displaying 'an inherent distrust of each other which all artists seem to possess'. The most influential gathering was the Seven and Five Society, founded in 1920, whose manifesto declared that 'A periodic explosion is essential in Art as in all other forms of organised activity, to blow away the crust of dead matter that time inevitably accumulates.' The Seven and Five offered liberty and variety, and until Ben Nicholson pushed it towards abstraction at the end of the decade it attracted a galaxy of innovative artists.

In November and December 1922, at the Seven and Five's annual show in Walker's Gallery in New Bond Street, a short walk from where Sybil and Cyril were studying at Heatherleys, one of the outstanding works was a linocut – Claude Flight's *Speed*. Flight already had a full life behind him. He had worked as an engineer, a librarian, farmer and bee-keeper and was thirty-one before he decided to study art at Heatherleys in 1912, where he became fascinated by the Italian Futurist shows at the Marlborough Gallery that year and in 1914. In the Futurist manifesto of 1909, Marinetti had turned brutally against the past, calling for the abolition of museums and libraries, glorifying war and violence, hymning danger and above all speed, seen in works such as Umberto Boccioni's drawing of a cyclist, *The Dynamism of Speed* (1913), whose radiating lines convey the thrill of being one with a machine. In London, in 1914, Marinetti composed a joint manifesto with the twenty-five-year-old C. R. W. Nevinson, who had been studying in Paris since he left the Slade two years before. In strong words they dismissed the retrograde, narrow vision of British artists. 'WE WANT', they wrote, 'to have an English art that is strong, virile and anti-sentimental.' This should be adventurous, heroic, embracing the dynamism of city life. 'Forward! HURRAH for motors! HURRAH for speed! . . . HURRAH for lightning!'

Flight met Marinetti and Gino Severini through Nevinson, and in the early 1920s, although he rejected the violence and quasi-fascist tone of Futurism, he was still drawn to the energy and rush of the city, and to sheer kinetic power. *Speed* showed three buses charging down Regent Street, their distorted forms echoing the curve of the buildings. The way they headed out of the frame gave a sense of rapid movement, the life-blood of a modern city. 'Time seems to pass so quickly now-a-days,' Flight wrote, and the speeding up of life, he thought, was psychologically important: 'Traffic problems, transport problems; everybody is on the rush either for work or pleasure, business is hustle, the Cinema, all movement . . . The Painter cannot but be influenced by the restlessness of his surroundings.'

———

Claude Flight, *Speed*, 1922

Sybil Andrews and Cyril Power fed on this energetic restlessness, but as yet their art had not changed: they were studying life classes, learning to draw better, absorbing what they saw. They were only on the fringes of the artistic world. Their own relationship was intense, but not yet settled. While studying, they turned to music, which through all their time together was almost as vital to them as art. In her early months in London Sybil went to the Proms at the Queen's Hall to hear Henry Wood conduct a programme of vocal pieces, making a special note of those by Rimsky-Korsakov. She was there, too, for the first autumn season of Sir Thomas Beecham's new British National Opera Company, and stood in the gods at Covent Garden to hear *Madame Butterfly*, *Carmen*, *Tosca* and *La bohème* and Colin Macleod Campbell's new, English-language, *Thaïs and Talmaae*.

When Cyril joined her they sought out good concerts, hearing Eugene Goossens conducting at the Albert Hall in February 1923, and Stravinsky's *Rite of Spring* at the Queen's Hall the next day. (Stravinsky had been in the audience when Goossens conducted the first British concert performance the previous June.) Although this was a pre-war piece, it still seemed like music for a modern world. Ten years before, when the Ballets Russes first performed *The Rite of Spring* in Paris, the wildness of the dance and the music, with its harsh dissonance and bewildering speed, provoked violent protests. In 1921, T. S. Eliot had suggested that its power lay in the jarring juxtaposition of primitive and modern. Such music, Eliot wrote, seemed to turn 'the rhythm of the steppes into the scream of the motor horn, the rattle of machinery, the grind of wheels, the beating of iron and steel, the roar of the underground railway, and the other barbaric noises of modern life; and to transform these despairing noises into music'. Here, in aural terms, was that discordant city rush that Flight identified in *Speed*. For Sybil and Cyril music and art came together: a few years later, both of them would make the concert hall the subject of their first linocuts.

8: PHOENIX PLACE AND DRYPOINTS

But Sybil missed Suffolk. It was not enough to see the sparrows on the pavements, to watch the clouds of starlings whirl over the roofs, to chart the slow bursting of buds on the great plane trees, turning the streets into a mist of green. Occasionally she went back to Bury, cycling out at Easter to find primroses. In London at the start of April 1923, with the city blanketed by fog, she painted all day while 'C did etchings etc.' Sybil was ill that month and Cyril took over the diary, recording her progress. They were not living together – he had rooms nearby – but they spent most of the time with each other. Throughout the year they continued to share the diary, and he noted the days when she bought a new hat, when her mother came down from Bury, when they went to the British Museum, as well as details of his own trips to Liverpool or to Mistley, and his rare visits to the family in St Albans. He called her 'Sandra', a phonetic shortening of 'S. Andrews', but also a feminised diminutive of Alexander – a woman of strength.

They now saw themselves as artists, not Sybil and Cyril, but 'Andrews' and 'Power', the names linked to their work. Andrews finished her spring course at Heatherleys at the start of May, 'one day over time', and a fortnight later she moved into her first proper studio, '1 Phoenix Place, Addison Avenue'. She lived here and worked here, and for Andrews, as for many women artists, the studio sealed her identity, giving her space, autonomy, a room of one's own. Her mother paid the rent. Andrews loved it, describing it nostalgically in her old age to Power's grandson Martin:

It was in a mews, a lane behind a row of larger houses. My landlord was the Police Doctor – he had turned the stables and coach houses . . . of earlier days . . . into his garage, and the upper floor, the coachman's quarters into a studio, and a jolly nice studio it was. It makes me smile to see it now. The table ex-Army 5/-, the two seats by the stove . . . seats from the old wooden aeroplanes mounted on a box with a petticoat. The couch was Tate & Lyle sugar boxes wonderful strong boxes which we never see the like of today, hidden by a piece of hessian.

This was not the Phoenix Place that survives today behind Mount Pleasant Sorting Office near King's Cross, but one of the many small, cobbled mews off Addison Avenue in Holland Park in West London: in 1937, when the Post Office was rationalising street names, the old name of 'Phoenix Place' was replaced by 'Addison Place'.

They came to know the area well. In January 1923 Power had made quick sketches of nearby streets, of workers mending the road at night, and later in the year he would sketch the greengrocers and local shops and draw his first evocative sketch of the London Underground at Notting Hill Gate (PLATE 19). Across the road from that Tube station, at 104 Palace Terrace Gardens, was the new Second Church of Christ Scientist, a grand, sombre red-brick building in Byzantine style completed in 1926. Andrews had gone to 'testimony meetings' at the First Church, in Sloane Square, the year before: she was not a formal member, but she used the Reading Room in Notting Hill Gate and 'picked up free copies of used journals and "Weekly Studies" donated by the congregation and given away for free in the front porch'.

Power sketched the First Church, by moonlight and gaslight, in December 1923. More intimately, he drew the studio, which they shared as their workplace. His rendering of the airy space with its rafters and beams and skylights, in swift pencil lines dashing across two pages of his sketchbook, is an architect's excited view, like an indrawn breath. The piano is there, and the table and seats. It didn't stay bare for long. There was an iron stove to keep them warm and Andrews made huge curtains to hang from the high beams, a patchwork of brilliant colours and patterns. She pinned up portraits and landscapes and filled the mantelpiece with old china and brass candlesticks. At the back of the room stood a heavy old carved chest and table, and they worked and ate at the plain plank table on trestles that Power had acquired after the war. In one corner, a real luxury, stood a wind-up gramophone with a large horn, like the one he had bought with his demob money.

The studio was vivid, makeshift and comfortable, defiantly different from the popular model of 'home'. The following January Andrews and her mother went to the Daily Mail Ideal Home Exhibition, two among that year's crowds of three hundred thousand people. To many of those visitors the show seemed a promise of a bright new world, full of striking designs, but at this stage Andrews and Power fiercely resisted the fashionable fusion of art and commercial design:

'Art and Artistic' are catchwords used as Commercial Camouflage.

If you want to get an idea of the Popular Idea of *Art* and things '*Artistic*' go to the Ideal Home Exhibition and read the chit-chat in the popular press.

And Wonder!

And Shudder!

In the summer they stayed in the city, sweltering through the August heat, while thunderstorms rolled over the streets. Power finished at Heatherleys in July but Andrews signed on for another short course, until early November. They were no longer students, and although Andrews had a studio, they had no solid income: Andrews was living on her savings and money from Beatrice, and Power sending his earnings back to St Albans. She remembered being hungry, unable to afford an apple a day, going down to the corner shop where they sold slices of ham and beef for sandwiches, and buying no meat, but

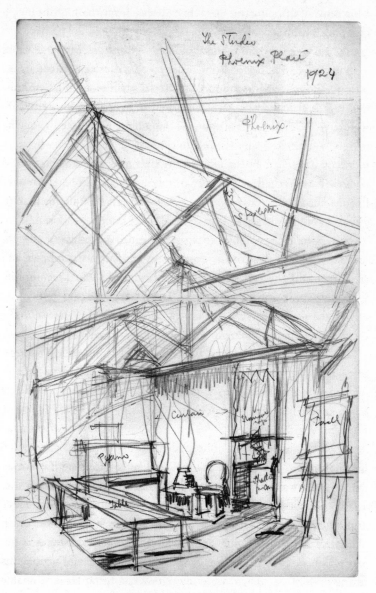

Cyril Power, *Phoenix Place*, 1924

a big bowl of dripping for 4d – it lasted her all week. Making a living became a burning concern.

One answer, they thought, would be to sell prints. Etchings were a good bet, a standby for print-dealers and galleries between exhibitions. Stepping into a Bond Street gallery, the hero of Aldous Huxley's satirical *Antic Hay*, published in 1923, 'found himself in the midst of a dismal collection of etchings. He passed them in review, wondering why it was that, in these hard days when no painter can sell a picture, almost any dull fool who can scratch a conventional etcher's view of two boats, a suggested cloud and a flat sea should be able to get rid of his prints by the dozen and at guineas apiece.'

Writers might scoff, but artists needed those guineas. Andrews and Power, looking at the market for prints among the professional classes and the well-off bourgeoisie, realised that they should exploit their interest in churches, landscapes and old buildings, rather than engage with modernity and machines. First, though, they had to learn to etch.

At Heatherleys Power had become good friends with Massey's second in command, 'Mac', the Scottish artist Iain Macnab. Mac was born in the Philippines where his father worked for the Hong Kong and Shanghai Bank, and spoke Spanish before he could speak English. As a boy, back in Scotland, he wanted to be a professional artist but to please his father he studied accountancy, leaving before his finals in 1914 to enlist with the Argyll and Sutherland Highlanders. His war was grim. Blown up by a shell at the Battle of Loos in 1915, he spent two years in hospital with hideous internal injuries, and on his discharge managed only a brief six weeks at Glasgow School of Art before going into hospital again. (His younger sister Jane, 'Chica', also studied art in Glasgow and taught print-making in the mid-1920s.) There were many other hospital stays later but in 1918 Mac came to Heatherleys as a student. Soon he was on the staff and within six months was deputy principal.

A proud Highlander, Mac came from a line of armourers and engravers, the Macnabs of Barachastlain, and had an intense interest in the past of his clan (and in good whisky). Power liked his energy and humour and understood his irritation with Heatherleys; his own feeling, unlike Andrews' wide-eyed admiration, that Massey was old-fashioned, lazy and full of hot air sounds through some quick doggerel:

> A theorist was H.G.M.
> Who was fractious & peevish & passé
> Work shy, he would slack
> & leave it all to Mac
> To run school, the secretary Cassie.

Mac was an exhilarating friend. Blue-eyed, mischievous, hating pomposity and always unwilling to conform, he was warm-hearted and good company, the kind of man, a friend said, 'you would go to see for half an hour and find yourself talking to three hours later'. But he also had a temper and when roused 'by dumbness or stupidity from people in authority', could flame a pompous bore with scorn 'devoid of tact, and loaded with acid'. In 1923 he was thirty-two, an impassioned promoter of modernism: his chief hero was Cézanne, but he was not doctrinaire – his 1936 book *Figure Drawing* includes examples from Michelangelo, Rembrandt and Rubens to Salvador Dalí and Picasso, Eric Gill and Henry Moore. Like Massey, he emphasised rhythm and harmony, noting how a curving line could bring movement into a print.

He had wanted to be a sculptor but his war wounds meant he could not stand for long hours, and he turned to engraving instead. In October 1922, rather than signing up for a five-year course he bought his own copper, tools and acid, and a book on etching: three months later, submitting six prints, he was elected an Associate of the Royal Society of Painter-Etchers and Engravers. Soon he became a leading figure in the wood-engraving revival of the 1920s.

Wood was no good to Power and Andrews. For their topographical and architectural prints they needed the finer lines of etching, or drypoint. Mac was a skilled printer, happy to give advice on etching processes, 'much easier than drypoint', and happy too, to make trial proofs for his friends. When they were satisfied with these, they took the plates to commercial art printers. In etching, a copper or zinc plate is treated with an acid-resistant wax: when the engraver draws on this with a fine tool, the lines expose the copper beneath. The plate is then dipped in acid that bites into the exposed metal, producing grooves and lines. With the waxy resist removed, the artist then rolls the plate with ink and wipes it off so that the ink remains only in the lines and the heavy weight of the press forces the paper into the acid-bitten grooves, producing the image. Drypoint is slightly different, one of the oldest of all print-making methods, more like drawing, where no acid is involved. This was the technique Power and Andrews used first, transferring their drawing to the plate with tracing paper, or drawing directly onto the copper itself (remembering that the image would appear in reverse when printed). As they cut, the hard, sharp-pointed needle threw up metal on each side of the furrow, giving a soft raised edge, the 'burr', its thickness varying according to the angle of the needle. When they wiped the plate, some ink would remain on the burr so that when the design was printed – using slightly damp paper to mould into the furrows more easily – the lines were softer, more velvety or feathery than in straightforward etching. Often, for effect, they combined the two techniques.

When they began to make prints in 1923, Power turned to the ecclesiastical architecture he had drawn so often. But technically, he was a novice. A view of the high altar in the Anglican church of St Bartholomew in Brighton became a mass of blurry lines – atmospheric but obscure, like an illustration for a ghost story. He went back to Westminster Cathedral, sometimes on his own, sometimes with Andrews or Macnab, and made etchings of the exterior, paying careful attention to the red and white band of bricks and Portland stone, the neo-oriental facade and the Byzantine domes and airy tower (PLATES 8, 9 AND 10). On one page of his sketchbook he drew a dizzying perspective looking down from the tower, with figures trying to dance the Charleston alongside.

There was also an element of the modern and unsettling at Westminster. Between 1913 and 1918, Eric Gill had carved a series of reliefs for the cathedral, of the Stations of the Cross. Gill converted to Catholicism shortly before he began these sculptures and their clear lines and stark colour, white on white with touches of gold, drew conflicting responses, some attacking them as grotesque, cold, hideous, primitive and pagan, others admiring them as dignified and restrained. Something of their hieratic simplicity – itself looking back to medieval sculpture – would come to haunt Power's work. But while Gill raged against the ornate Edwardian decoration and the 'snobbery' and 'pomposity' of the building, Power loved the cathedral's theatrical tone. His prints of the interior, looking up towards the altar, had a mysterious quality, as if he was seeking some spiritual truth that the sharp etching tool would let him reveal.

Power knew, however, that he and Andrews had to earn money. With an eye on the market he made prints of other London churches, and they both etched studies of colleges in Oxford and Cambridge, designed to attract academics and nostalgic former students as well as tourists. In the scorching summer of 1924 they took cheap Sunday tickets on the train and spent a day in Oxford, drawing furiously, and another in Cambridge: 'Finished Christ's Coll. Cambridge, C on All Souls all day', Andrews noted in November.

Beyond London and the old universities, Power engraved scenes of Canterbury: the Norman staircase in King's School and the Tudor gateway to the cathedral close, with its elaborate decoration, niches

Sybil Andrews, *Merton and Corpus Christi, Oxford*, c.1924

and statues. Andrews, meanwhile, worked on landmarks in the East Anglian towns she knew: the Norman Tower in Bury, Wolsey's Gateway in Ipswich and King's School in Ely, with the cathedral behind. From further afield she made prints of the Roman baths at Bath and of 'Scholars Lane' and 'The Olde Grammar School and Almshouse' in Stratford-upon-Avon. In the same faux-antique style, five years later, she printed the 'Old Shambles in Manchester', with rough figures in period clothes.

The prints were sold in batches of thirteen, a baker's dozen, to print shops like Bell's and Forster's in London and to others in provincial towns. On later holidays in Normandy and Brittany, Andrews and Power would find still more subjects for good, selling prints, for tourists and lovers of old buildings. These were accomplished works, full of atmosphere, but nothing marked them out as original or daring. It was closer to home, in their drypoints of London, that both artists came into their own in this medium. In *The Portico, Covent Garden*, Power used dark lines to make the loggia of the market seem a slightly threatening place, standing out against the elegant buildings behind, with boxes and buckets on the ground and porters loading goods and pushing barrows. When he looked beyond the picturesque to the structures of the industrial, commercial city his work acquired an intensity that was distinctively his own. A drawing – or rather an exercise in perspective – of Lots Road Power Station, which they went to see in November 1924, made the building monumental, an almost abstract arrangement of curves and straight lines. Looking up from street level, the great chimneys reach into the sky: on a grid to find the vanishing point, Power marked out the tall windows, gables and sheds, emphasising the building's height by including the terrace houses across the street, with a figure or two to add a touch of human life.

Power liked these unusual viewpoints, from below, or at an angle, so that shadows loom and curve, a pattern of cylinders and cubes – suggesting that he had been looking carefully at the sharp viewpoints, dusky shadows and towering forms of Nevinson's bold lithographs of London and New York from the early post-war years. In Power's *The Goods Siding*, the round concrete pillars catch the light, contrasting with the dark right angles of the bridge and the diagonals of the ironwork. The tapering lines of the rails mirror the wooden planks above and also seem to rise towards them, as if destined to meet on some distant horizon. Here, and in a scene of a railway station with its huge arches, the people seem small, mere tokens of life, dwarfed by the structures around them.

These London railway views were dramatic and highly structured. *The Viaduct*, also from 1924, was an almost abstract composition, with the circle of the viaduct and train casting long shadows down the steep embankments, the curve counterpointed by the opposing bend of the rails beneath. Andrews' *Cannon Street Railway Bridge* has a similar mood: its startling array of dark columns and rails, almost running over our heads as if we should duck, casts shadows on the river beneath and dramatises the act of bridging, as much as the bridge itself. As they became more technically competent, they could be bolder artistically. In both *The Viaduct* and *Railway Bridge*, the atmosphere came partly from leaving a thin layer of ink on the plate, giving a shimmering light that contrasted with the deep, velvety pigments caught by the burr.

Often they explored the alleyways leading down to the old wharves. Sometimes they asked the owner if they could paint in the yards, as Andrews did when she approached 'R. Edy & Co, Wharfingers', who ran their business from the Providence Wharf at the bottom of College Street in Battersea. Permission given, she etched the lorries in the cobbled yard, silhouetted against lamplight. Mac lent them frames, and they showed their prints in Heal's in April 1924 and at the Goupil Gallery in Regent Street that November. They also tried provincial shows and print shops. Power took their drypoints with him on his trip to Liverpool, where the Walker Gallery showed them in their 1924 Autumn Exhibition. That

Cyril Power, *The Goods Siding*, 1924
Sybil Andrews, *Cannon Street Railway Bridge*, 1924

September Andrews had sent prints to Ipswich and a few weeks later was waving a letter, 'saying both framed prints sold & ordering another print of each'.

It seemed that they had found a way to live.

9: WEMBLEY

Phoenix Place was full of oddities. The sofa made of hessian-covered boxes was soon backed by an extraordinary wooden panel, with stylised carvings of figures and birds and crocodiles. Over one corner Andrews hung heavy, woven African fabrics. The carved panel was a prized 'Benin door' from Nigeria, which Andrews and Power bought jointly at the British Empire Exhibition in Wembley in 1924. This sophisticated work, the coded language of a high culture, was glibly labelled primitive in 1920s London. One superb door, carved by the Yoruba master Olowe of Ise for the Ikere Palace ten years before, was bought by the British Museum, but the artist's name was not acknowledged for many years.

The Wembley exhibition – a £12 million, morale-boosting exercise to trumpet the glories of Empire, promote trade and boost increasingly shaky political bonds – was opened by George V on St George's Day, 23 April 1924. After the football stadium rose in the leafy North London parkland, building after building had shot up, using the latest material, reinforced concrete, then styled 'ferro-concrete'. The pavilions in this concrete city, one for each dominion or colony, or group of colonies, used crudely stereotypical forms: towers and domes for India, Arab forts for West Africa, a temple from Burma, Dutch gables for South Africa. Alongside them marched imperial-style palaces of Industry, Arts, Engineering and Government. In the first six-month season, and a second in 1925, twenty-seven million visitors trooped through, paying 1s/6d entrance fee or 9d for children. They gazed at the sights, went boating on the lake, whirled on the roundabouts and roller-coaster, crashed on the fantastically popular American dodgems and queued

The 'Benin door' at Phoenix Place

at the many restaurants run by J. Lyons & Co. (graded from A, posh, to E, 'Lyons' Teashop Service').

Andrews and Power went back at least three times, taking visiting friends or family, including Andrews' young brother Hal, who saw 'many wonderful and strange things' on his first visit and collapsed with food poisoning on his second, carted off to hospital with a crowd of fellow sufferers who had all scoffed Lyons' veal and ham pie. Power loved the funfair – the subject of future prints – and was intrigued by the array of machines, but even more by the structures themselves, the new materials (on his sketches of the Underground, he often scribbles 'ferro concrete'), and the photos of industrial buildings overseas. In his sketchbook he drew the vast grain silos at Fort William and Midland, Ontario, calling them 'The Temple of Ceres'. These fitted his preoccupation with London power stations, gasworks and railway stations, yet the huge tubular columns of the silos, ranged in great rows beside the quays, did indeed look like temples from some ancient land.

Andrews and Power were fascinated by the different cultural traditions on show. They were particularly gripped by the West African display, the 'Walled City' or 'The City of U-em-Bhili', modelled on Kano. This contained the pavilions of Nigeria, the Gold Coast – modern Ghana – and Sierra Leone, with a host of objects made by Yoruba, Igbo, Fulani and Kanuri artists. (Key exhibits were the tall door panels, carved with figures that on closer inspection included caricatures of colonial officials themselves, in pith helmets on motorbikes.) Craftsmen and their families had their own workshops, making and selling their goods in a 'village' within the walls: a bead polisher and his wife from western Nigeria, a potter, silversmiths and weavers from Kano, leatherworkers from the east of the country and woodcarvers from the south.

Exploring the exhibits and workshops, Andrews and Power showed no hint of discomfort at colonial prejudice or public condescension. Yet the programme, entitled 'Races in Residence', made the people themselves into exhibits. The Africans in particular faced racist articles and cartoons in the press, while some London hotels refused to put them up. They protested vehemently, in vain, to the Colonial Office: far from forging bonds, the exhibition became the spark for West African student protests against the Empire. The situation was more complex still with regard to the India pavilion, modelled on the Taj Mahal and Delhi's Jama Masjid mosque. Although Indian troops had fought and died throughout the war, Britain was still refusing India self-government, and nothing had resolved the furious sense of betrayal aroused by the Amritsar Massacre of 1919, when over four hundred unarmed demonstrators, protesting about the suspension of civil liberties, were shot by troops under British command. Several Indian provinces had called for a boycott, yet still the show went on. To Virginia Woolf, the whole of Wembley was a botched attempt to bring the world into a London park and claim sovereignty over it all. Everything seemed packaged and cheap, not only the bread and ham but the avenues of new cars, the machines for crushing gravel, the 'dress fabrics, rope, table linen, old masters, sugar, wheat'. When a summer thunderstorm swept through it was as if the colonies themselves shivered with rebellion: 'Pagodas are dissolving in dust. Ferro-concrete is fallible . . . Cracks like the white roots of trees spread themselves across the firmament. The Empire is perishing; the bands are playing; the Exhibition is in ruins.'

But Andrews and Power were enthralled, most of all by the African pavilion. Since 1900 African sculpture had been a powerful influence on avant-garde European artists: Matisse, Picasso and Modigliani in Paris and Jacob Epstein in London had adapted its stylised forms of the human figure, and had responded, without deep understanding, to its spiritual power. But could Andrews and Power convey the essence of the walled city in prints, ignoring the concrete and the crowds, the Lyons tea houses and the dodgems? They could at least try. In their prints the heavy burr of the drypoint is densely atmospheric. In 'The City of U-em-Bhili', Power made the African pavilion

The Bhuli. Gate. U-em Bhili.   Cyril Power

Cyril Power, *The Bhuli Gate, U-em-Bhili*, 1924

seem like a desert town on the edge of the Sahara, with its walls standing starkly against a black sky, as if lit by the moon. In another print, he drew a figure leaning in an arched gateway as if guarding the entrance to an ancient realm, with embroidered banners hanging from high, sandy walls. Power's subjects were often places of ritual, glimpses of a world beyond, of shadowy places, enshrining secrets. Andrews was more down to earth: she too etched the city's high walls, but also a street within the artists' village, more domestic in mood, with clay houses and thatched huts.

Although they sold some to the commissioner in charge of the Nigerian exhibition, they made few impressions of these prints. Several of Power's early prints, like these Wembley subjects, were deliberately exotic, exploring ritual and faith. He and Andrews had been spending time in the British Museum and reading *The Arts and Crafts of Ancient Egypt* by Flinders Petrie (with whom young Hal Andrews hoped for a job). In 1923 Power etched 'The Temple of Isis', showing a statue of the bare-breasted goddess poised on a flight of steps, high in her square temple, with a kneeling supplicant below and smoke from a torch curling up around her. The first trial print was beautifully printed by Mac, who also produced trial prints of those from the British Empire Exhibition. In one of these, called variously 'The Topaz Mosque' or 'Pilgrims', perhaps inspired by the buildings within the Indian courtyard, Power let his imagination roam, depicting a line of worshippers watching an imam being carried beneath a canopy towards a mosque. The hazy crowds of men suggest a sense of awe, as if individuals are insignificant compared to the mosque and the towering minaret.

Power was always curious about different forms of faith and ritual, reading widely, and, perhaps, keen to travel further beyond Europe. In the small collection of papers handed down to his grandchildren is a brochure advertising trips to Algeria in 1923 and 1924 organised by the Polytechnic Touring Association, attached to Westminster Polytechnic. In thirteen days this would take him to the

Atlas mountains and to Bou Saâda, with excursions to Biskra, Constantine, Tunis and Carthage – but it seems he did not go. He could at least collect some of the crafts on sale at Wembley. He bought the Benin door jointly with Andrews, but in a rush of extravagance he also acquired a carved stool and chest, black pots and an embroidered marriage cloth, while Andrews added a loom from Sierra Leone, complete with yarn, a helmet, and two small curved swords to hang above the fire at Phoenix Place. Their greatest purchase was the door, carved in high bas-relief with heavy scrollwork borders. Andrews could run her fingers over the wood and feel stylised people, birds and animals come alive.

Etching and engraving, Andrews felt, bore a relation to these arts of bas-relief. In years to come, irritated by critics hunting for influences on her linocut, she burst out that she had never seen or discussed these 'influences'. 'The most important for me', she wrote, 'was the Han Dynasty carvings & reliefs in the BM which Power had shown me . . . The simplicity, the lack of fuss – the sense of movement & action which appeared & all that they did has remained vital to me & that must have been 1919 – before ever I went to London to study.' Those brick and stone reliefs (of 200 BC–AD 220), with smooth figures standing out against a rough background, were usually carved as funeral offerings, showing scenes of court life, warriors, peasants and craftsmen, as well as gods and monsters, dragons and lions and the spirits of thunder, rain and wind. Because they were hard to see clearly on the soft stone the Han artists made rubbings, pressing sheets of wet paper into the grooves and carefully inking the surface. To Andrews these were works of art in themselves, forerunners of prints.

Her feelings were close to those of Iain Macnab, who would talk intensely in later life about the recently discovered Lascaux cave in south-western France, where people had cut into the rock face, pressing earth pigments of red, yellow and black into the grooves, creating images of animals and the hunt, full of energy – the first engravings, charged with meaning. Thinking along these lines, Andrews began to see her own work as part of a long tradition, in three dimensions as well as two. Carving was the most potent form of making. Later, when she demonstrated her linocutting, she always referred to the first lines she dug out of the soft lino, not as 'cutting', but as 'carving'.

10: 'THE ART OF TO-DAY'

In May 1924, a month after the Wembley exhibition opened, Andrews was fetching some of her prints from the printer Jo Wilson. She was wearing an odd hat, Dutch-style, with curled-up corners. 'I saw this man,' she said, 'and felt him looking at me, looking and looking, peering right through me.' As he was leaving he said, 'I draw you. You come?' and invited her to his studio. This was the Polish sculptor and print-maker Henry (Enoch Henryk, or Enrico) Glicenstein. Famous in Europe, Glicenstein had gained a gold medal for sculpture at the Paris Exposition of 1900 and had exhibited with Rodin, but then moved to Italy with his wife Helena after winning the prestigious Prix de Rome. In 1921 he came to England, staying for three years. On his arrival, the Ben Uri gallery, founded in Whitechapel in 1915 to help Jewish artists, organised a great celebration and the Jewish community raised funds to help him move, buying several works.

Bearded, bespectacled and forthright, Glicenstein took to Andrews and Power. A week after their first encounter Andrews went round to see him and he etched a portrait of her, laughing, wearing her hat, with one earring dangling and bobbing over her shoulder: not beautiful, but strong, bold, full of life. She hung a copy on her wall at Phoenix Place. Glicenstein's studio intrigued her, full of sculptures, paintings, models, blocks of wood and chunks of marble, and she watched him with amazement, scratching away, 'drawing from life direct on great chunks of copper . . . right off the bat'. He came to supper and met Mac, with whom he got on wonderfully well, and Ba Holloway, whom he sketched in *Antony and Cleopatra* in June. The group saw each other often, and in July he made three sketches of Power. Andrews was grateful for his teaching her drypoint, and for the way he stressed

Henry Glicenstein, *The Laughing Girl*, 1924

the value of cutting, reducing and simplifying form. Like Massey and Macnab, he made her think about her own approach to her art.

At the time, Andrews and Power were thinking hard about the kind of art they admired. This year they wrote a joint manifesto, directed at the Grosvenor students: 'Aims of the Art of To-day'. They were interested in theories of culture, in the works and ideas of Picasso, Braque and Cézanne, talking long into the night, hammering out ideas between them. Their demand for an art 'true to its period . . . reflecting the ethos of today' followed a tradition of manifestos, a marked feature of artistic movements before the war, calling for freedom of expression and rebelling against set conventions. In the wake of the Futurists, Cubists, Vorticists and Dadaists, they adopted the now conventional soapbox tone and iconoclastic rhetoric, if with less confrontational bravado and wit. Writing possibly for a lecture at Heatherleys, they built on the ideas of Roger Fry, amplified in Clive Bell's 1914 book *Art*, a text all art students would know. What is the quality that makes a 'work of art'? Bell asked, couching the question in terms that spoke to Andrews' and Power's interest in the art of the past, from Chinese reliefs to medieval architecture.

What quality is shared by all objects that provoke our aesthetic emotions? What quality is common to Sta. Sophia and the windows at Chartres, Mexican sculpture, a Persian bowl, Chinese carpets, Giotto's frescoes at Padua, and the masterpieces of Poussin, Piero della Francesca, and Cézanne? Only one answer seems possible – significant form. In each, lines and colours combined in a particular way, certain forms and relations of forms, stir our aesthetic emotions. These relations and combinations of lines and colours, these aesthetically moving forms, I call 'Significant Form'; and 'Significant Form' is the one quality common to all works of visual art.

Bell was building on Fry's insistence that in a work of art it is the formal qualities – line, mass, overall design – that condition the viewer's emotional response, and that artists should 'dispense altogether with the idea of likeness to nature, of correctness or incorrectness as a test'.

These ideas appealed to Andrews and Power, but in their manifesto they moved from a purely formalist approach, where the work of art was autonomous, an end in itself, to the idea that art also had a function, communicating some spiritual, social or even political truth. It could not be detached from its context; it had to be integrated and engaged in some way with daily life. Reading works like Wassily Kandinsky's *Concerning the Spiritual in Art*, translated into English in 1914, Andrews annotated and underlined particular passages, on 'the principle of the innermost necessity', the spiritual hunger and the search for pure colour and form that drives the artist to create, and the public to appreciate, art.

Looking round the galleries and exhibitions of early 1920s London, driven by a desire to clear the decks, the two artists rejected the 'progressive' mode of Sickert and the pre-war Camden Town Group, as 'an artificial, false and aggressive imitation Bohemianism' with its scenes of 'unfinished meals, uncooked edibles, compositions of sordid intimicies [sic] emanating from back bedrooms of Camden Town attics'. With equal ferocity, they damned the 'self-sufficient smugness' of Victorian narrative paintings and still-lives: 'Oh! The Tate is full of these commercialised horrors, sentimental sob stuff and misapplied technique gone mad, wonderfully painted but oh so sickly! And superficial.' But while they argued that the Impressionists, transfixed by the search for light, had lost their way in a 'formless, shapeless, Polychromatic haze', they hailed the rise of the post-Impressionists, led by Cézanne, who they saw as seeking solidity in design, pattern in reality. Post-Impressionism, they held, 'went back to Primitive and Essential Form and the study and understanding of it, restoring the 3rd dimension (depth and recession) as part of the design'. And, they added, 'Note that the *Primitive* is always *Modern* and *Eternal*.'

Modern art, they argued, cannot help reflecting the ethos of the time, and although it was outside the scope of their paper, that ethos included ideas developed earlier in the century, notably Freud's theories of the unconscious and Einstein's theories of relativity which changed ideas about space and time for ever. In this new, anxious, fast-moving age they felt art must try to steer a path that would avoid both the 'cult of the crude and ugly' and the 'cult of sugary prettiness'. The railway stations, bridges and power stations that Power had been drawing and they had explored in their London drypoints needed a bold approach: 'True it is an ugly age, judged by the beauty of past periods, but our factories and industrial building have a majesty all their own, a titanic, savage, satanic strength that calls for simplicity and sternness of treatment, and cannot be represented by prettiness and picturesqueness of handling.'

Even in this industrial age, however, the artist must aim to find the 'essence' of a subject. Here their enquiry merged Fry's focus on form and feeling with the search for a deeper truth beneath material reality, a quest that underlay Power's Catholic faith and Andrews' Christian Science belief that surface appearances were mere illusion. It was a question that applied to all arts, neatly phrased by Vaughan Williams in his essay 'The Letter and the Spirit' in 1920:

> . . . may we take it that the object of an art is to obtain a partial revelation of that which is beyond human senses and human faculties – of that, in fact, which is spiritual? . . . The human, visible, audible and intelligible media which artists (of all kinds) use, are symbols not of other visible and audible things but of what lies beyond sense and knowledge.

Clumsily but passionately, Andrews and Power expressed their credo in almost religious terms. Art was not national, or even international but 'Supra National': its spiritual field was global and cosmic, deriving from an ancient language of symbols and patterns that expressed a 'real' substance veiled by material things.

We are 'out' now to search for and try and express *the big things behind outward visible facts*; – the *Eternal Spiritual Reality* behind material things that no camera can give. The Camera has no soul.

We are out to paint what we FEEL rather than what we SEE . . .

The disdain for the camera was one of their blind spots. In the early 1920s pioneering photographers like Man Ray and Dora Maar were using their cameras to create haunting patterns of form, light and movement that certainly exposed a reality beyond the mundane. But at this point Andrews and Power looked firmly at 'art' in terms of canvases and prints and sculpture in the galleries.

Trying to find works in London exhibitions in the past couple of years that expressed feeling, and conveyed an 'essential' truth in the way they advocated, they cited Nevinson's *La Mitrailleuse*, painted when he was on leave from ambulance service in 1915. In this dark close-up of French machine-gunners in the trenches, with the sky above netted in barbed wire, the men with their featureless faces seem as impersonal and mechanical as the gun itself. This work, wrote Andrews and Power, was a brave use of 'savage' technique suited to the brutality of warfare: 'To express the revolting horridness and noisy, incessant vibrating rattle he has used sharp angular shapes and drabby crude colour which hurts to look at.' Looking for other examples of an artist conveying the essence of a scene or subject, they noted 'Van Gogh's *Wheatfield*, a very free and strangely revolutionary way of painting. But you can hear the wind rustling through the wheat stems, and feel the breeze and open air. Or his "Chair". Here you get "form", the "chairness" of the object painted – it has reality and life.'

How could artists reach this essential reality? The secret lay in form. Modern art could convey the dynamism of the age by showing action and movement through 'stressed exaggeration' of lines, shapes, masses and colours. With hindsight Andrews said that from the start she was aiming at 'the personal suppression of the non-essential', and her first interest was 'in the shapes and rhythms and the patterns of things'. This was a shared aim. Among their friends, Mac suggested the same goal in his book on figure drawing, in terms of classical aesthetics 'first propounded by Plato':

That certain arrangements of curved and angular shapes, and of solid and linear form, will give pleasure to the eye, and that the pleasure experienced in contemplating these designs cannot be accounted for by associating them with the visual appearances of natural forms . . .

The pleasure which the artist experiences in drawing from the figure comes first from the perceptual discovery of these abstract qualities; secondly, from their emotive conception in his mind; and thirdly, from arranging his symbols in an ordered design which will exteriorise his conception and make visible his sensations.

Such severity and reduction called for bravery on the part of the artist, Andrews and Power declared: 'The greater the abstract convention the greater is the artistic creation! The further you go from realism, the greater the risk of failure from the popular point of view.' They were ready, almost, to risk all.

From time to time in this manifesto they included personal comments and definitions, marking them with their initials. While Andrews' were emphatic and personal, Power wrestled more coolly with ideas that chimed with those of their friends, Massey, Macnab and Glicenstein:

FORM . . . When we say a work of Art has *form* we mean that it is *instinct with Life*, whether executed graphically in Stone, Paint or Line and in a like measure by musical notes, dramatic characterization, written or spoken word. C.E.P.

. . . The same difference as between a living and a dead object. It is *Reality not Realism*; – by Realism I mean mere imitation or copying. S.A.

RHYTHM . . . is the pulsating arrangement of lines, spaces, masses, colours, emphasis, etc., running through a design or work of Art, which carries the design along and makes it live. C.E.P.

DESIGN. Is the arrangement of the component selected objects, co-ordinated and sub-ordinated and interrelated into a coherent Unity. C.E.P.

The voices weave in and out, Power untangling concepts, Andrews challenging students to think afresh. The dominant voice is hers, displaying the eager impatience and impetuous emphases and capitals that would always mark her writing, as in these questions written for her students in the last decade of her life.

WHAT DO YOU MEAN, UNDERSTAND – BY REALITY

Likeness?

Appearance?

Reportage?

Representation?

A copy?

A photograph?

Descriptive?

All these might be a good picture OF something, but that is not what the creative Artist means by the word REALITY.

REALITY

Is the underlying basic spiritual thought,

the life of the work

the essence,

the heart.

To gain the reality, you are forced to eliminate, give up the material likeness. Shape, detailed drawing is not enough. It is the spiritual content which gives the form.

11: THE GROSVENOR SCHOOL

The studio at Phoenix Place was a welcoming space, a meeting place for friends and for the whole Andrews family when they visited London, as they did on Hal's twenty-first birthday in May 1925. On a clear blue day, as hot as midsummer, after lunch at the Trocadero they went to the Zoo – Hal's favourite place – and had tea at the studio.

Andrews was energetic and happy, and Power had new work to keep him going. As the summer rolled on, he was often in the country, designing and supervising a library extension for Stour Lodge at Bradfield, near his sisters' farms at Mistley: the delivery notes for timber and materials came to him at Phoenix Place. The work carried on for the next four years, and his trips to Mistley gave him great pleasure. One evening at the end of August 1925 he sketched the men at work on the small quay, making notes on the opposite page for a watercolour, with keys to letters on his drawing: the glow of the setting sun on walls and wood, the shadows and reflected light, the shifting colours on the water. 'This was a wonderful effect of pure brilliant colour,' he wrote,

(A) The reflection of the yellow building was molten orange & gold, & the water (B) shaded from pale blue down to deep (B2) liquid blue in the foreground & then (C) faded away to a patch of light at the right hand corner.

Close to this 1 highlight was the patch (D) of Deep Olive Green shadow of the quay walls of Greenish Grey cement & stone.

In the middle of the Reflection (A) was the shadow of pale Grey Green tone.

As Power sketched and painted, he and Andrews were preparing for another move. Early in the year, Mac was back in hospital, 'put out of action by a too vigorous pull at the etching press', spending three months with his back packed in ice. While he convalesced in a nursing home, he decided on a radical change. Having had enough of running Heatherleys for Massey, he would start his own school. He handed in his notice and took a lease on 33 Warwick Square in Pimlico. Then he roped in Power as a lecturer on architectural form and ornament, and architectural drawing, while Andrews came too, as the school secretary – a typical example of the expected roles, which she slowly came to resent. When Mac came back from holiday in Holland in late summer, got the keys and brought the builders in, he wrote briskly to her: 'Have possession & King's merry men are working like Trojans. Could you start in your capacity as Secretary on Monday & inaugurate it by brewing vast cauldrons of stain? & we'll start staining & polishing on Tuesday, if possible?' He had already designed and printed the writing paper with 'The Grosvenor School of Art' in green and the phone number 'Victoria 1972' beneath a logo of a stylised eye and eyebrow.

On 19 October 1925, the Grosvenor School opened. Everything was happening fast, and Power worried about the costs. Thanking him, Mac assured him that he was doing fine: 'I hasten to reassure you that I am watching the expenditure and so far everything (except of course all the King's horses and all the King's men which will amount to more than his estimate owing to extras such as electric lighting, repairs to conservatory &c) is running under scheduled cost.' He had decided against a long lease of twenty-seven years (though in the end he stayed there for much longer) and this left him a reserve of a thousand: 'Of course there is a decidedly sporting element in it all but it's the kind of gamble I like, with the odds in my favour. However I think it's going to pan out well.' Which it did.

The school stood on a corner opposite the neo-Gothic St Gabriel's church, at the end of a long, white-stuccoed Regency terrace, typical of the area. When these Pimlico streets were built by Thomas Cubitt in the 1820s on the marshy land between the later Victoria station and the Thames, the area was planned as an extension of Belgravia to the north, but it was never as popular or smart. In the 1920s, the squares were cluttered with stalls on market day and the streets behind the station were full of small shops, greengrocers and butchers, hardware stores, bakers and bookshops, their awnings hanging over the pavement. Between the shops stood pubs, chophouses and cafes – and artists' studios. No. 33 Warwick Square had its own eccentric gentility. One of the first purpose-built studio houses, built for the Scottish society portrait painter James Rannie Swinton in 1859, it was a curiously shaped mansion, with an almost blank street wall, ending in a brick tower, slanting across the corner of the building. Inside, the house unfolded like a shell. It was big enough to contain Macnab's home and studio as well as a large airy room for life classes with a 'sculpture room' at one end and a 'still-life room' at the other, and printing workshops for etching and lithography in the basement. Students remembered the grand staircase beneath a domed ceiling and the huge conservatory, still with the original glass roof. In 1900 the dancer Isadora Duncan had used one room as a studio, and in the late 1930s, when Mac married the dancer Helen Mary Tench (who performed as Helen Wingrave, using her grandmother's maiden name), the grand ballroom upstairs became her dancing school.

Andrews and Power both moved, separately, to the Grosvenor School, living there and using the studio. 33 Warwick Square was the address on the front of Power's next sketchbook, and he is here on the electoral register for 1926–7. Towards the end of 1925 Andrews left Phoenix Place and moved to rooms at 34 Warwick Square, which also seem to have been part of the school. In a photograph labelled 'my quarters', the long plank table and the Nigerian door are there, and the African weavings and the old blue plates on the mantelpiece. By December, in her office at the school, she was tapping away on a new typewriter in bold blue ink, sending promotional material to organisations and clubs, which she asked them to display 'in a prominent place', and signing her letters with a flourish 'Sybil Andrews, Secretary'. All her drive was needed to get the school underway, and judging by a reference from Macnab a couple of years later (which she typed herself) she did every job that was needed, having been 'entirely responsible for and had complete charge of the office, dealing with all correspondence, advertising and publicity, organising of Lectures and Exhibitions, interviewing of clients and models, the ordering and sale of materials, together with keeping the cash and writing up the books and Registers of the School'. He added that she was absolutely trustworthy and efficient 'and accustomed to dealing with every contingency'.

There were many contingencies to cope with, but to Macnab's relief there was plenty of cash coming in. Admission was open to all, with no entrance test, and students could enrol for any length of time they wanted. As at Heatherleys the set-up followed the flexible French atelier system, and students bought books of tickets for the courses they preferred, day or evening classes in painting, drawing, design and art theory. Like the house with its skylights, winding stairs and glass doors, these courses were fluid and open, in tune with Macnab's declared aim in the prospectus, 'to encourage students to express their own individual ideas rather than be forced to accept worn-out academic theories'. At the same time, however, he wrote, 'to be sure that their ideas are worth expressing, students are made familiar with the basic principles of all Art, whether contemporary or belonging to the past.'

Mac had postcards printed, showing the still-life room, sculpture and painting studios full of keen students. The Australian artist Ethel Spowers, who studied here in early 1929, explained that the chief work took place in the life room, where the hard-working model posed 'from 10–1, from 2–4, and from 4.30–6.30 for quick sketching, and again from 7–9.30 every evening'. The pose stayed the same

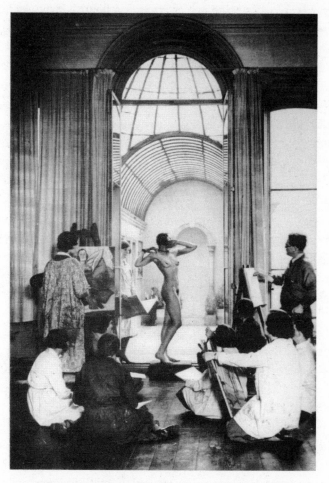

Eileen Mayo posing at 33 Warwick Square, early 1930s

Cyril Power, life study, c.1925

for a fortnight, with students moving their easels around to sketch different aspects. Sometimes students themselves were the models, a way to earn extra cash: a photo from the school's early years shows the artist Eileen Mayo in a determinedly classical pose beneath the airy arches.

Andrews and Power both went to the life classes, and practised life drawing in their studio at Phoenix Place. Power's sketchbooks from this year contain a tender nude study of a young woman. She leans on her arm, her bracelet dangling over her wrist, her thighs and breasts heavy and relaxed, her bobbed hair flicking out at the side. She looks remarkably like Sybil Andrews.

———

At Warwick Square the mood was easy-going. Before classes, students met for coffee in the downstairs drawing room with its long French windows opening on to the conservatory: there were few rules, apart from paying in advance and providing your own materials, although the prospectus did note that 'Students are requested not to talk during classes. The Lounge is provided for the talkative as well as for the hungry.' If you were indeed hungry, the school's restaurant provided lunch, tea and supper at a shilling for students and friends, and dinner for an extravagant three shillings.

One secret of the school's success was Macnab's attitude to teaching. The landscape painter and engraver Guy Malet, who came as a student in 1927, spoke of his incisive advice, patience, charm and 'uncanny, yet apparently effortless ability to draw a student out and inspire keenness to progress'. The painter José Christopherson noted how he guided students to find their own style, 'giving them complete freedom of expression without forcing his own style upon them . . . he ran the school in a free and easy way,' while the wood engraver Gwenda Morgan added that 'he always had a tremendous sense of humour, and he was always encouraging . . . Once a month in the evening there used to be a Sketch Club meeting and students' work was hung in the upstairs ballroom and Mac used to get a well-known artist to come and criticise it. I remember very well one evening when Mark Gertler came.'

The Tasmanian artist William Kermode, who had taught at Heatherleys, came in to teach from time to time, and a succession of speakers gave lectures, including Frank Rutter, art critic for the *Sunday Times* and former curator of Leeds City Art Gallery, who ran a course called 'From Cézanne to Picasso'. The first year went well, with more students enrolling. Life seemed peaceful until May 1926, when Britain was thrown into turmoil. From 3 to 12 May, the General Council of the Trades Union Congress called a general strike, hoping to force the government to stop the cuts in wages for the coal miners whose pay had been almost halved since 1919 and who were currently locked out of the mines. Over 1.5 million workers joined the strike, from Scotland to Cornwall. Special constables patrolled the streets, volunteers ran buses, there were tussles with the police in Southwark and Bermondsey, and the army marched into the London docks. Although the strike was called off after nine days, it was hailed as a triumphant show of workers' solidarity, and three years later the Labour Party under Ramsay MacDonald gained power in the general election. The epicentre was Pimlico. The TUC and Labour Party headquarters, where dispatch riders on bikes and motorcycles gathered to take instructions across the country, were in Eccleston Square, five minutes from the Grosvenor School.

At the end of June London streets were quiet again, and that summer Power jotted down a timetable for a holiday in northern France. They would take Andrews' mother Beatrice, who showed no anxiety about their relationship, and he booked rooms for them in the Hôtel Moderne in Rouen and the Hôtel Chomel in Paris. In his plans for the Paris stay he filled every morning and afternoon with classic sites: Notre-Dame, the Musée de Cluny and the Luxembourg gardens, 'Opera district & shops; aft. Versailles'. It was an exhausting itinerary. This was no Grosvenor School trip in search of modern art – no mention of Picasso or Braque, no avant-garde plays, no trips to see stars like the nineteen-year-old Josephine Baker in *La Revue nègre*. In Rouen, Power's list of places visited included the cathedral and several churches as well as the Musée d'Art Normand. When they arrived, while Beatrice explored the city, they sketched the churches, streets and courtyards and old buildings with their spiral staircases in crooked towers. On this working holiday, they revelled in the markets with their stalls piled with cheeses and charcuterie, eggs and cabbages and beans; in the breakfasts of fresh bread and homemade jam; in Normandy meals of pork and apples and cream; in the scent of coffee and Gauloises from the cafes.

There were other holidays to come. In the spring of 1928 Andrews went to Bruges and Ghent, and in mid-August they both returned to Normandy, this time without Beatrice. Starting at Caen they drifted on to Bayeux and Lisieux and back to Rouen and Le Havre, stopping in small towns and ports along the way. Power made over fifty detailed sketches of subjects ranging from towers and churches to back streets and courtyards. Back home, they used these studies to engrave atmospheric drypoints in which women with their baskets, awnings over market stalls, cafe signs and shuttered windows are as vital to the scene as the great churches that loom behind them. But there was modern life too. Power found contemporary subjects in the ferro-concrete tanks at Mézidon, in the Calvados region, and the art nouveau Gare Rue Verte (now Gare Rive-droite) in Rouen, opened in 1928, with its canopied platforms and overlapping semi-circles of walls, bridge and tunnel.

While the French holidays brought new scenes, London never lost its allure. In 1926 they etched the city's stations, buildings and streets, and the bridges and wharves of the Thames, in a new series of dramatic drypoints. As always, Power sketched as they went, filling one book with rapid, dramatic drawings of cranes at Wapping and boats in St Katharine's Dock, and making several studies of the

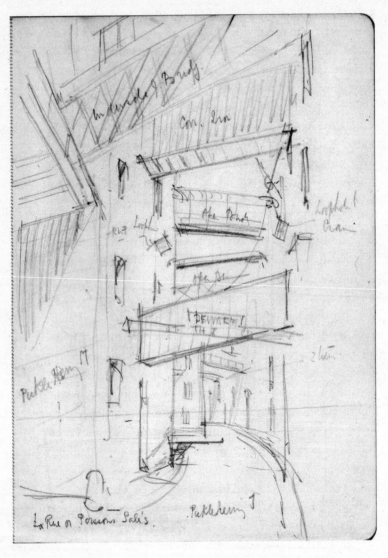

Cyril Power, sketch of Pickle Herring Street, February 1926

Sybil Andrews, *Pickle Herring Street*, 1928

shadows cast by the ramshackle walkways across the narrow alley of Pickle Herring Street in Bermondsey. Andrews followed his drawing closely in her drypoint, *Pickle Herring Street*, one of her favourites, where the tall, angular shadows make the old warehouses look like huge creatures with robotic legs, and the walls slope inwards, driving forward round the cobbled street.

This narrow street of warehouses (lost when the area was cleared in the 1980s, and now the site of City Hall) ran along the south bank of the Thames opposite the Tower of London, as far as the tunnel under the approach to Tower Bridge. Behind it lay Tooley Street, where George Orwell would stay as a tramp in a 'kip' in 1931, writing his notes for *Down and Out in Paris and London*. In their waterside prints, the viewpoint was inevitably from the waterline, on the shore at low tide. We are almost in the Thames, the great artery of the city.

The London drypoints won their first critical acclaim in April 1927, when Andrews and Power showed a selection in the prints section of the Royal Society of British Artists exhibition at the Suffolk Street Galleries. Frank Rutter, who knew them at the Grosvenor School, singled them out in the *Sunday Times*, welcoming Andrews as 'a new woman etcher of conspicuous gifts', admiring her sensitive drawing and 'rhythmic orchestration of light and shade', while Power's print of the railway station, he thought, 'combines in the happiest manner a passionate interest in life which rouses our attention, and that decorative value, due to skilful composition, which holds the attention once roused.' Rutter picked out two other London plates, *The Viaduct* and *The Goods Siding*, as offering further testimony of Power's skill in design 'and his gift of finding beauty amid the turmoil of modern industrial life'. In black and white, they were on their way.

12: THE ARRIVAL OF FLIGHT

In the late summer of 1926 Mac invited a new visiting lecturer to the Grosvenor School: Claude Flight. The following year, Flight joined the staff, his name appearing beneath Power's on the first page of the prospectus. The programme for that autumn included his weekly classes on 'Colour Block Printing': a month for two guineas, or three months for three. Power and Andrews signed up straight away.

Power and Andrews knew Flight's work from exhibitions of the Seven and Five Society and from magazines like *Artwork* and *Colour*, as well as *Ray*, which introduced several European artists to Britain, including Kurt Schwitters, Naum Gabo and Hans Arp. From September 1926 to March 1927 he edited the *Arts and Crafts Quarterly*, running a six-part series on colour linocuts. When he came to the Grosvenor School he was forty-four. Another former Heatherleys student, he had studied art in Paris after the war with his wife Clare, causing a stir as 'the caveman artist' when he bought a Neolithic chalk cave to work in, forty miles from Paris in the cliffs by the Seine at Chantemesle. (The famous cave was the centre of later sketching parties, recorded in cheerful photos of semi-naked artists and students, cavorting with garlands of flowers.) Returning to London, Flight left Clare and his two daughters for the artist Edith Lawrence, his partner for the rest of his life. So far, he had painted oils and conventional watercolours and it was apparently Lawrence, a prize-winning student at the Slade who worked in many media, who persuaded him to try his hand with lino.

Linoleum had been used for flooring since the late 1860s and offcuts were cheap to buy and easy to cut. By the end of the century linocutting was seen as a minor art, a diversion, an afternoon's fun for children, like potato printing. Yet some European artists began to take its possibilities seriously. The German Expressionist Ernst Kirchner made rough-looking black-and-white portraits and landscapes; in 1907 Kandinsky printed mosaic-like scenes of fairy tale and folklore, while his pupil and lover Gabriele Münter cut bold designs in flat, jewel-like colours. Linocuts became associated with innovative work: in 1915 the Russian Cubo-Futurist Olga Rozanova used brilliantly coloured cuts based on playing cards to illustrate abstract, experimental poetry. A year before that, in London, the Australian artist Horace Brodzky started playing with leftover lino scraps instead of wood blocks. He shared the idea with his friend Henri Gaudier-Brzeska, who cut the dramatic, entangled forms of his only linocut, the black-and-white *Wrestlers*, as a card just before Christmas 1914. Months later Gaudier-Brzeska was killed in the trenches, aged only twenty-three.

Flight knew the work of Brodzky and Gaudier-Brzeska, and was also inspired by the Austrian artist and teacher Franz Cižek, who had organised classes for students and schoolchildren at the Vienna Arts and Crafts School. In 1920 linocuts by these children were included in an exhibition at the British Institute of Industrial Art in Knightsbridge, which then toured the country. The following year, Flight made a dizzying linocut, *Swing Boats*, a pattern of fairground curves. In 1922, his linocut *Speed* was hung in the Seven and Five exhibition, and more speeding vehicles, increasingly abstracted, appeared in his *Paris Omnibus* of 1923. Although his work still kept a dynamic Futurist mood, in 1925, the year before he arrived at the Grosvenor, he was also inspired by the great Paris *Exposition Internationale des Arts Décoratifs et Industriels Modernes*. 'Art deco' turned the signature elements of Cubism and Futurism – angles and curves, flat primary colours, geometrical forms and zig-zag flashes – into a language of design. Its influence on Andrews' and Power's own work is evident, although 'deco' was a label Andrews hated. Just as important was the idea that 'decorative art' could inform

Henri Gaudier-Brzeska, *Wrestlers*, 1914

daily life: soon Flight and Lawrence were running their own design business, using their clear, colourful style on everything from murals to pyjamas. They believed, with other avant-garde artists of the inter-war years, that 'art' should not be the preserve of the elite, to be contemplated on gallery walls, but could be integrated with commerce and domestic life: Paul Nash, Ben Nicholson and Barbara Hepworth also designed furniture and rugs. In 1926, an article in *Colour* looked back to Ruskin, who 'did at least make the artist part and parcel of the social system': 'This metaphysical business can be overdone. Art is made of sterner stuff, of more substantial matter. It can and does exist in lower regions, where common mortals dwell and earn their living and where even "trade winds" cannot extinguish the Flame of Genius. Leonardo invented a sausage machine.'

Yet in the mid-1920s 'the attempt to express the spirit of today in terms of harmony and simplicity', as Flight put it, seemed a bold venture:

In England 'the movement' has started . . . We have but to look
at a modern poster to realise how universal is its appeal . . . little
bands of 'modern' English painters are valiantly braving the scorn
and abuse which always assails anything new in their endeavour
to express freely and without restraint, and in terms of their
individual experiences, the collective spirit of the times.

Linocuts, Flight thought, could help to dispel this scorn for the new. Modern architecture and urban living would encourage people to buy prints, works of art small enough to suit a modern flat, and the prints themselves, full of colour and vitality, would make people at ease with modern art, overcoming the notorious philistinism of the British. 'People live in smaller rooms, and the pictures they buy must necessarily be smaller,' he wrote in 1925, 'and the colour print being a simple colour scheme can be chosen to suit the colour scheme of the particular room to be decorated.'

Flight was ahead of the trend. In 1932 *Good Housekeeping* would declare that the 'plain, light-coloured modern wall' was no place for old masters. What was needed was 'a picture bright in colour and composed of simple, pleasing shapes, welded together into a harmonious design. In a word, modern walls require modern pictures.' Yet while linocuts were 'modern' they were also approachable, combining near-abstract design with representation of people at work, playing sport, dancing, running. They both fitted an urban, mechanised world and demonstrated a return to craft, to the unique handmade object. Lino itself was a modern, 'democratic' material, machine-made, efficient, cheap. Linocuts could be sold, Flight wrote airily in 1927, 'if only the interest in and the demand for them could be stimulated, at a price which is equivalent to that paid by the average man for his daily beer or his cinema ticket' – a comment that showed how far removed from a working life he was. The vital 'handmade' element ruled out mass production, and the price of a pint that year was 10d, less than a shilling, while a print usually cost two or three guineas, almost a week's wages for many people.

However impractical, Flight's utopian ideal intrigued Andrews and Power. They were inspired by his classes: 'Claude Flight did good work when he began to teach – being full of beans himself, his students responded to his enthusiasm.' When the Australian painter and print-maker Dorrit Black arrived at Warwick Place in September 1927, she sent a brisk description home:

> He is a small man with very bright eyes, little bits of side-curls, and one feels instantly at one's ease with him. During the summer he lives in a cave in France, a very attractive cave apparently, but still a cave; and in the winter he comes out of his cave to teach lino-cutting to students of the Grosvenor School, and perhaps, elsewhere.

Black stayed for three months before leaving to work with the Cubist André Lhote in Paris. When her fellow Australians Eveline

Syme and Ethel Spowers arrived the following year, Syme said that Flight made them feel immediately at ease:

> Sometimes in his classes it is hard to remember he is teaching, so complete is the camaraderie between him and his students. He treats them as fellow-artists rather than pupils, discusses with them and suggests to them, never dictates or enforces. At the same time he is so full of enthusiasm for his subject, and his ideas are so clear and reasoned, that it is impossible for his students not to be influenced by them.

He was certainly 'clear and reasoned' about the geometric principles he adopted, advocating the use of intersecting lines, circles and triangles, so that the design seemed to radiate out from particular points, 'with one or more of the curves equal to some proportion of the frame'. This, he maintained, created a rhythmic pattern and play of line and curve that gave the work both harmony and dynamism. It was partly this geometric element that led critics of the 1930s like S. C. Kaines Smith to see him as 'the only true futurist that this country has produced'. He had adapted and developed the Futurist aesthetic, Kaines Smith argued in 1934: 'seeing that the effect of kaleidoscope movement achieved by Severini was due to the presence of a geometric rhythm in the arrangement, he has reduced the rhythmical element to rigidly controlled order.'

Andrews and Power took this to heart, covering loose papers and notebooks with precise drawings, using compasses and triangles, angles and squares, showing how lines could intersect or radiate out from a central point. They built on Flight's theories of the way that intersecting triangles and circles could create a harmonious whole, finding something similar in their reading of Kandinsky, who argued that 'Form alone, even though totally abstract and geometrical, has a power of inner suggestion':

A triangle (without the accessory consideration of its being acute- or obtuse-angled or equilateral) has a spiritual value of its own. In connection with other forms, this value may be somewhat modified, but remains in quality the same. The case is similar with a circle, a square, or any conceivable geometrical figure [having] a subjective substance in an objective shell . . .

The mutual influence of form and colour now becomes clear. A yellow triangle, a blue circle, a green square, or a green triangle, a yellow circle, a blue square – all these are different and have different spiritual values.

Flight's emphasis on order and rhythm also fitted the stress they placed on design and simplicity in 'Aims of the Art of To-day'. Other influences overlapped in the designs of Flight and his followers: the bold geometric designs of the Cubists and Vorticists; the contrasting planes and angles of the Russian Suprematists and the abstract, austere Constructivists with their emphasis on the industrial and urban worlds, including Naum Gabo's scintillating, shivering abstract sculptures reflecting the laws of physics. Since the war, a startling new way of seeing movement – and modernity – was also felt in films, still silent, that explored the bounds of the real: René Clair's *Entr'acte* and Fernand Léger's *Ballet mécanique* were both screened in 1924, and so was F. W. Murnau's *The Last Laugh* with its swooping camera work. Three years later Fritz Lang offered a Gothic nightmare of a towering, rushing Futurist city in *Metropolis* and Alfred Hitchcock directed his first great success, the ominous, claustrophobic thriller *The Lodger: A Story of the London Fog*.

There were experiments, too, in their own field of prints, with different techniques. At Heatherleys Andrews had been intrigued when Bill Kermode, another fine wood-engraver, gave a lecture on wood-block printing. This technique, popular since the interest in Japanese colour woodcuts in the 1890s, was slow, tricky work, technically very difficult, involving printing from blocks 'brushed with

Claude Flight pulling a proof of his linocut *Women and Washing*, c.1925
Cyril Power, *Woolpit*, c.1926

a mixture of powdered colours and rice paste'. The introduction to block printing, as opposed to the linear cutting of their drypoints and etchings, was invaluable to Andrews and Power, but this particular art form, which often took decorative or landscape subjects, was already beginning to feel old-fashioned. The *Original Colour Print Magazine* launched in 1924 lasted only three years: in the first issue, readers were warned that the main threat to this art came from works mostly 'printed on linoleum, or by crude and coarse methods' – as if the two were synonymous.

Another Kermode class introduced Andrews and Power to this 'crude and coarse' art. Scrawled across Andrews' diary for Monday 12 February 1923, and long before they met Claude Flight, was a single word: 'linocutting'. In its black-and-white form a linocut worked like a woodcut, with the areas dug out remaining white against the black of the inked surface. In keeping with the schoolroom mood, Andrews made a single print, 'The Chieftain', showing a warrior complete with helmet, shield and beard – 'that was Macbeth, from Shakespeare', she said – while Power cut a Roman centurion. They already knew how to control curve and line.

Power was the first to take lino more seriously. In early 1926, experimenting with the black-and-white style shown by Kermode, he made complex linocuts of buildings, like the beams and gables and bow windows of houses in Lavenham. The physical flexibility of lino let him cut swiftly and easily, and he found that the hand's natural tendency to cut in a curve imparted movement and energy. He liked the roughness of linocut, the way it displayed the hand of the maker so directly. It seemed suited to vernacular architecture, the stoutness of beams, the grain of wood and knobbliness of plaster.

One of Power's black-and-white linocuts was of a cottage on the corner of a village lane, with a steeply sloping roof and a side door under a porch. This was Beatrice Andrews' new purchase. In May 1926 – almost coinciding with the general strike – in a grand auction of a farm and sixteen houses in Woolpit, a few miles from Bury, she bought Lot 6, a fifteenth-century cottage, with a carved oak gable and overhanging beamed front, on the corner of Mill Lane. From the start Power found Woolpit full of promising subjects, such as 'Elmer's Mill', an old post-mill, rotating on its wooden post to catch the wind, leaning like a ship against the rolling clouds. The mill, the cottage and the village were force fields, breathing energy, like the wind, into the lives of Andrews and Power.

13: HAY LANE AND BROOK GREEN

In 1927 and 1928 Andrews and Power were finding their own style, building on their vision of what art should be. Soon they would move into a different artistic milieu, and widen their interests still more. But Power had personal obstacles to deal with, including his family, about whom he worried, intermittently. A couple of years earlier his eldest son Toby had moved to work in the Midland Bank in Letchworth Garden City. Here he felt at home among the families of the original supporters of the Garden City movement – 'quakers, theosophists, arts and crafts stalwarts' – including the printer and book-binder Sandy Cockerell, of the Cockerell Press. But to his surprise, after two years there, 'as a result of a request from my father to the bank, I was transferred to London to enable me to rent a house in North London where my mother, my sister and my two brothers could live while he continued his pattern of artistic life in central London, visiting the family every two months or so'. It's a mark of the ruthlessness beneath Power's genial, easy-going surface that he could move his family so airily without consultation and expect Toby, at twenty-one, to look after the family. All their concerns, to which he closed his eyes, were secondary to his art, to the Grosvenor School, to life with Sybil.

This was the second time Toby's life had been disrupted by his father, and he felt it hard, but in the spring of 1927 he dutifully rented a detached villa in Hay Lane in Kingsbury Green, a leafy North London suburb looking down on Hendon aerodrome. Although Toby's banked-down impatience occasionally filters through, the memoir he wrote in later years is understandably more concerned with his own life and interests. At every stage he paints a picture of his mother as a model of restraint. During these years, he remembered, Power 'was able to finance the family on a minimal and precarious basis. My mother naturally suffered, but without bitterness and never once did I hear one word of reproach.' He and Dolly seem to have viewed Power's absence and fitful interruptions as a trial they had to bear: Dolly did not complain of the latest move, although, rather defiantly, she did name the new house 'St Alban'. One consolation was that the new Catholic church, begun in 1926 and still unfinished, was only three minutes' walk down Hay Lane. Toby was more fervently devout than his father, even taking an early train so that he could go to mass before work at the bank's branch in Fleet Street.

Peggie and Kit were at school, but Power's elder children had moved on, reacting to his absence in different ways. His second son, Cyril, 'Boisie', was perhaps the most rebellious. Seeing that his father could do nothing to help him in any career, in July 1927, aged eighteen, he took an assisted passage to Australia. His plan was to work in a vineyard near Adelaide belonging to an uncle, his mother's elder brother, but it was not a good time to emigrate. Australia was in the midst of the Depression and after a couple of years hunting for work, he gave up and came home to drive buses in England.

———

While Power moved his family like chess pieces, Andrews worked on at the Grosvenor School. She made lifelong friends there, among them the painter and print-maker Ursula Fookes, then in her early twenties, and her mother Amy and aunt Maud. One of Sybil's closest friends, however, Sam Butler, was not a student but a teacher and fine portrait painter who often came into the Grosvenor School to paint. Butler had been an observer for the Royal Flying Corps in Mesopotamia during the war, and was now working in Egypt. In 1927 he was home on leave. This deep but unstated friendship, with a powerful undercurrent of attraction, would last all their lives.

All this, plus Flight's lessons, made the Grosvenor School a lively place to work. There were parties at the Fookeses', teas at the studio and dances at the school. But the school was also a constraint and Andrews needed to feel independent. In 1927, when Power's family were settling down at Kingsbury Green, she began to look for a new studio. On Saturday 8 October, she wrote, 'Moved to B Green.'

Brook Green Studios were in the building of the former Hammersmith School of Art, now converted into seven studio flats, a mile south-west of her earlier studio at Phoenix Place. The flats on the corner of Brook Green Road and Dunsany Road were in a bustling, mixed area. Dunsany Road itself ran down from the shops in Shepherd's Bush to the long, wedge-shaped Green (through which the 'Brook' had once run), with tennis courts, elms and great horse chestnuts. From there she could walk south to Hammersmith and the Thames. Her studio was No. 2, on the ground floor, an airy room with a ceiling fifteen feet high. All the familiar furniture and objects were carted over here. Power drew rapid sketches looking up from below at the mantelpiece with its pewter jug, and a rough sketch for a still-life of a yellow melon, dark blue china and purple and golden glass against a green silk hanging.

They shared the studio, although Power's official address was still 33 Warwick Square, followed by a room in the old Adelphi buildings near Charing Cross. Baliol Holloway, on tour in a season of Shaw plays in Canada and the USA, trying to sell their drypoints to New York dealers on the side, wrote sympathetically to them both, as 'My dear Sybil and Cyril',

How are you both, my dears? I hear that you have got a new studio at H'Smith. I hope it is awfully nice and that you will work most happily and comfortably there. I have an idea that you are both terribly pleased to be on your own again! At least more or less, for I hear that Sybil is still in charge at Warwick Sq.

Andrews was indeed still in charge, although she harboured plans to leave the Grosvenor School, briskly typing up the reference from Mac. She was earning her living, or just about. She had her hair bobbed, and at the end of April 1928 set off to Ghent and Bruges for a week with Ursula Fookes, as a modern woman. It seemed a good time to make changes. But she kept her job at Warwick Square for another year or so, doing office work and going to Flight's classes. She also learned wood-engraving and in 1929 she made three affectionate wood-engravings of Macnab's cat Ferdinand, 'The Grosvenor Cat', cleaning himself diligently in different positions. He was a big tabby, and 'the spot he most preferred', she remembered, 'was the hearth rug in front of the office fire. Macnab used to wear him round his neck like a stole, head & forepaws on one side, tail & back legs on t'other.'

That year, in her office, she painted a large portrait of Power, leaning forward with his hands on his knees: 'It was so easy, he came in about tea-time and just sat down.' She took an old canvas that was leaning against the wall, a painting of a lovely nude. It belonged, she said, to someone on leave from Egypt (presumably Sam Butler) who didn't want it any more, so she turned it over and began. 'Don't you move,' she told him. 'It was a wonderful easy position, so loose and easy. So I said "Don't you dare move", and I kept him there till about 9 pm.' The large portrait hung on her studio walls until her death.

Power went on teaching at Warwick Square and stayed there from time to time. They remained close to Mac and the Grosvenor School, and to Flight, who gave his classes there until 1931. Brook Green brought an extension of their circle, rather than a break.

———

Many of their friends were artists and actors and musicians, but one couple, Cuthbert Greig and Doris Holmes, came from a different milieu altogether. Cuthbert was an economist with an office in

Kingsway, concerned with the growth of credit and on the council of the National Association of Trade Protection Societies, while Doris came from a wealthy Norfolk shoe-making company. At the time both were married to other people, but they were already insepara-ble, living together nearby in Kensington. Eventually, in 1944, they were able to marry. They would remain good friends of Andrews and Power, meeting almost every week over the next few years. Briefly, bolstering her interest in working lives, Andrews thought she should learn about credit herself, writing an earnest list of books.

Brook Green appealed to Power partly as a Catholic district. Its old nickname was 'The Pope's Corner' and the eastern end of the Green was dominated by Holy Trinity Church, built in the 1850s on land donated by Cardinal Wiseman, to cater for the large population of Irish labourers. More important, Brook Green was a city village, full of artists: some became famous, others gave up, many have been for-gotten over time. Artists of different kinds occupied the other studio flats in Andrews' building: Stanley Royle Davies, related to the British Impressionist Stanley Royle, and his wife Elizabeth were in No. 3; John and Idalia Littlejohns in No. 4; and Louis Kasha, the son of a Polish painter, and his wife Mabel in No. 7. Davies and Kasha were both struggling artists who turned to other things, while John Littlejohns taught art at Westminster City School, and Idalia was a well-known figure in the Arts and Crafts world. In 1927 she had just published *Ornamental Homecrafts*, and her other books covered painted fab-rics, gesso, batik, prints and patterns, all subjects dear to Andrews' heart. The most obviously successful resident at the time, however, was Birket Satterthwaite, who came to live here with his wife Ber-tha: he worked in oils and drypoints, exhibited at the Royal Academy, and engraved portraits of Philip Snowden, Labour Chancellor of the Exchequer, and the actors Sybil Thorndike and Nora Robinson.

All these neighbours were trying to make a living through art, and Andrews and Power now found themselves surrounded by crafts-men and artists. The Silver Studio at 84 Brook Green sold designs for wallpapers and textiles to Liberty and Sanderson. The Anglo-French lithographer Ethel Gabain had a studio here, and nearby in Girdlers Road the sculptor, painter and print-maker Leon Underwood, one of the founders of the Seven and Five group, opened his Brook Green School of Art in a former architect's studio in 1921.

Underwood's classes were inspiring, unconventional and informal, attracting outstanding talents: pupils in the early 1920s included Henry Moore, the Surrealist Eileen Agar, and the wood-engravers Blair Hughes-Stanton and Gertrude Hermes. This young, dynamic crowd joined other artists and writers in the neighbourhood for parties and projects, forming the English Wood-Engraving Society in 1925, and producing the short-lived magazine *The Island* five years later. Underwood taught that the command of line was vital, and believed in working fast, getting his students to catch movement and outline at once. His interests were wide and like many artists of the time, he was fascinated by the ritual of different cultures: he travelled to Poland, Iceland, the caves of Spain, and Mexico, and collected superb examples of African, Native American and Mexican art. The primitive outlines of his carved reliefs and sculptures, flat yet mobile, resembled those of Eric Gill and Gaudier-Brzeska, and he was convinced of the spiritual power of art, taking it even further than Andrews and Power in seeing it as a possible replacement for religion. In *Art for Heaven's Sake: Notes on a Philosophy of Art*, he wrote, 'Art alone is capable of satisfying the need of the masses, for whom reality is material and touchable, and also for those outside the masses, for whom reality is immaterial and spiritual.'

These convictions were in tune with those of Andrews and Power, and the move to Brook Green made Andrews in particular want to learn more, to seek out new teachers. Spending what little money she had, she took life classes with the Russian émigré artist Boris Héroys, whose studio was not far away, in Holland Road, and who was then teaching at the School of Art in Chelsea Polytechnic. They met in the summer of 1929, when she was staying in Chelsea for a few weeks.

A man of great charm, enthusiasm and humour, Héroys probably appeared to his students, as his grandson says, 'an exotic, eccentric, bearded middle-aged foreigner'. He came from a military and administrative family of French origins. A forebear, Claude Héroys, one of many professional experts who flocked to the expanding Russian empire, had taught architecture at Catherine the Great's new Academy of Arts: ironically his son, Boris Héroys's grandfather, fought against Napoleon's French troops. Boris himself, like his father and elder brother, became a soldier, Professor of Military Science at the Imperial Staff College and a leading major general during the First World War. He learned to draw, he said, at military schools and at meetings of an amateur club, which held 'evenings of an unconstrained Bohemian character' where guests could draw from life, 'usually from a model in an interesting costume'. (It was his life drawing that most impressed Andrews, and he was known in London for his portraits.)

When he fled Russia after the Bolshevik revolution, crossing the Finnish frontier in the frosty moonlight of New Year's Eve 1918, he carried in his pack, 'instead of a Field Marshal's baton, my old paint box with English water-colours and brushes. Almost my first call in London was at the shop from which these colours came, in order to refill the box.' After a time as head of the White Russian Mission, he enrolled at Chelsea and later joined the staff, giving private lessons on the side. At this time he was in a situation rather like Power's. In 1927, aged fifty, he left his Russian wife to live with his student Dorothy Barkworth, twenty years his junior; it was a lifelong relationship, in London and then in Paignton in Devon. He was a fine artist, respected by Henry Moore and Graham Sutherland, who were both at his farewell dinner when he left Chelsea in 1938. Sybil thought him a superb teacher: 'It was he who really made me realize what drawing was,' she wrote; 'to make a few lines do the work, to feel the form under my chalk.' One tip his son quoted, which she certainly followed, was 'Draw a *bold* line.'

Around the same time Sybil also met the artist Edna Clarke Hall, who worked in a completely personal style in watercolours, pen and ink, lithography and etching. Clarke Hall, like Héroys, was nearly fifty. She had studied at the Slade under Henry Tonks and was one of the talented group around Gwen and Augustus John and Ida Nettleship. She and her husband, William Clarke Hall, were close friends with the poet Edward Thomas (it has been suggested that she is the 'Woman', the muse of his poems). But William opposed the idea of an artistic career and although she had a show at the Chenil Galleries in Chelsea in 1914, after the war the tension took its toll. She was haunted by the atmosphere of Great House Farm, their fifteenth-century, half-timbered house on Upminster Common: it reminded her of Emily Brontë's *Wuthering Heights* and she drew scenes from the novel over many years, dramatising the anguish of Heathcliff and Cathy and the destruction of the wild creative instinct. After she suffered a breakdown in 1919 her husband, with Tonks' help, set up a studio for her in South Square, Gray's Inn. When Andrews met her she had published her first book of poems and had held two exhibitions at Redfern Gallery, prompting *The Times* to call her 'the most imaginative artist in Britain'. Her impressionistic drawings had a passionate, ferocious atmosphere (they have been compared to those of Balthus, or Paula Rego), and she worked fast, as Andrews did, seizing a subject quickly. Very different in subject and style, Clarke Hall matched Andrews in determination and intensity. As with Héroys, her command of line impressed Andrews most. 'Such splendid drawings of utmost simplicity,' she remembered admiringly, 'each line doing all it had to do, and I said to her "How do you *do* it?" And she replied, "it's just practice and practice and practice".'

Surrounded by the artists in Brook Green, discovering inspiring teachers and working at the Grosvenor School, Andrews and Power felt part of a true avant-garde: 'A break away to a fresh awareness . . . a general unfoldment all round.' And in the late 1920s a new era was arriving in their lives with the development of the form that would bring them fame – the colour linocut.

III: MAKING

Cyril Power, *The Giant Racer*, 1930

14: COLOUR

The move from black-and-white drypoint and etching to colour lino-cutting called for clear vision and hard work. The key difference was the need to combine boldness of lines with the idea of blocks. As Andrews remembered it, Bill Kermode's demonstration of wood-block printing at Heatherleys had given her a starting point, 'so I had already been thinking and working in terms of blocks when I met Flight and I immediately saw that his method was what I want-ed for my ideas.' Through Flight, she discovered Franz Cizek's work and books: 'Just up my street, all his big strong lines . . . full of move-ment, so we were all right . . . to see his work was always exciting.' As far as Andrews was concerned, it was 'full speed ahead'.

Flight taught them that when working in colour, they needed a separate block for each tone, and this demanded more stages than black-and-white printing. They made preparatory drawings, first in pencil and then in coloured pencils or crayon to try out the effect they wanted. After planning the overall design and working out how many colour blocks they needed, they had to create separate plans for each block, seeing how these would come together or overlap. Other print traditions, like lithography or colour-block printing, used a whole range of blocks, achieving an almost watercolour effect, but they followed Flight's advice and began simply, starting with only two blocks, progressing to four or five at most. Flight's approach, how-ever, made the design stage more complicated than traditional colour printing because he dispensed with the key block commonly used to outline the main features. Instead, he asked his students to think not in terms of outlines, but of an arrangement of line and mass, produc-ing work 'that builds up block by block to a perfect whole'.

Once they had worked out their designs, Andrews and Power laid out their lino on the bench, then drew, or used carbon paper, to apply their pencilled designs to the block for each colour – perhaps red, blue, yellow, black – remembering that the image would print in reverse. Then they began to cut, or 'carve', using a sharp metal tool. Wooden handles were available to fit interchangeable cutters, but their tools did not have to be specialised or expensive and in Andrews' view the most efficient cutter (something Flight suggested in his first manual, *A Handbook of Linoleum-cut Colour Printing*, in 1927) was the shortened metal strut of an umbrella, sharpened to a point, with a wooden handle attached that would fit into the palm of the hand. After that they used wood-engraving tools, and gouges for larger areas, suggesting texture by stippling and cross-hatching. The areas cut out of the lino would remain uncoloured by the paint.

They made colour tests, keeping careful notes of how the different colours looked together, and what happened when they overlapped. This became a key point for Andrews, who made elaborate colour wheels and charts. Their 'paint' was sticky, shiny printing ink or matte oil colour, sometimes thinned with Vaseline or linseed oil, or (Andrews' preference) squeezed straight from the tube. Sometimes they used both, the shiny ink contrasting with the matte oil. Then they smoothed each block with a gelatin roller. Next, very carefully, they laid a sheet of paper over the block and rubbed it, over and over again, with the hand, or the back of a spoon – this was slow, patient work and as they became more experienced they applied different pressures to give varying intensity of colour. Finally they peeled back the paper and put it over the next coloured block, and so on, until the image came together. Along the way they made proofs, testing various colour combinations. It was easy to make mistakes, to let the paper slip and blur the whole (though they cut a little notch in the corner of the blocks to help keep it steady), and many proofs were crumpled up and thrown in the bin. For the final print, the paper itself was important – Flight recommended Japanese mulberry paper, whose long fibres made it almost transparent yet very strong, and whose sheeny surface held the ink without running or bleeding.

Power's son Kit described his father's technique, which he saw as a teenager on visits to London in the mid-1930s:

> We would have breakfast, then work through, stop for lunch, restart and probably by 9 o'clock I would have made about eight prints. They were all done manually. We would take a piece of Japanese tissue paper and lay it over a block, which we would ink, say, yellow and green and red and blue, with our fingertips, and if you wanted to get it heavier, say a very dark green, you'd use the back of a spoon. We would print one colour after another, usually four colours in all. There'd be a trial copy, and some copies had to be thrown away. It would take a good day's work to get eight copies.

Technical knowledge was vital. But the main point, for Flight, Andrews and Power and the other artists of the Grosvenor School, was that this was something new and direct, demanding boldness and imagination. Linocutting pushed Andrews and Power quickly towards a radical simplicity. Three years before, in a drypoint of *Low Water, Limehouse*, Andrews had composed a relatively busy scene, looking across to moored boats with houses on the quay beyond them, carefully delineating ripples and gleams on the water. In the centre the huge dock rose like a monster from the Thames, with cranes above seeming to touch the clouds. Now, beginning her lino-cutting career by using only a single block, she made a cut of *Lime-house*, homing in on the dock itself, casting aside the details of boats and quay and water. Instead, the print was dominated by texture and pattern: the contrast of rough beams with smooth metal; the opposition of straight lines and curves, shadow and light; the ropes and hawsers holding the scene together, mooring it within its frame.

In another experimental linocut from 1926, using only two blocks, in blue and black ink, she played with stripes and squares, curving

Sybil Andrews, *Low Water, Limehouse*, etching and drypoint, 1923

forms and horizontal bars, quickly grasping the abstract potential of the medium.

If Andrews liked geometry and design, Power was slower, more meditative, more visionary. In 1926 and 1927 his black-and-white linocuts had dramatised the way that shadow and counter-shadow made contrasting images, conveying movement. When he moved to colour he explored this patterning again.

Power began by returning to one of his favourite buildings, Westminster Cathedral, ignoring the elaborate decoration and looking at the light and shade of arches, vaulting and windows. Two years before, on Maundy Thursday, he had made a quick drawing, noting 'Shadow pattern in S aisle Westminster cathedral, Ap. 1st 1926 during Tenebrae. Nave lit up. Aisle and chapel dark'. Shadow patterns always engrossed him, but the Maundy service itself prompted a

Sybil Andrews, *Limehouse*, linocut, 1926

depth of emotion he found hard to express in words, a return to light and life from darkness and despair. Dating back to the monastic ritual of the ninth century, the Tenebrae services, held on the last days before Easter, follow the progress of Christ's Passion from the agony in the Garden of Gethsemane to the Crucifixion and entombment. They are themselves about shadows, as the name makes clear. In the form that Power knew in the 1920s, the services were divided into three 'nocturns', the first with readings from Jeremiah's Book of Lamentations, the second from St Augustine's responses to the Psalms, and the third from Paul's Epistles. With these went Psalms sung to Gregorian chants and polyphonic compositions, from Palestrina and Tallis to modern composers. Held in late afternoon, Tenebrae generally ends as dusk falls. Gradually fourteen of the fifteen candles in the sanctuary are extinguished, plunging the church into darkness, but the last candle is hidden, sometimes behind the altar, sometimes in a special lantern. Then a book is slammed loudly on the floor or on a pew, making a great noise, a *strepitus*, like the earthquake after Christ's death. Finally, when the hidden candle is shown to the people, they leave, in silence.

It was a commitment for Power to begin his coloured linocutting with something that meant so much to him. In *Westminster Cathedral, Evening* he transferred the shadow pattern onto different blocks, cutting bold lines for columns, vaults and window arches and finer lines for the tracery, getting texture from scoring and cross-hatching. First he used three blocks, in ochre, Prussian blue and cerulean, a rich azure blue, emphasising the formal aspects and merging to convey both the shadow and the candle-lit glow across walls and floor. Another version used four blocks, with still greater richness. Then he went further, reducing the image to its essentials, leaving only the outline shapes and one small window, with stairs leading up to the left. In this form he produced *The Crypt*, using only two blocks, so that the shadows fan out on the floor, and the vaults arch above, while the simplified columns stand out against dark alcoves.

Andrews was also noticing how shadows within a building formed abstract patterns. For her first major prints she returned to quite different places that had meaning in their lives, the concert hall and the theatre. The first print, *Concert Hall* (PLATE 11), was of the Queen's Hall in Langham Place, where they heard Stravinsky in 1923 and where they returned often: in 1927 the BBC broadcast its first season of the Proms there, with Sir Henry Wood conducting, and the Berlin Philharmonic gave sensational concerts. The huge hall, built in 1893, could seat 2,500 people. You could get cheap standing-room tickets for 2d or 4d, and standing at the side, looking up, Andrews remembered, 'It was a tremendous sight, the whole place crammed with people – tremendous swirling patterns, with rows of lights, a huge storey swirling up to the next storey.' The repeated curves, she felt, gave a dynamic motion, above the heads of the crowd below.

Andrews left out all the lavish decoration, giving no hint of the painted cupids on the ceiling, the gilt mirrors and portraits of composers, the fountain with goldfish in the auditorium (into which, Beecham said, 'some fascinating young female' fell every three or four minutes and had to be rescued). But the way that the galleries bulged out and then curved back towards the stage still made the scene immediately familiar to concert-goers, and she conveyed its superb acoustics by showing all the levels flowing out from the stage, open to the music like a window to the sky. The grand tier, the gallery and the lines of the ceiling soar up above the stylised audience, ranged in widening rows below. The print succeeds in a different way, as an abstract design, an array of curves, of dark struts and pale triangular shadows. It is clever, a static scene that is somehow full of movement, both fluid and precise. She used four blocks – yellow, light blue, viridian and black – and instead of white oriental tissue, she chose a buff colour, adding warmth to what would otherwise have been a cooler symphony. 'I had been watching the big swirling lines of the upper balconies and the rows of lights and people below,' she explained later. 'I'd been trying to get it in paint and couldn't. And then along came linocuts.'

A rival to Queen's Hall in their affections was the Old Vic, where they knew many of the company and backstage crew. After Toby began working in London, Power often took him there to see Shakespeare. 'We only paid sixpence for what my father called his "radiator stalls", standing in the pit,' Toby said, remembering his father as a constant theatre-goer who became friends with actors like Baliol Holloway, Bernard Miles and Horace Sequiera. 'They were regular visitors to the studio. Once more I was often embarrassed by his loud "bravos". All his life my father quoted widely from Shakespeare and other literary sources.' Years later, Bernard Miles wrote to Sybil, remembering the old days and wondering what had become of her.

The Old Vic had always been a far more intimate, amateurish place than the Queen's Hall, and Andrews' 1929 print, *Theatre* or *Au théâtre* (PLATE 12), reflects this. The colours are warmer, printed in three blocks of orange, viridian and dark blue. The tall columns supporting the gallery (very like Power's arches in *The Crypt*) spring from the centre of the print, with the audience ranged below, in lines of eyes: the viewpoint is on their level, on the edge of the stalls, gazing not at the stage but at the audience and the circling spaces above. The Old Vic closed for nine months in 1927 for modernisation, replacing the gas lights with electricity, mending the crumbling facade, putting in more toilets – before, there was only one for all the stalls and gallery – and reopening triumphantly with *Romeo and Juliet* on Valentine's Day 1928. Meanwhile Lilian Baylis was building a new venue north of the river, a ferro-concrete theatre at Sadler's Wells, which would eventually house the Old Vic's opera and dance. Just as Andrews made a print of the old theatre before refurbishment, so Power drew a flurry of sketches to remember the effect of the old gallery at the Wells: 'Sadler's Wells, before rebuilding 1929.' The theatre was a teacher, as Andrews had said. Both artists used lino to convey drama, making physical space itself a chief actor.

Working in colour was difficult, but when it succeeded the effect was striking, and a range of tones appeared when the different blocks overlapped. To keep track they began to share a 'print book'. This was a simple notebook where they wrote down the date each print was made, the number of trial proofs and numbered impressions, and who they were sold to, adding to the list over the years, the fading pencil overwritten by later biro. It took hours of patient work to create a finished print and although Andrews and Power planned editions of up to fifty impressions, they never finished complete runs in a single go, scribbling notes on colour in the print books to remind them when they wanted to make a new impression. Sometimes they pasted in examples of the colour trials, or the brand of oil paint they used.

But colour was not all. They realised, too, that the spaces were as vital as the blocks. Andrews kept a clipping – still pinned up in her Canadian studio many years later – of an article on composition in the Han dynasty reliefs that Power had introduced her to. 'Open spaces are not voids,' it said. 'They are active participants in the whole pattern.' In tune with this, she cut the blocks to leave parts of her print blank, so that the white of her paper created streaks and dazzling spots of light, throwing the action into relief. Learning about colour also meant learning when to leave it out.

15: THE FIRST SHOW

To begin with, as they continued to experiment, lino was a sideline, an enjoyable challenge. The sign that they were beginning to take it seriously came in early 1929, when they sent a couple of linocuts to an exhibition of the Royal Society of British Artists. It was not until Flight began putting together an exhibition, to open at the Redfern Gallery in early July, that they were really catapulted into action. Flight had been planning this for over a year, asking colleagues, friends, present and former pupils to send in their prints, or to come and make more. The basement studio of the Grosvenor School was heavy with the smell of oil paint and ink and newly cut lino. Japanese tissue paper was stacked in piles, finished prints went to be framed. Everyone compared their work and wondered where their prints would be hung.

Andrews and Power gave some test proofs to Flight and others to Power's son Toby, and then sent their prints to the Redfern. The gallery on the top floor of 27 Old Bond Street had been launched by two well-off men, Arthur Knyvett-Lee and Anthony Maxtone Graham, but by now the driving force was a young New Zealander, Rex Nan Kivell, who had joined in 1925 and was more than ready to promote and push new art. Plausible, energetic and exuberant, he was 'an archetypal outsider – illegitimate, homosexual, self-educated and antipodean'. Born Reginald Nankivell, he constantly reinvented himself and was currently strolling through town as a debonair connoisseur with a grand name, Rex de Charembac Nan Kivell. Although he claimed to have been gassed on the Western Front, he had in fact joined the New Zealand Expeditionary Force in 1916 and served in hospitals and at the New Zealand command depot, a time 'marked by delinquencies such as insolence, stealing and using a travel warrant, and masquerading as an officer'. On leave in London, he pursued his two great interests, antiquarian collecting and modern art. Flight's new linocuts, with their sharp deco lines and bright colours, were right up his street.

It was Knyvett-Lee, however, not Nan Kivell, who invited Flight to put on an exhibition after he saw a linocut show at the Grosvenor School and heard Flight lecture, presenting it as a major launch, the 'First British Exhibition of Lino-cuts'. Flight marshalled his artists and wrote a flyer, a 'Foreword' explaining the novel technique: how the pictures were all hand-printed 'from blocks cut in the common linoleum of our floors', how the oil paint and printing ink were put on the blocks with a roller, and the colour transferred 'by means of rubbing on the back of the paper', how the printed editions were limited to fifty, each numbered and signed – a good investment. 'Having no tradition behind them', Flight wrote,

lino-cut artists are not hampered by any cult of technique, but have invented one of their own which enables them to approach, because of the necessity of simplicity, unity and harmony, nearer to the spirit of their age than is usually found in the work of the older forms.

We who are accustomed to looking to the past for inspiration in our visual arts accept the films and the wireless on their face values, so let us also encourage the votaries of the lino-cut in the perhaps somewhat unusual expression of their experiences in this changing art-world of to-day.

The bravado of that paragraph suggests some nerves.

The exhibition ran from 4 to 27 July 1929. Eager to show the development of lino as an art, Flight included Gaudier-Brzeska's *Wrestlers* and two earlier prints by Horace Brodzky, cut in 1914. In all there were ninety-four linocuts by thirty-three artists and the bulk of the prints were new, produced over the last couple of years, many in response to Flight's classes. Priced between one and three and a half guineas, they were a bargain compared to watercolours, which cost up to £20, let alone to expensive oils. The number of exhibitors was designed to make people feel this was a growing movement and the varied styles showed that all kinds of artists could succeed in this new form. Here, for example, was Polish-born Stanislaus Brien, better known afterwards for his posters for London Underground and Shell; Oxford-educated Julia Mavrogordato, well-bred artist of hunting scenes, dogs and horses; seventeen-year-old Diana Drew, whose *Archer* compressed into a circle seemed disconcertingly strange and primitive. Flight's partner Edith Lawrence showed four prints, her fluid *Skating* standing out against her Cubist landscapes, and Bill Kermode also showed four, cheap at a guinea because they were in black and white. Dorrit Black's work stood out with its rhythm and panache: an acrobat balancing in the air, a Spanish dancer raising her arms to the click of castanets, and naked, Matisse-like dancers spinning against vibrating colour in *Music*, inspired by an evening in London's Dominion Artists Club. There was energy here, a feeling of life in motion.

Flight's own best prints continued his obsession with speed, with a print of racing at Brooklands and a fairground image of swing boats, with elongated figures, high in the corner, pushing the arc of the swing perilously close to the edge. Yet speed was not his only subject. He also showed a scene of men fishing, quiet and still, with diagonal lines of rain cutting across umbrella-carrying figures, and in two more prints, called *Persuasion* and *Discussion*, he showed how linocuts could convey relationships through simplified body language – something Andrews took to heart.

As well as *Theatre* and *Concert Hall*, Andrews showed three very different prints, confident statements of versatility. *Oranges* (PLATE 13) and *Haulers* took up a favourite theme of manual work, while in *Straphangers* (PLATE 14), the most formalised of these early linocuts, printed in June 1929 in red, burnt sienna, cobalt blue and black, Andrews made a pattern of office workers, swinging to work as if in a boat or riding on a crescent moon, the arms of their suits flying up like wings as they cling to the straps of the Tube. The following year she took the formal reduction even further in *Rush Hour* (PLATE 15), showing only the feet and legs and flaring coats of three commuters riding up and down the escalator.

Power's three prints were starker, more daring, and although they were all concerned with the world around him, with building, the city and speed, they seemed governed by a more complex emotional response than Andrews' brisk formal patterns. One was the austere, eerie vision of the shell of the library he was building, a dazzle of diagonals and receding perspectives. The other two prints pointed forward to one of his most potent subjects, the London Underground. But the trains and stations that he had often drawn in his sketchbooks were not yet on show. He was approaching the subject obliquely, concentrating on the stairs and the escalator, the descent into the underworld, the ascent towards the light. In 1927, drawing the spiral staircase leading up from the platform at Russell Square station, he had noticed how the beams of light played on the stairs, the way the corner of each step was hidden as it twisted round the central steel pole with the shadows varying under each rung. In *Tube Staircase* (PLATE 18), delicately printed in yellow, cobalt blue and black, with the pressure in printing varied to suggest the variation of light, the whole spiral seems to twirl slowly in space. In the upper section the handrail on the right has disappeared altogether, making the descent – or ascent – feel still more perilous. Yet there is safety here too, and harmony: the intricate staircase is a Fibonacci spiral, an oriental Tao, balancing dark and light.

Two days after the opening Flight wrote to Dorrit Black: 'People are pouring in and liking it and we've sold 7 or 8 so far, one of Miss Lawrence's and my "Brooklands".' Knyvett-Lee was delighted, 'and hopes to get it taken round the country . . . I really do feel we are on the way now to having a yearly lino-cut exhibition.' In press interviews Flight stressed the points he had made in his book the year before, that this was a democratic art, using a humble material, easily available – there was no need for fine tools. 'Works of Art on Linoleum' was the *Star*'s headline: 'All you need is a knife, rib of umbrella, and a toothbrush.'

Many papers took this up in an amused, condescending manner, as if linocutting were a passing show of fireworks. Some fell back with relief on Julia Mavrogordato's hunting scenes and dogs, naming them, to Flight's irritation, as the stars of the show and even 'quite distinguished little works of art'. Other critics were more impressed, although the mix of representational scenes and geometric designs led to puzzles over the relation of realism to abstraction. In a finicky review in *Apollo*, criticising Flight's *Fishing in the Rain* as too realistic, Herbert Furst noted that 'the difficulty of using a natural scene as a jumping-off board for design is very subtle'. Andrews had 'pulled it off' in *Au théâtre*, he thought,

> but not in 'Straphangers', which looks like a design for a merry-go-round; again, her 'Haulers' are successful but not subtle enough. A good example of the 'trickiness' of this kind of design is Mr. Cyril Power's 'Tube Staircase'; as one sees it, it is almost realistic, and in that sense not quite right; turned upside down, it becomes immediately satisfying as a purely abstract rhythmic design.

Frank Rutter in the *Sunday Times* found no need to turn it upside down, declaring Power's *Tube Staircase* to be one of the most original exhibits and at the same time 'an illuminating and intimate study of the beauty to be found in an aspect of hyper modernity'. The *Star* agreed, singling out *Tube Staircase* and *Straphangers* as 'the very soul of modern London'.

Just as important as the reviews were the sales. In October Flight reported gleefully to Dorrit Black that the show had now sold over a hundred works, with the British Museum and V&A buying four each, though none of hers, he was sorry to say. Working through the Redfern, he felt, was a better route than starting a linocut society as the wood-engravers had done, 'as societies always get stuck & the wrong people get in.'

The following year, when Flight organised the second display of prints, new artists joined the list, including some whose names would always be associated with the Grosvenor School, such as William Greengrass, then working as a museum keeper at the V&A, nineteen-year-old Lili Tschudi from Switzerland, and the Australians Eveline Syme and Ethel Spowers. Another addition to the party was the beautiful Eileen Mayo, now in her early twenties. After graduating from the Slade, Mayo had been modelling for Laura Knight and Dod Procter among others, and for the Grosvenor School life classes. When Flight met her, according to Rex Nan Kivell, he asked her to take part in the next show before she had ever done a linocut, giving her instructions over the phone. The result was the soft and sexy *Turkish Bath*, the first of many linocuts in her long career.

By the time the second show was staged, in July 1930, Grosvenor School linocuts had reached a wide audience. In 1929 the Redfern arranged for the exhibition to tour Britain, and over the next two years it travelled north, to Burton-on-Trent and Blackpool, Manchester, Carlisle and Gateshead, Darlington and Sunderland, where Flight said that over twelve thousand people came to see it, and to Swansea, where the Art Gallery bought prints. A separate exhibition toured cities in the USA in late 1929 and 1930. Then on the shows went, to the Shanghai Arts Club in 1931, Melbourne in 1932, Brooklyn in 1934, Ottawa in 1935, Bucharest, Vienna and Prague in 1936. Linocuts, as Flight had prophesied, were a global hit.

16: WOOLPIT

Sybil had no time or spirit to revel in the success of the first linocut show in 1929. While crowds and critics gazed at the prints in the Redfern, she was at her mother's bedside. Beatrice Andrews had fallen ill the previous autumn, apparently with cancer. The winter of 1928–9 was ferocious, said to be the coldest in Europe since the ice age: the Danube was frozen, snow blanketed the Riviera and wolf packs were rumoured to hunt children in eastern Europe. Over the icy winter and long-awaited spring Beatrice's condition worsened. In late June 1929, seriously ill, she came down to London with her daughter Mike for treatment, staying in a flat by the river in Cheyne Row. For a while she seemed to rally, but by late July it was clear that she was dying. 'Sat up all night with mother,' Andrews wrote on 1 August. She sent a note to Hal, who had gone back to Bury to be with their sister Joy: 'Mother is laying, quiet and peaceful, and her time will not be long now.' For the next few days she took turns with the nurse at the night watch. Slowly Beatrice slipped into unconsciousness. On 7 August, a clear, hot day, Andrews sent a wire to Bury to say that Beatrice had died at 9.45 that morning, 'very peacefully and quietly'. With Mike and Geoff she brought her mother's body home by train. The funeral took place in Bury two days later.

Beatrice had felt that Sybil, of all her children, would understand her love of history and past cultures. In December 1928 – 'her last Christmas', Sybil noted under the inscription – she gave her a copy of *Piers Plowman* edited by Walter Skeat for the Early English Text Society in 1869. The well-thumbed volume, which may have belonged to Beatrice's own father, had many annotations plus occasional pencil translations of the Middle English poem, and scholarly comments comparing the three variant texts: 'There is a remarkable passage here in C but not in B', Beatrice had written, carefully copying out the passage on a separate sheet. The gift placed Sybil in the medieval world Beatrice herself loved, in Langland's 'fair field full of folk' – a world away from the commuter crowds of London, from art deco and the determinedly modern linocuts.

The urge to look back, in reaction to the exhortations to abandon the past in strident manifestos from the Futurists onwards, was felt by many artists, writers and musicians in the inter-war years. This would be increasingly so in the 1930s, when, as the critic Alexandra Harris notes, 'There were church murals, village plays, campaigns to save historic buildings. There were Paul Nash's megaliths, the erotic dramas of Graham Sutherland's landscapes, Vita Sackville-West's old roses at Sissinghurst, Edward Bawden's copper jelly moulds.' With these came a revival of pageants, Cecil Beaton's photographs of his cronies in period dress, Mortimer Wheeler's excavations at Maiden Castle, John Piper's and Myfanwy Evans' photographs of Early English sculptures in rural churches, Vaughan Williams' folk songs – and more. Planning the Shell Guides, on the grounds that 'there are at present no adequate guide-books to any part of England', the young John Betjeman, always tongue in cheek, asked, 'What books are there on Oxford in the seventeenth, sixteenth, fifteenth, fourteenth, thirteenth, eleventh, tenth, ninth, eighth centuries?' and noted that Devon would be a rich subject: 'Devon is still great on witchcraft, I found.' In their backward glance, Andrews and Power were not alone.

———

In her will, Beatrice Andrews stipulated that if Sybil stated within a month that she would like to buy the Woolpit cottage and its contents, it should be sold to her for £250. Drawing on some of the cash and bonds that formed her share of the legacy to all four children, she bought it straight away, without the slightest objection from her siblings.

Andrews and Power both loved Woolpit and so did Hal, whose life became closely bound to theirs. In his mid-twenties Hal was restless, and although he travelled to France and Algeria and would later go to the Levant, the Caribbean and East Africa, his current dream was to live in the open, in wild England. He taught himself to ride and became passionate about hunting, particularly otter hunting – an odd, brutal obsession in a gentle nature lover. On camping holidays, he fell in love with the New Forest and in the year before Beatrice's death had bought a gypsy caravan there, which he called 'the Holt', the name of an otter's den. In the spring he gave in his notice at the bank in Bury where he had worked for eight years. He would have to live simply, he noted in his diary, but 'my real riches will be FREEDOM . . . In future when I enter a bank it will be as a customer not a wage slave.' (The staff gave him a pocket barometer and altitude measurer.) In June he set off to find a new site for his caravan but almost straight away, on 26 June, as his mother grew frailer, he was called back to Bury. When Beatrice seemed to rally, he went back to the Forest and moved the caravan. 'START OF A NEW LIFE', he wrote. It lasted just over a month.

In the weeks after the funeral the Andrews siblings slowly cleared out all the familiar furniture, books and china from the family home in Northgate Street. Most of Mike's and Hal's things went to the cottage at Woolpit, while Sybil's went to London and Geoff took his share in cash. Joy was left in a nearly empty house, echoing with memories, until she rented a flat in the town. On 24 August the house was sold for £1,050. 'The last of 117 Northgate Street,' wrote Hal, 'our home for 20 years.' At the end of September, when Sybil bought the Woolpit cottage, Hal packed up the caravan and moved to Woolpit with Mike. 'Cottage very effective with our furniture, pottery etc, – from home (that was) – and very comfortable o'night with fire going & lamp alight.' They stayed there through an autumn of torrential rain and gales, and Sybil joined them for Christmas. 'Awful day,' she wrote on 21 December, perhaps because of the day's heavy snow, perhaps because it seemed bleak without their mother.

Although they stayed close, the family was scattering. Geoff and Sybil were both living in London. Hal went back to the New Forest in February 1930, setting up his caravan at Puckpits, a clearing in the middle of the woodland, where Sybil stayed with him in late summer, and again in the autumn. Mike stayed in Woolpit until the autumn, when she moved to a house named Lords Waste in another medieval village, Bredfield, near Woodbridge: from late 1934 she ran a cafe in a big department store in Ipswich, becoming a much-loved figure in the city. Until he moved into rooms over the old Andrews and Plumpton shop in Bury in February 1931, Hal stayed in Woolpit over the winters, going back to the Forest or setting off on other travels in the summer.

The Woolpit cottage had two bedrooms upstairs, with 'church windows' and soaring oak beams and rafters, like an upside-down ship, sketched ebulliently in a small watercolour by Power. The sitting room below had a beamed ceiling, a brick and tile floor, an old stove and corner cupboard. Behind it was a scullery with a stone sink and a copper to boil clothes. This was all, plus a small lean-to box room, a brick coal shed and outside lavatory. Andrews noticed, however, looking at the gap beyond the big gable, that there must have been a second gable, destroyed by a fire. Between the two, once forming the centre of a whole house, was another 'poor, lost cottage'. The first time she called there, she said, an old lady opened the door, 'and there – it was a shock – there was a wonderful room, all oak beams – much better than my own . . . I could have bought it for £150 shortly after but where was I to get £150?'

The original house was typical of a village that had grown rich on brick-making for over four hundred years. Pale 'Woolpit whites' were famous, used for local mansions and exported across the country and overseas, with a special tramway built in the nineteenth

Cyril Power, *'Up', Woolpit, c.*1927

century to carry them to the station in the nearby village of Elmswell. Of four brick-making sites known from the seventeenth century, two were still going in the 1920s. Long lines of bricks were stacked up to dry, and the smoke from the small Suffolk kilns – fired three or four days at a time – hung in the air above the trees and fields, wafting across the village on windy days. Between the wars Woolpit had its own school, fire station, police station and four pubs – the Bull, the Ship, the Plough and the Swan – as well as boot-makers and butchers, carpenters and thatchers, blacksmiths and millers. Yet it felt like an ancient place: Roman coins were found here, the stump of a Saxon cross stood in the churchyard, and the village records dated back to the tenth century. Its name was not linked to wool – the basis of so much Suffolk wealth – but to the wolves in the nearby forests.

On the back of a postcard of her cottage on the corner of Mill Lane, Sybil wrote: 'its old name was WULFPETA.' This, she added, meant the place where the king's bailiff paid out a bounty on the head of every wolf brought to him. This was a familiar belief, although the name Woolpit probably derived instead from the warrior Ulfketel (whose name means 'wolf trap'), a counsellor of King Aethelred, who granted the manor to the shrine of St Edmund in Bury in 1005. From the twelfth century on people crowded into the Cow Market and Horse Market in September, and pilgrims prayed at a statue of the Virgin in the chapel of the Blessed Virgin Mary, or Our Lady. There was a family connection here: on a slip of paper Hal recorded that in 1574 'Dame Elizabeth Andrews' had left 'one of her two diamond rings to Our Layde of Woolpit'. Henry VIII ordered the statue removed and the chapel was destroyed, but centuries of gifts had enriched the church, and carved angels still looked down from the decorated hammer beam roof.

Beatrice called the cottage Tyrrells, after ancestors on her mother's side. Her maternal great-grandmother, Anna Maria Browse, born in 1772, was the illegitimate daughter of Edmund Tyrell (or 'Tyrrell') from Gipping Hall, nine miles to the east. In 1931 Sybil and Hal walked over to Gipping to see the manorial chapel built by Sir James Tyrell in 1482, with its flint-work and fine Perpendicular windows and carvings of Tyrell knots. 'Could not go in', Hal wrote, 'but studied the beautiful exterior of Tyrell devices etc.' The name had shadows attached. In 1462, Sir James Tyrell's father William and elder brother Aubrey were executed for conspiring against Edward IV. Forty years later, in May 1502, Sir James himself, a supporter of the House of York in the Wars of the Roses, was executed for treason by Henry VII: during his imprisonment, according to Sir Thomas More, he confessed to the murder of the Princes in the Tower. The shadows stretched even further back, to Sir James's ancestor Walter Tyrell, who shot the arrow that killed William II when they were hunting together in the New Forest in August 1100.

Fascinated by the stories, Andrews made a wooden coat of arms, and a matching one for Power, of the Irish Power family. On his part, Power followed up the Tyrell links in the manuscript of Matthew Paris's thirteenth-century *Historia Anglorum*. Sitting at seat 19, under the great dome of the Reading Room at the British Museum, he copied the Latin account of Tyrell and the arrow, making little sketches of the illuminated borders. Although his own family had no such lineage, for years he had traced the family tree of his wife Dolly, whose maternal forebears ran back to the Roper family and thus to Margaret Roper's father, Sir Thomas More. Power returned on and off to this, exploring church registers and deeds, gravestones and wills. He and Dolly added 'Roper' to the names of their children: in years to come their granddaughters would get into trouble at school for referring to 'St Thomas More', instead of 'Sir Thomas'.

———

Woolpit was a retreat from the city and from the news. Britain's economic recovery after the war had slowed drastically since the disastrous return to the gold standard in 1925 – the exchange rate was so high that this devastated industry, and unemployment soared, especially in the north. Then in October 1929, Europe dived into recession following the Wall Street crash. As countries put up tariffs to protect their trade, British exports collapsed, firms closed and unemployment rose still higher, queues built up at soup kitchens and families were evicted from their homes.

In Suffolk Andrews and Power stepped back in time, away from all this: 1929's Christmas present list included Urquhart's translation of Rabelais and Lord Berners' translation of Froissart's chronicles. At odd weekends and in the summer, they bought pewter jugs, plates and ewers in local markets and ranged them on the oak dresser, with huge pottery flagons underneath. They put rag rugs on the floor, and a year or two later they hung Andrews' unfinished tapestry of St Edmund on the wall, showing the saint, as the story demanded, 'as full of arrows as a porcupine is full of quills'. She began this in 1930, working in Liberty silks on hand-spun, hand-woven linen. Around the figure of St Edmund were other scenes: the wolf guarding the saint's head, the Danes in their longboats, pilgrims with their staves, the abbots in their robes, and a famous needlewoman of the early thirteenth century, Mabilla, 'Mabel of Bury St Edmunds'. It was a work of art, but years later in Canada, when a student admired a photograph, 'Just darning, my dear,' Andrews said.

Inspired with a renewed historical interest at Woolpit, in 1930 Cyril wrote an article for the Antiquarian Association journal, on 'Adventures in Archaeology', intended to woo a new generation of addicts. 'Most people seem to think that archaeology is dry, dull and uninspiring,' he admitted, its study 'the mark of a reactionary mind, one blind to the joys of present day progress and hostile to the trend of current ideas. Fuggy and fogeyish!' This was understandable in the present age, a wonderful period when 'the hectic speeding up in progress, the rapid extension and ramification of scientific knowledge is proceeding at a rate which makes one dizzy.' How could a study of bones, dust and ruins appeal to young people 'dancing through life with pulses racing high'?

Power's answer, echoing 'Art of To-day', was that the 'primitive' is always modern, ever young. Each age built on the past, yet records and remains were constantly being lost or destroyed: it was a duty to record and protect a heritage of which the people of the present were merely the trustees. Cars could now let people travel to more sites and if cameras could help them to record, study would sharpen observation:

> Don't look at these buildings, records, or whatever it may be as a dry, dead specimen like a bottled snake in a museum, but realize that your subject was created by living human beings, was the outcome of human activity, and try and get back to the ethos of the period and picture the lives of the people of the time in your imagination. And you will find it so wonderfully fascinating and stimulating.

In urging others on, Power expressed his own passion: 'There is so much to be done. Think of all the manuscripts which have never been thoroughly examined, Parish registers which have perhaps never been thoroughly searched, Archives of Towns, and Documents in private hands, which may be full of information.'

Immediately before this in the journal, another article, 'The Pyx Veil or Sindon at Hessett', displayed the kind of research he meant, using extracts from wills and parish registers, documents and inventories from across the country. In the middle ages a portion of the consecrated bread was often kept in a pyx, or box of precious metal, suspended by a cord in front of the altar, covered with a long veil (sometimes called a 'sindon'), often with a canopy above, 'something like a cone or umbrella'. The veil belonging to Hessett Church, only two miles from Woolpit – where Dolly Power's uncle had been vicar – was apparently the only remaining example in England.

The conversational style, careful research and confident exposition of ecclesiastical practices, and the heartfelt lament that iconoclasm should have swept away such treasures in the sixteenth century, are typical of Power's writing. Yet the article is signed 'Sybil Andrews'. Later Power crossed out Andrews' name and wrote his own in emphatic capitals. The attribution was probably to evade the ruling against two articles by the same person in one issue, but it was more than that. Just as they sometimes printed each other's work, used each other's sketchbooks ('we often grabbed one another's by mistake', Andrews said) or even borrowed a design, so their names appearing in the same journal acknowledges a shared interest. Andrews, the craftswoman, is present in spirit, to the extent that the article seems written for her, if not by her. The pyx veils, Power suggests, 'must have been lovely specimens of the needle-craft of English women. How sad that so much has perished or been destroyed.' He mentions the embroiderer Mabilla, whom Andrews was currently including in her tapestry of St Edmund, so skilled that she worked a chasuble for Henry III in 1241 and was made a king's pensioner. The article includes an intricate diagram of drawn thread work, dating from around 1440, which is very like the pencilled diagrams of stitches and weaves from across the world that appear in Andrews' scrapbooks and in Power's sketchbooks. This was another of their many shared subjects: from linocutting to historical research, they fired each other's interest, talked eagerly, hunted down examples, tried things out themselves. One reason why they had liked each other so much from the start was their sense of a joint venture, and this deepened over the years: by now they were equals, each bringing their own perception, sparking ideas in the other, spreading their net wide. Exploring craft and pattern, for example, they both drew sketches of stitching techniques and patterns from Turkey, Syria, Palestine, Mesopotamia, as well as Celtic plaitwork, Turkish ceramic designs, African weaving, Persian rugs (including some seen by Power in Liberty's window in September 1920), Arabic counter-change tile patterns, and Byzantine and medieval embroidery.

They had seen the veil together at an exhibition at the V&A, when, Power wrote drily, 'a person came up and vacantly gazed at the Hessett Veil and remarked "Humph! Looks like a Victorian antimacassar!"' For Power and Andrews, by contrast, the veil embodied the faith, passions and pains of the past. It was said, Power noted, that when Mary, Queen of Scots was executed a veil like this was used to blindfold her before she laid her head on the block. His final image was of the veiled pyx swaying in the air, silhouetted against the glowing glass of the east window behind the altar, 'as if the Blessed Sacrament were surrounded with an aureole of glowing radiance.'

17: UNDERGROUND

At the start of 1930 they were busier than ever. One Saturday in March, Andrews wrote, 'printed 36 prints between us', needed for the Redfern's American linocut tour. As they worked, everyday life carried on: trips to the dentist, a flood from a burst pipe, bouts of flu, dinners with Ursula and Amy Fookes, teas and suppers with friends, a string of names: 'Horace', 'Tom', 'Flavia', 'Cuthbert & Doris'. In London they watched the Boat Race, took long walks along the towpath and went upriver to Hampton Court and Kew, where Power made notes on the riotous colours of the rhododendron walk. There were the usual trips to the theatre, the ballet and the cinema. Out of town, there were the weekends and summer stays at Woolpit – blossom in spring, blackberries and elderberries in autumn – and Andrews went down to the New Forest to see Hal in his gypsy caravan. In June 1931 they went to Brittany, filling their sketchbooks with drawings of narrow streets and overhanging houses, Gothic churches and chapels, forts and ramparts and markets, harbours and rocky bays and the grandeur of Mont St Michel across the wide sands.

From time to time, Power caught up with his family. In April 1930 his son Toby, now aged twenty-four, was promoted to a post in Hertford and a few weeks later Power went up to oversee the family's move to the village of Bengeo on the edge of the town. It was now several years since he had left his family, and his children, if reluctantly, had accepted the situation. Yet although the pattern of London life was established, an inner unease in Power seems to surface in his work. With his architect's hat on Power was still working for Lord Iveagh and taking on new commissions, and was also now invigilating for RIBA, the Royal Institute of British Architects, to bring in more cash. One of his first linocuts was *Carcase*, inspired by work in progress on the library extension at Stour Lodge, Manningtree – a pattern of light falling through planks, with beams and shadows forming angles and diagonals that recede into the distance.

There were several periods of intense work, particularly for the summer linocut shows that would impose a timetable on their lives. Visitors seeing their work in exhibitions were faced with a variety of subjects. It was hard to tie Andrews or Power to a single theme: a print of the Crucifixion might appear next to one of show-jumping or a Tube station or umbrellas in a gale. Yet each strand mattered to them in different ways – the London Underground; the physical beauty of the body in riding, swimming, dance, skating, sport; the thrill of speed; the hunt for spiritual meaning – and it's worth standing back to look at these separately, one by one.

————

The films of 1930 included *All Quiet on the Western Front*, based on Erich Maria Remarque's harrowing novel describing the experience of German soldiers at the front. A cluster of works about the First World War appeared, like Remarque's, at the end of the 1920s, among them Robert Graves's *Goodbye to All That*, Richard Aldington's *Death of a Hero*, Siegfried Sassoon's *Memoirs of an Infantry Officer* and Ernest Hemingway's *A Farewell to Arms*. It seemed that ten years had to pass before writers could begin to face the horror of war, trying to make sense of it. Something of that existential anxiety entered Power's drawings and prints. The Grosvenor School had given him a radical change of direction and Flight's teaching had encouraged technical daring that one would never have expected from his watercolours a few years before. In linocuts he found the perfect medium for subjects that had long preoccupied him – railways and stations, light and shadow – re-visioned and intensified so that they seemed to become allegories both of his own doubts and dislocations and of the excitement and unease of the post-war city itself.

For years, the London Underground, known since the late 1860s as 'the Tube', had been a site of experiment, under the partnership of Alfred Stanley, later Lord Ashfield, the jovial, diplomatic Anglo-American who ran the finances, and the shy, brusque, idealistic Frank Pick, at first in charge of publicity and then Commercial Manager. In the late 1920s the web of tunnels expanded rapidly, with lines reaching into the countryside and new suburbs springing up around them. Rush-hour trains were packed – by 1930 Londoners were making twice as many journeys across town as they had in 1914, for work, shopping, leisure. The scale of the expansion made the Tube an icon of modernity, remapping the city from below.

As the network grew Pick brought it up to date with daring designs, hiring the architect Charles Holden to design new stations and replace old exteriors in a streamlined modernist style. In the refurbished Piccadilly station, opened in 1928, the circular walkway below road level glowed with art deco lighting and the banks of escalators became the Underground's showpiece. At 55 Broadway, near St James's Park, the new London Underground headquarters was a towering ziggurat, adorned with Jacob Epstein's Egyptian-inspired sculptures *Day* and *Night* and with bas-reliefs of the winds by artists including Eric Gill and Henry Moore. The sculptors here worked directly on the Portland stone facade, rather than making their works in the studio, inspiring the *Architectural Review* to describe Broadway as 'a Gothic workshop. In Westminster seven good men have been hacking and chipping stone; creating images in the way this sort of thing was done up and down England from the thirteenth to the sixteenth century.' Yet Epstein's 'primitive' sculptures with their mix of Egyptian and Mexican influences, especially the heavy male figure of *Day* embracing a naked boy, shocked Londoners so much that newspapers ran campaigns to remove them. In the uproar Pick offered to resign. The scandal calmed, slowly, so it is said, after Epstein agreed to remove half an inch from the penis of the small naked figure.

Symbolic images like those that inspired Epstein were of huge interest to Power, and the direct carving at 55 Broadway struck a chord with a man who valued pre-industrial craft and had written about English Gothic architecture. But his own vision of the Underground was Gothic in a different sense: a realm without daylight, governed by a hidden, electric power, whose tunnels and stairs turned people in crowds into isolated beings, atoms funnelled through the dark. He found the speed of the trains hurtling through the tunnels with their burden of bodies both exhilarating and disturbing, a darker version of Marinetti's vision of the Tube as foreshadowing a future where men would become 'non-human and mechanical . . . constructed for an omnipresent velocity'.

The formal qualities of life below ground had their own peculiar appeal. Power had always been drawn to curving forms of construction, from circular tanks of gasometers at St Pancras to the mansion blocks behind the Albert Hall, and he found this circling movement in the tunnels and platforms below.

He was fascinated, too, by the interplay of light and shadow, finding patterns even in daily surroundings, from 'Shadow pattern from W.C. Seat turned back' to the shades cast by the jugs above him on a mantelpiece. This feeling permeated his airy *Tube Staircase* and was even stronger in a second Underground print, *The Escalator* (PLATE 20), based on a sketch made at Charing Cross station the year before. The perspective is distorted, receding sharply so that we seem to be sucked into the funnel of the stairs. He had urgently wanted to get this right, as Andrews always remembered:

he wanted the drawing of it so went on the downward direction staircase & turned round & kept going up – !! – trying to maintain position while moving & walking – he looked so funny & people came rushing up & down, 'Oh Sir! Oh Sir! You are walking the wrong way' & he was so annoyed at being interrupted. I laugh now when I think of it.

Cyril Power, 'Pattern Rhythm, Albert Hall Mansions', August 1928

Cyril Power, 'The man who went up the escalator
the wrong way', 1928

In his sketchbook Power drew 'the man who went up the escalator the wrong way', its comedy offset by the unbalanced fury of the small stick figure. It was an enormously bold move to put the escalator smack in the middle of his print, like a Romantic painting of a great waterfall. The colours are yellow, Chinese orange and viridian, and the contrast of red and greenish tints adds to the swooning effect. In the print book Power wrote detailed notes, both on the colours and the pressure that should be applied in particular places to make the tone paler or more intense: graduating the steps, making the ribs of the ceiling deepest in colour and 'edges of man as hard as possible'. What he wanted, he noted, was 'a subtle gradation of values'. The patterns are dazzling, yet in the finished print there's a feeling of danger, heightened by the forward thrust of the dark figure at its foot, like a man in an early gangster movie, desperate to flee his pursuers. But something is wrong – instead of rising, the escalator seems to cascade down towards him, baffling his escape. Nothing resembles it, until one comes to a photograph of people sleeping on the escalator during the Blitz, like a stairway of the dead. It has the feeling that Jinny, in Virginia Woolf's *The Waves*, published in 1931, expresses so powerfully:

'Here I stand,' said Jinny, 'in the Tube station where everything that is desirable meets – Piccadilly South Side, Piccadilly North Side, Regent Street and the Haymarket. I stand for a moment under the pavement in the heart of London. Innumerable wheels rush and feet press just over my head. The great avenues of civilization meet here and strike this way and that. I am in the heart of life. But look – there is my body in that looking glass. How solitary, how shrunk, how aged! I am no longer young. I am no longer part of the procession. Millions descend those stairs in a terrible descent. Great wheels churn inexorably urging them downwards. Millions have died . . .'

She lives, and moves, but among the crowds she is alone, asking, 'But who will come if I signal?'

The unease is even more intense in Power's next escalator print, made for the second linocut exhibition. This time the moving stairs carry a column of faceless, anonymous people, ferried down from the daylight into the hurrying, worrying underground. On a wax crayon sketch of this escalator, at Tottenham Court Road, he wrote: 'The Robottomless Pit, Homo Mechaniens'. As he worked he called his linocut 'The Cascade' and in the show itself, which ran from late July to 23 August 1930, it bore the questioning title *Whence & Whither?* (PLATE 22). The flow of humanity, trailing into the background, with no obvious starting point or destination, seems endless, mindless, almost despairing. Time slows and stops even as the column moves on. The hoops of the ceiling curve like giant teeth and the commuters' dark bodies lean forward, hats tilted down, arms outstretched. Across the assertive central rail, the skyward escalator is empty. Once again Power made insistent notes in the print book: the Chinese orange should be 'heavy on the centre rail, rather medium on figures'; the viridian, too, should be heavy on the rail, and, like the permanent blue, 'pale on roof and steps'. All the focus was on the great central band swooping down from above. The invisible city above is like a pressure on their heads.

He returned again to the Underground in *The Tube Station* (PLATE 21), shown in 1932. He had drawn so many stations in his sketchbooks, noticing the double bands of the roof, the position of the lamps and their reflections, that he could play with the scene with scintillating confidence. He focused on the narrowing perspective, the tunnel circling and retreating, creating a vortex towards the distant vanishing point. In a clever, rhythmic composition the platform sweeps round, widening out from the dark mouth of the tunnel, and as the train rushes out of the frame to the left its red carriages seem to fan out towards the viewer, missing us – but only just. Everything is slightly distorted. The walls curve in with the air of an oriental temple. The shadows on the platform form triangles within triangles, like crowns, while those on the ceiling make a canopy of spikes and clouds, their elegance broken by harsh rectangular signboards. A single figure, perhaps a station guard, waves the train off. We are left with emptiness.

The Underground had burrowed into the psyche of city dwellers. It gave them freedom to move yet herded them like cattle. This feeling had been building for a decade: in 1921 an announcement on a 'stentorphone' during rush hours at Charing Cross, the busiest station, chivvied people on the escalators: 'Please keep moving. If you must stand, stand on the right. Some are in a hurry. Don't impede them.' In a pamphlet of 1924 analysing overcrowding, Lord Ashfield concluded that 'One contributory cause has been the emancipation of women, who are tending to travel as freely as men . . . Another contributory cause is the addiction to pleasure' – too many people going to shops and shows, sporting events and funfairs. Hurry, sex, unfettered women, the lure of pleasure: the Underground was at once a circle of Dante's Inferno and a metaphor for the buried unconscious, a train of dreams and nightmares and unacknowledged impulse. In novels and films it was also an image of the city itself, where people lived in crowds yet were always alone. *Underground*, made by the young Anthony Asquith in 1928, followed the lives of four Londoners, ending in a chase over Lots Road Power Station, which Power had drawn so carefully in his sketchbook. In the opening sequence of Hitchcock's *Rich and Strange*, released in 1931, city workers crowd down to the Tube at the end of the working day, scuffling to get on the train, glimpsing a poster that asks, 'Are you satisfied with your present existence?'

In these prints the whizzing, optimistic spirit of the early Futurist vision of the city has been transmuted into something darker and more mysterious. In 1931, Power reduced this paradox of exhilaration and danger to abstraction in a print called *The Vortex*, where two opposing spirals roll furiously together, like an inhalation of flame, one pulling us into the dark core, the other thrusting us out into the light. A year later, perhaps spurred by his new friendship with the puppeteers John and Doris Bickerdike, Power put some of this confusion into rough verse:

MAN
Puppet!
Dangling!
Decked with gifts of borrowed glory
By external art
whence?
and whither?

Dancing in a frenzied animation
Not with movement of itself
Urged by circumstance external
Taken, for a brief space
from the darkness into light
and then?
Put back in a box.

18: ACTION

The men and women in Andrews' linocuts are robustly physical. They work at great machines, brace umbrellas against a storm, swim in tumbling waves, soar over fences on high-bred horses. She wanted her pictures to be active scenes where there was 'always something *happening*'. Her interest in physical labour, in particular, was part of her rebellion against prettiness. 'The Victorians', she said, 'didn't care for the man with a sledgehammer doing something in the road, doing the hard work of this world.' This is hardly the case, if one thinks of Courbet's *Stonebreakers* or the navvies in Ford Madox Brown's *Work*, or the ideas of Ruskin and William Morris – but in the 1920s, it was true that she was unusual in granting real dignity to men loading lorries or working a heavy machine. She respected the rhythms of manual labour, the balance and strength, the precision and force – the inner dynamic – excited her: 'the curve of the movement, the curve of the machine, the curve of their arms', she said of *Sledgehammers*. 'It's the *action* I am always looking for.'

In *Oranges*, exhibited in the first linocut show in 1929, men carry their boxes of fruit like a line of dancers. They work while dawn breaks, their long shadows curling like ribbons as they carry the heavy crates on their shoulders to the man on the lorry, whose bent back reflects the arched struts above him that would hold the tarpaulin cover. *Haulers*, in the same show, also celebrated manual labour: facing away from the viewer, the men stand in a line, straining as they pull, their bent backs and bowed legs contrasting with the taut, straight lines of the ropes. She was proud of this print: 'See how the rope is held differently by each man,' she said, looking at it again in later life. She wanted to convey the feeling of a scene and the emotions of the characters simply through movement and line. Once, she remembered, a friend looking at her work exclaimed that the figures had no faces: 'I told her, "if you can't get the emotion into the whole body why bother sticking the emotion on the face?"'

In several prints in the first exhibition, she showed the action from behind or from the side, so that the faces are hidden. In *The Winch* (PLATE 16), which she sent to the 1930 show, the single figure is almost at one with his machine. The cogs of the hand-crank, pulling in the cable in the centre, seem to make the whole print turn, as if energy were diffused into the air like the orange bands encircling it. We can't see what the cable is pulling – it could be barrels, or bricks, or steel bars for building, but we can see how considerable the weight is from the tautness of the cable and the way the man's feet are flexed against the floor. Every sinew strains. His whole body leans back, in balance with his partner, in a near-abstract, bending shape. In another print, *The Giant Cable* (PLATE 17), shown in 1931, the tug of forces is even stronger: the men on the ground heave on a straining cable, while those up above wrestle with a huge drum and pull a heavy zig-zag crank. Their heads tilt back, their arms reach forward, orange against their green overalls and the iron base and the drum. Everything throbs with the pulling of gears and levers. The group is a triangle, a rising mountain of effort. She had made a sketch of the men when they were installing a huge cable, to run beneath the streets from Parliament Square to the new Piccadilly Underground station. She remembered watching them, a whole big team, one group after another, as far as she could see, coming across the square from the Houses of Parliament before the cable went underground, all working together: '"*heave* ho", "*heave* ho". We had a chance to see exciting things in those days – and it made you ask questions: *how* do you pull? *how* do you tug?'

She studied the angles, the tension, the movement of muscles. Three years later she showed a different bodily effort in *Flower Girls* (PLATE 23) of 1934, one of her own favourites. Taking her sketchbook, she

Sybil Andrews, *Haulers*, 1929
Sybil Andrews, *Steeplechasing*, 1930

went to Covent Garden and drew the women arriving early in the morning, captivated by their old-fashioned costumes, their Victorian hard hats, shawls and button boots and the way they carried their baskets. In her print she made their bodies flat, almost two-dimensional, echoing the straight lines and hard angles of their legs and arms in the triangles of their patterned shawls and skirts, and the sideways slant of their rectangular feet, planted firmly on the rising steps. Their heavy baskets, by contrast, are round and full, with red tulips spilling out like a song. The tilt of their heads and the stretch of their arms, counterbalancing their load, tell us all we need to know about the strength required as they puff up the stairs in the dawn.

———

The synchronised movements in Andrews' prints of working remind one of the patterns of bodies in dance, or of groups of swimmers in Busby Berkeley movies. Sometimes the solo dance becomes a duet, as with the umbrellas in *The Gale*, sometimes a rhythmic chorus, as in *Winch*. In *The Gale*, the familiar curved bodies are braced against the wind and rain, their feet firmly on the ground. She knew what effect she wanted, writing in her print book about the colour permanent blue: 'keep lower part of first umbrella light as background & graduate to dark. Keep clouds very light to top of picture where they join'.

Another of Andrews' subjects in the second show, in 1930, was horse racing, which became a key theme. She knew its excitement from the point-to point races at Ampton, four miles out of Bury, where the racecourse was on a hillside and the last two fences were pitched on a steep climb. At point-to-points the amateur jockeys rode everything from farm horses to thoroughbreds. The races were on open country with the course marked by flags. Walls, fences and ditches formed the obstacles, not specially constructed jumps, and crowds gathered even if it was windy and wet, bristling with anticipation.

In Andrews' *Steeplechasing* leaping, elongated horses trace the arc of the jump, while the jockeys fly above them. The design, using three blocks of orange, purple madder and deep Prussian blue and reducing the horses to simple black and gold shapes, was brilliantly simple. Later, asking her students to look at the art of different cultures and periods, she stressed how a simplified form could be at once stylised – 'abstracted' – yet recognisable at once:

> Almost every period and every century has looked at life and the world in a different way and using a different convention to express themselves:
>
>
>
> Chinese horses
> Byzantine horses
> Munning's horses
> Assyrian horses
> Greek horses
> Disney's horses
> Prehistoric Man's horses . . .
>
>

All differ, but we know them as symbols of horses.

The following year, she returned to the jump more elaborately, and to the hunt, not the race. *In Full Cry* (PLATE 24) showed horses leaping a country hedge after the yelping hounds. The leading horse is a blackish-green shape, like a cipher: the beauty is in the line, not in accurate representation. The rider's blue coat lifts like wings as he flies off the saddle, peering ahead to see the fox. 'I don't draw the horse jumping,' she said, 'I draw the jump' – the moment of flight. Another print, *Water Jump*, has the same flowing movement, with the black horse rising over the high fence while the leading white horse, formal as a paper cut-out, lands across the dappled water, its lengthened front legs describing the trajectory. Formal details bring the riders alive: their tight, light-coloured jodhpurs, their bowler hats and peaked caps, the tawny underside of their boots as they fly over the fence.

Sybil Andrews, *Water Jump*, 1931

Sybil's brother Hal, who had taught himself to ride, spurred her interest in riding, jumping, on racecourses or across wilder country, and in hunting – not always on horseback. In 1932, Hal wrote a vivid account of cycling out in his green riding clothes to join an otter hunt on the River Brett near Lavenham. As men guarded the river downstream, shouting and brandishing their poles, the hounds closed on the otter. The hunters crossed on the weir-race, 'ankle deep in swirling water with the dark depths of the pool below', tracking their prey to its holt among the branches and roots. When they saw the tell-tale air bubbles rise they thrust in their poles, trapping the beast, with the whole pack baying above, pouncing, tearing and biting.

Hal's account was startling in its ferocity, especially at a time when Henry Williamson's recent novel, *Tarka the Otter*, with its lyrical descriptions of the otters in Devon rivers and horror at the violence of the hunt, had brought an outcry against its cruelty. Something of this ambivalence haunts Andrews' *Otter Hunt* (1933; PLATE 25). The print shares the same powerful centripetal force as *Sledgehammers*, where the men swing their hammers, aiming all their blows at the anvil in the centre. In *Otter Hunt*, with its hint of surrounding hills and rough stubble, the panting hounds form the circle, jaws open, noses twitching at the scent of the prey. The centre is not the glowing fire of a furnace, but the watery hole beneath the tree roots. Among the hunters a single man, in the green of Hal's hunting clothes, looks like a medieval knight, his otter-pole a lance piercing the darkness.

The narrowing circles of these powerful prints are recognisably 'Andrews', like a signature. As a teacher she would emphasise the importance of the underlying structure, 'scaffolding', she called it, or 'bones'. But she also knew how to inject drama and emotion through the use of a powerful focus – the anvil, the dark burrow – or through the drama of the perfect line – the horses in the air. Sometimes, as in *The Bathers* or the swirling orange *Sculls*, the pattern implies the action. Elsewhere geometry and action fuse. *Steeplechasing*, for example, is composed of circular arcs rising and falling within a triangle, with the jump at its base. She contrasted these approaches in a page of notes for students, headed 'Focus Point'. This, she said, means

> That the lines and curves of your design and the tone, especially the dark and light tones, all lead the eye to that point in your picture where the eye comes to rest.
> Usually we find, at that point, the lightest light and the darkest dark.

BUT –

> If the design is not of a pictorial nature but is an IDEA, a THOUGHT, there is no single focus point.

INSTEAD –

> Every line, curve, shape and tone must express the emotion of that idea, that thought.
> Find the curve or line which expresses your thought and build your whole design on that.
> Though the body is made up of joints – action is a curve, one clear curve.
>
> Find the curve of that particular action.

As her hand guided her cutting tool through the pliable lino, Andrews found the curve.

19: IN THE BODY

Walking from Brook Green to the Thames, Cyril and Sybil watched the crews rowing on the river, passing beneath Hammersmith Bridge. The Boat Race between Oxford and Cambridge was always a big day and almost every year they joined the crowds lining the bank, with Andrews fiercely supporting Cambridge, her local city: 'Cambs won boat race', she wrote triumphantly on 21 March 1931. Power made many studies of the crews, particularly when they were practising for the Head of the River race two weeks before the Boat Race. One sketch showed the boat from behind, with the eight rowers trying to synchronise their strokes and the cox in the stern, arms akimbo, urging them on through his megaphone. Everything was rather hard – square heads, square shoulders, knees bent at a tight angle, oars straight.

As he worked, the design became more formal, a pattern on a page. In his print of *The Eight* (PLATE 26), the hardness of the drawings has vanished. The crew urges the boat towards us, working in harmony, utterly in control. The prow and the cox at the rear, even the blades of the oars, are all outside the frame, so that our view homes in on the crew's unity. They lean to each side and their arms are taut: Power catches them just after they have pulled the oars back, swishing above the surface of the water, and are now dipping them in again, ready to pull and begin the stroke. It's all there, in anticipation: the oars sweeping through the water, gradually accelerating, driving their boat forward. Fine orange webs, lines of force in the air, suggest the action of pulling the oar back and then driving it forward again. Power took great care over the printing. For the rowers' shirts he usually left the creamy white paper unprinted, although in a few impressions he printed them lightly in yellow. He wrote notes on the colours: chrome orange, 'Fairly heavy on men, medium pressure on oars'; permanent blue, 'full pressure, pale on backs of men'; pale chrome, 'not too heavy'; Chinese blue, 'rather light pressure except for accents of Heads and Shadows, take care not to make oars too dark'. There is something almost Chinese about this elegant print, but it also has a yearning poetry. As the boat glides towards us into a deeper blue and the black oars curve downwards, the water parts in rays of gold that fan out behind. Everything is in continuous, smooth, fluid motion.

Three years later, Andrews too made a linocut of rowers: *Bringing In the Boat* (PLATE 27). At the time Power had been asked for more prints of *The Eight* for the Redfern's travelling show and they treated their two prints as a pair. In late April 1933, Andrews noted, 'C printed 6 eights, S finished & proofed Bringing in Boat, Putting the Boat away', crossing out both titles in a fit of indecision. Her print shows the oarsmen lifting the boat above their heads to bring it on shore. Like Power's it is a study of working in unison, but with a marked contrast in style and mood. This is not a vision of men in harmony in a watery world, but a version of Andrews' images of men at work, of leverage, co-ordination and stress, all angles, effort and tension. The racing shell, the boat's delicate frame, is a glowing gold in Power's print. In Andrews' it is solid, black against the sky, with the riggers, the metal supports that hold the oars, sticking outward like triangular scaffolding, and a spiky zig-zag of light and space separating the square-headed men with their blue-green kit and their brown legs from the dark silhouette of their partners opposite.

While Andrews offers an essay on strength, Power's response is less mechanical, more musical. He found a magic in the mixed restraint and liberty of rowing and other sports, and he was sensitive both to the elation and to the effort. Moving through the air, over water, across the ground, his sportsmen and women are themselves artists in motion. Sport appealed to his kinetic sense and his delight in rhythm, 'the pulsating arrangement of lines, spaces, masses, colours' that he felt should run through a work of art. He often went to the White City Stadium, a walk of three quarters of an hour from Brook Green, which had cycling and running tracks and pitches for rugby, football, lacrosse and hockey. The Amateur Athletic Association Championships were held there from 1932, and when he printed *The Eight*, Power also made linocuts of women running, hair flying, feet kicking from the blocks in a spurt of dust, their speed evoked in a flare of lines as if the air was rushing past behind them. In another print of 1932, *Acrobats*, he showed the graceful flight of trapeze artists at Bertram Mills Circus, defying gravity.

Like Andrews in her scenes of hunting and racing, Power caught moments of action. The curves that came naturally with the hand's movement in cutting lino suited bodies in motion, a topical theme when sporting events drew huge crowds, and when dance, from ballet to folk and jazz dancing, was growing ever more popular. Several Grosvenor artists took up these themes, in particular Lili Tschudi, whose Redfern prints, sent from Paris and then Switzerland, showed sledging, ice hockey and skiing as well as runners, gymnasts, circus tumblers and the cyclists of the Tour de Suisse. In a list of possible subjects towards the end of their first print book, Power and Andrews jotted down a host of ideas featuring rapid, high, athletic movement: leapfrog, cartwheels, hurdling, long jump, high jump, tug of war, skipping, tennis and 'Palais de dance'.

One of the biggest crazes was for skating. Figure skating had been a centrepiece of the first Winter Olympics in France in 1924, the only event which had a women's category. It was both sport and dance, combining balance, precision and speed, always with a touch of danger. Its synchronised movements could also, at a pinch, be reduced to near-geometric diagrams. In 1921, when the Swedish Bror Meyer, a former Olympic figure skater, published a book of instructions, he illustrated the changing positions with diagrams made with the help of a cinematograph, using the movie camera to catch each action in turn, then freezing them in stills so that individual figures dance before one's eyes, the blades biting into the ice the way a lino-cutter's point forges its circles and lines.

Indoor skating took off in London after the Ice Club opened in Westminster in 1927 (in what is now John Islip Street, just behind Tate Britain). On the opening night the cream of society, in evening dress, left their cars stuck in traffic jams and walked in the rain to get to the club. Hundreds of onlookers were turned away. The club ran glamorous events and hosted the Women's Figure Skating World Championship in 1928 and 1932, with Sonja Henie of Norway as the great star. By the mid-1930s there were indoor rinks in Richmond, Streatham and Hammersmith, with ice dances ranging from the waltz to the tango. Prints of skaters appeared in almost every Redfern show. Power's decorative 1932 trio, *Skaters* (PLATE 46), with their bell-shaped skirts and waving scarves, form blue and green silhouettes against the ice, whirling in circles. Yet he found it hard to get exactly the effect he wanted: it was difficult to print the thin red outlines to their skirts, legs and scarves and to trace the delicate aerial curves of their swishing skates, especially when he tried rubbing the paper with the back of a spoon. Across the bottom of the page he wrote:

Note: the Red does not want to be too heavy or the cobalt too juicy else the green will go dirty; the rubbing mixing the colour too spreading. Wipe the spoon and print the Green girls coats etc first.

   & print the green over red last, all very careful that the red does not spread into the blue or green.

The thrill of ice dance was matched for Power and Andrews by the excitement of opera and ballet. Andrews kept well-thumbed programmes for the 1928 season of Diaghilev's Ballets Russes, and for Sir Thomas Beecham's six-week 'Grand Season of Russian Opera and Ballet' at the Lyceum in 1931. Beecham's programme was a sensation, with striking sets and costumes, starring the veteran tenor

1 Cyril Power, *Air Raid*, 1935

2 Sybil Andrews, *The Star Inn from the back*, watercolour, 1920
3 Cyril Power, *The Star Inn from the back*, watercolour, 1920

4 Sybil Andrews, *Greyfriars*, watercolour, 1921
5 Sybil Andrews, 'The Martyrdom of St Edmund', tapestry, 1930–75

6 Sybil Andrews, *Market Day*, 1936
7 Sybil Andrews, *Sledgehammers*, 1933

8 Cyril Power, 'Westminster, shadow
pattern, 1 April 1926', drawing

9 Cyril Power, *Westminster Cathedral,
Evening*, 1928

10 Cyril Power, *The Crypt*, 1928

ABOVE:
13 Sybil Andrews, *Oranges*, 1929

OPPOSITE:
11 Sybil Andrews, *Concert Hall*, 1929
12 Sybil Andrews, *Theatre*, 1929

14 Sybil Andrews, *Straphangers*, 1929
15 Sybil Andrews, *Rush Hour*, 1930

16 Sybil Andrews, *The Winch*, 1930
17 Sybil Andrews, *The Giant Cable*, 1931

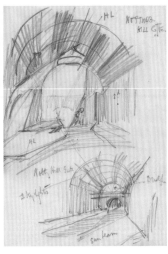

ABOVE:
18 Cyril Power, *The Tube Staircase*, 1929
19 Cyril Power, 'Notting Hill Underground', drawing, 1923

OPPOSITE:
20 Cyril Power, *The Escalator*, 1929
21 Cyril Power, *The Tube Station*, 1932

22 Cyril Power, *Whence & Whither*, 1930

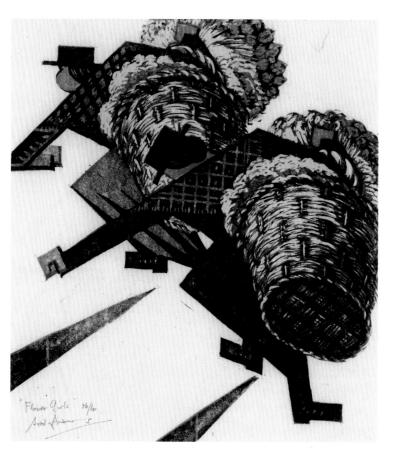

Flower Girls 36/60
Sybil Andrews

23 Sybil Andrews, *Flower Girls*, 1934

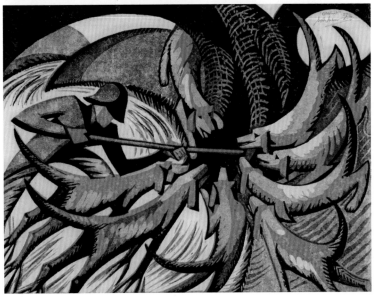

24 Sybil Andrews, *In Full Cry*, 1931
25 Sybil Andrews, *Otter Hunt*, 1933

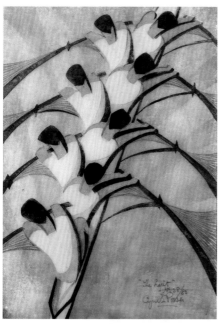

26 Cyril Power, *The Eight*, 1930

27 Sybil Andrews, *Bringing In the Boat*, 1933

28 Cyril Power, *Divertissement*, 1932
29 Cyril Power, *Folk Dance*, 1932

Chaliapin with the Opéra Russe de Paris and drawing over a hundred thousand people. That June, Andrews noted, 'Tried for Igor, but too full'; they soon got tickets, however, and she marked her programme with fierce ticks for Borodin's *Prince Igor*, Mussorgsky's *Boris Godunov* and Rimsky-Korsakov's *Sadko*. Meanwhile Ninette de Valois, who had danced with Diaghilev in the early 1920s, became the choreographer for what was known as the Vic-Wells Ballet. Their first performance was at the Old Vic on 5 May 1931, moving to Sadler's Wells ten days later. With Anton Dolin and Alicia Markova as stars and Constant Lambert as musical director, de Valois showed that dance, too, was a cutting-edge art: her first masterpiece, *Job*, was performed this year, followed by *The Rake's Progress* four years later.

Pioneers of modern dance, reacting against classicism, felt that theirs too was an 'art for today', full of feeling but based on pattern, fluid geometry verging on abstraction. As long ago as 1914, the innovative Margaret Morris had claimed that 'the machine age with all its technical rapidity, efficiency, accuracy and rhythm can also be expressed in beautiful dance movements'. Three years later she said, 'I look at dancing from the visual point of view of the artist, seeing movements as combinations of shapes and lines, and ballets as pictures with the possibilities of actual movement added.' Photographs of set pieces emphasised the line, the circle, the timing, qualities Power acknowledged in two spirited prints. In *Divertissement* (PLATE 28), awash with colour, the heads and torsos of three dancers are framed in the bright circles of their orange and lemon skirts. These flare up behind them as they pirouette against a background of jagged lines, as if wild jazz music is blaring from the band. They dance in a widening funnel of light, springing from the deep V of the dark green on the front of the stage, a bodily language of movement.

Other dance forms caught his eye. Cinema-goers would soon be enraptured by the flawless routines of Ginger Rogers and Fred Astaire, their glamour a release from unemployment and hunger. In the dance halls, throughout the 1920s and 30s, new dances arrived from the United States and Latin America – swing, tango, the one-step, the Lindy hop, the Lambeth Walk – and at the same time there was a revival of folk dance. So Power shared the mood of the times. But there is something odd about his 1932 print, *Folk Dance* (PLATE 29). Instead of the usual flowing forms, he used a hard-edged style and cut out the original background patterns to make it even sharper: '*Note*', he wrote, 'Rays and shadows have been cut away and omitted.'

Still, in *Folk Dance*, as in *The Eight* and *Skaters*, there's a real sense of delight. Andrews had a horror of 'prettiness' and even her beautiful Flower Girls are all angles and elbows. But Power was unabashed: his runners and rowers, skaters and dancers have an easy musical grace, a lyrical charm. His playful prints have a fizz of joy and amusement, due partly, perhaps, to the amazement and awe of a stout, un-athletic man in late middle age – how do they do it? In *Folk Dance* the men in black and blue and the women in black and red dance in couples rather than the traditional sets, squares or rounds: with their bent knees, tapping feet and stiffly angled arms, they seem to be jiving, rather than dancing 'Strip the Willow' or 'The Bonny Broom'. Their stomping, bending, rhythmic movement is at once universal and intensely physical, and supremely modern.

20: FALLING OR FLYING

Power was fascinated, too, by the lure of heights and depths and the scary exhilaration of sheer velocity, in trains and fairgrounds, races and speed trials. The mood of 1929 had been one of wild speculation followed by crash. Power's *Whence & Whither?* had shown a dark line of people gliding down to the depths. But in other prints of the early 1930s he looked up, to elevation rather than descent. In 1929 his sisters' brother-in-law Harold Champness, a partner in the London lift firm of Hammond Bros & Champness, had commissioned him to design an advertisement for the company's new lifts. This appeared in *The Builder* in January 1930, with an acknowledgement to the artist for the 'impression of Modern Lift Speed after his visit to King William St House', which had five of their high-speed lifts. Modifying his advertising design, cutting out the dark blue block he had used to delineate the cables, Power simplified it as *Lifts*. In that print the lifts burst from the depths of the shaft below, rushing up of their own volition, into open space. The air behind, like a jet stream, shows how fast they come. As he developed the work, Power cut even more. Using cheap, thin paper so that he could see the effect when the sheets were placed on top of each other, he printed one proof in green and laid over it a proof with an extra block printed in red, showing a red bar under each step. Feeling this was too heavy for the streamlined effect he needed, he cut the red bars, leaving the green steps floating in space.

The downward and upward thrust in *Lifts* was rendered even keener, more abstract, in a print called *The Giant Racer*. The inspiration was the 'Great Racer' switchback at the Wembley funfair in 1924. But here the ride takes place in pure space, detached from its

Cyril Power, *Lifts*, 1930

original. The car is poised on the top of the fairground ride like a surfer breasting a wave, about to dive into the trough ahead and then swoop up again. Simplicity is key. Power showed the rising curve and the way it descends and curls up again, using only two thin blocks, as if he was drawing with a pen or a brush, adding sweeping curves to ground the ride on its frame and backward waves in the sky to emphasise the forward motion.

He made two more vertiginous fairground prints, based not on the Wembley funfair but the famous Easter Fair on Hampstead Heath. This had been held since the mid-nineteenth century – Karl Marx apparently rode a donkey there, 'with more fervour than skill' – and the crowds grew even greater after Bank Holidays were introduced in the 1870s. Among those crowds in 1927 Power had drawn a pencil sketch of the merry-go-round, like an upside-down spinning top. This was the basis for another 1930 print (PLATE 30). It looks back to Mark Gertler's *Merry-go-round* of 1916, also based on a Hampstead ride. But while Gertler's soldiers and citizens had spun on the old, stately carousel, frozen on their horses amid the horrors of war, Power's roundabout was the aerial 'swing-ride': his peacetime riders are launched into a space that has its own dangers.

The swing-ride was airborne, a 'wave-ride' with the riders in seats suspended by chains. As the top section of the roundabout spun on its central column the chains stretched out almost to the horizontal, and the roof also tilted as it spun. The thrill came from the danger as well as the spinning, hurtling, dizzying sensation. This Hampstead ride can still be seen in a British Pathé film of the late 1920s, with women in gloves holding hard to the chains, reaching up to pull down their cloche hats, their mouths open in delighted shrieks; elsewhere in the film men, women and children slide down the helter-skelter, ride donkeys in the falling dusk, buy lemonade and ice cream, and stream up and down the hill.

Merry-go-round is like a fairground version of the Woolpit *Elmer's Mill*, powered by an engine rather than driven by the wind. The viewpoint is on the ground, staring up from below at the massive, tumultuous sphere. The figures spin in a pulsating vortex of mechanical energy, a frenetic, frantic movement and counter-movement. Like a moving train passing another going the opposite way, the speed appears doubled: the merry-go-round spins to the left and the ground and air spin to the right. The people hang down, tipped to the edge of their seats, or even sailing in mid-air – far higher than the actual seats would go – their forms losing all definition as they cross the centre, flying past the viewer's eyes. Around them, dark tongues of shadow climb up like black flames.

A third print also draws on this London holiday, made famous in 1902 by Phil May's 1902 *Punch* cartoon, 'A Cockney Carnival', where riotous women dance while a balloon-holding child screams as loudly as she can, and, even earlier, by an 1890s music-hall song from Albert Chevalier:

> The toffs may talk of Rotting Row,
> There ain't no place on earth
> Like 'Ampstead, 'appy 'Ampstead for
> To get yer money's worth.
> The bloke as owns the cocoa-nuts
> 'Twon't break yer to support,
> Three shies a penny's wot I calls
> A find old English sport!
> Oh, 'Ampstead!

Power's *'Appy 'Ampstead* (PLATE 32), cut in 1933, with its oscillating back-and-forth dynamic, takes the feeling of being almost out of control to its extreme. The figures seem on the edge of a force field that might fling them into space. Against the tents of the showground behind, the two-seater swing-boats hurtle up and out, down and over, in a double oval of lines, while the scaffolding that supports them is like a skeletal bowl tossing them up and out – almost, one feels, in full circle over the top – as near to flying as you can go.

The urge to go faster and faster was a mark of the time. In the Futurist manifesto of 1909 Marinetti had proclaimed the arrival of 'a new beauty: the beauty of speed. A racing car whose hood is adorned with great pipes, like serpents of explosive breath – a roaring car that seems to ride on grapeshot is more beautiful than the *Victory of Samothrace*.' That belief had rippled through Claude Flight's *Speed* in the early 1920s and in 1928 Flight made a very formal, geometric print of the latest sporting craze, dirt-track racing, an abstract design of enlarged crash-helmet shapes whizzing round a circle. Then he turned to motor racing, with *Brooklands*, celebrating a phenomenon much in the news, the 'Six Hour Sports Car Race', first run in 1927 at the steep-banked Brooklands circuit near Weybridge, south of London, a test of speed, skill and endurance in front of packed, cheering crowds. Many of the drivers were amateurs, like the famous 'Bentley Boys', described as '"race hard, play hard" gentlemen racers'. Flight's cars in their headlong chase suggest intense competition but also the repetition, the endless rounds of the track. The leading car is almost out of the frame and the waves of coloured lines, thick and thin, seem to flicker on the eyes as they roar past. To make the illusion even stronger, he used ultra-thin paper mounted on backing paper flecked with metal, so that the cars seem to shimmer and move, burning the tarmac.

Writing about *Brooklands*, Stephen Coppel, an expert on the Grosvenor School, quotes Marinetti but also, aptly, Evelyn Waugh's *Vile Bodies* (1930), which takes the race track as a metaphor for the ruinous social whirl of the twenties. Speed is, literally, a nightmare, as Agatha Runcible relates her hallucinatory dream after crashing a racing car:

> I thought we were all driving round and round in a motor car race and none of us could stop, and there was an enormous audience composed entirely of gossip writers and gate-crashers . . . all

Claude Flight, *Brooklands*, 1929

shouting to us at once to go faster, and car after car kept crashing until I was left alone driving and driving – and then I used to crash and wake up.

There was something heroic, though, about the Brooklands drivers in their elegant, streamlined cars. In 1929 Brooklands introduced their '500 Mile Race' – the fastest long-distance race on the globe: the drivers, it seemed, were all after records of speed, or distance, or both. Malcolm Campbell, for example, who had raced at Brooklands, was determined to set the world speed record. Power's linocut *Speed Trial* (PLATE 33) depicts Campbell's attempt at Daytona Beach, Florida, on 5 February 1931 where he reached 246 miles per hour in his supercharged 'Blue Bird', with its cowled radiator and aerodynamic tail fin. On his return, Campbell was knighted. The following year he broke the record again, reaching five miles per hour faster.

Power must have seen the pictures that filled the papers, and perhaps the Pathé news feature, where crowds gather on the Daytona sand dunes while Campbell insouciantly explains the virtues of car and crew, and then Blue Bird itself whizzes past with sand streaming behind, a blur as it passes. This is exactly the impression that Power achieves. In his print there are no solid lines at all. The sinuous shape of the car, like a great cat leaping, is conveyed in a series of flowing lines, curling round the wheels and indicating the bump of the driver's head. We feel the speed in the sharp rays above the bonnet and the swoop of the air behind, like a speedboat's wake. The ground too seems in motion, rolling backwards under the wheels, and the colours – blue, green and white, the colours of water – emphasise the fluidity of the whole. Life, like the car, is racing on, sometimes too fast to see.

21: 'OUR LADYE'

In the spring of 1932 Power was working at RIBA, giving evening classes and invigilating, with Andrews writing his appointments in her diary. Meanwhile, in the Brook Green studio both of them were busy: 'hard at linos all week', wrote Andrews in March. The next Redfern exhibition was planned for 21 July, but it was slow work producing the prints and as summer came their schedule intensified: 'finished work at 4.35 am', she wrote on 25 June. At last, on 9 July, they could take the prints in to the gallery. Three days later, they were off to Woolpit. They were back and forth all summer. The freedom and exuberance of their life in the village shone in a water-colour sketch that Power painted of the main street with the church spire beyond. The colours were those of a child's palette: bright red and blue striped awnings over shops, a ladder leaning against a green wall, a hay-cart in a blue shed, an arc of trees mirroring the curve of the street below. The whole village was held in an oval, pulsing with life.

On one long weekend at the end of July, Hal joined them. Perpetually restless, in 1931 he had met the archaeologist Sir Flinders Petrie, hoping to join the team excavating in Palestine, but was told they were short of funds and could not pay his expenses. Later that year he walked the East Anglian coast, pitching his tent along the way and persuading the skipper of a smack to take him on board for weeks of fishing. He belonged to no group, yet his love of camping and hiking was typical of British movements that sprang up in the wake of the First World War, especially the Kindred of the Kibbo Kift – a name from old Cheshire dialect, meaning 'strong'. John Hargrave, known as 'White Fox', had founded the co-educational movement in 1920 as a breakaway group from the Scouts, rejecting Baden Powell's militarism. (The educational wing of the Kindred, the Woodcraft Folk, broke away in turn five years later.) Sybil too was interested in this movement. The Kindred had a strongly pacifist, co-operative, anti-capitalist ethos, promoting the outdoor life and pre-industrial crafts, with the utopian ideal of eventually creating a world free of war and poverty. It was also rife with oddities, loving flags and banners, carved totems, decorated tents and clothes – its members wore Saxon cloaks, used old dialect names and were hot on ceremonies, especially Native American and Egyptian, inspired by an enthusiastic reading of James George Frazer's *Golden Bough* and the classicist Jane Harrison's writings about the ecstatic impulses behind ritual and art.

The Kindred went in for dressing up – and dressing down. Hal would have fitted in. Unselfconscious and theatrical, he loved going without a shirt, having bare feet. In Woolpit in July 1932 he had 'a new garment' made by the tailors of Bury: 'a medieval jerkin of bottle green flannel – zip-fastener & belt – very fine indeed.' He wore this with shorts, bare legs and canvas shoes until the middle of October, feeling that he had 'effected a considerable emancipation from hideous & unpractical modern costume',

> but most of all I have got on to many new subjects and an
> increased & wider interest in old ones, viz. – Symbolism, art, music
> (flute), poetry, history, pre-history, archaeology, social history
> etc . . . . I have also been giving myself Maori rhythmic exercises
> for the middle of the body, & am developing so as to need all my
> breeches etc. to be let out!

Maori rhythmic exercises had little appeal to Andrews and Power, but they were amused and interested in Hal's medievalism and music, his concern for symbol and ritual. When he came over to Woolpit in July the sun shone and they saw kingfishers in the stream and tawny owls in the willows. Hal and Sybil went over to Gipping to see the Tyrell chapel, walking the eight miles there, eating bread and cheese in a sun-soaked field and persuading a cottager to bring them a tray of tea to drink on a bench in the churchyard. In the next few days the rain set in, but still, Hal wrote, 'We have been very busy & keen on finding out the history of Woolpit, & connecting it with prehistory via the Holy Well.' In a field north of the church a perpetual spring, the Ladywell, bubbled with clear, cold water known for its healing powers, strengthening weak children, good for the eyes, rich in sulphates. (Tracking down another holy well, 'Our Lady of the Sacred Grove', a natural spring at the nearby village of Badley, Hal crowed with delight at 'a pond shaped like a *phallic symbol*!') In her diary, Sybil put their investigation briskly: 'To Our-Ladye's well. Explored field.' But when she remembered it in later life, she explained how they had searched for the well and found it 'in one corner of the little field, much trampled by cows – so unrecognisable', imagining a much greater flow of water in the spring in past days. 'In the moonlight it was magical,' she wrote, '– a little amphitheatre, remains of a moat, surrounded by trees – just the sort of place to set Power's imagination working.'

When Power sketched the pool beneath the trees he remembered the story of the wolves linked to the village's name. 'The trackway runs twisting, twixt the Pit & the Pool', he wrote in quick notes above a rough sketch:

> Pit of Death, the pool of life
> Blood soaked & fang sown
> Pit of retribution, Pit of revenge.

He wrote a poem, in a neo-pagan mode, to the Lady of the Holy Well, no Virgin Mary or saint, but a stronger, more primitive spirit, 'Primal Earth-Mother/Vengeful yet creative'. Power was no poet, and his verse was partly a Gothic pastiche, but the feeling is deeper than playful spookery. In a cloud-laden dusk, a weary traveller staggers down the track, 'ringed round with fearsome forms/elusive and shadowy'. Kneeling in the ring of trees he appeals to the spirit of the well:

> Savage yet tender
> > Fecund yet destructful
> O unknown Mother Spirit
> > Would I could placate thee.
> How the wolves howl!

As the final verse moves to 'Today', there is a sense of real fear. Power's linocuts had been hailed as true to the spirit of modern life, finding beauty in speed, the funfair and the Tube, the neon-lit underworld of the city. But his poem hints at the dangerous, 'destructful' edginess also present in those prints:

> Past the world rushes on, bewitched by speed
> Shrieking by day & making night more hideous.
> Stabbing the darkness with their spears of light.
> Here in thy lonely scarce-remembered sanctuary,
> Only the birds & flowers nestle round thy shrine.
> > Well overgrown & muddy.
> Water soiled by cattle.
>
> > Rending & tearing
> > In sacrilegious manner.
> > Pity & pardon them.
> > Timeless Eternal Mother.
> How the wolves howl!

Often at Woolpit, an intoxication with the middle ages blurred with a fascination with older traditions and beliefs. A year or so after they explored the well, Power wrote a haunting, rhythmic tune for recorder and drum. Below a transcription of this, Andrews copied her own short poem 'The Holy Well':

> Midnight
> On the night of the full moon. Samhane
> The silver moonlight
> flooding the green sward,
> and the dark, black water,
> of the Moat
> beneath
> the tangled undergrowth

One of the four Celtic fire festivals, Samhain, or Samhane as Andrews wrote it, marks the end of harvest and the beginning of winter, the dark of the year. It takes place at the end of October, halfway between the autumn and winter equinox, at the same time as Halloween, or All Souls, when pagan and Christian traditions both held that the veil between the living and the spirit world was thin. The dead walk. Bonfires are lit to chase away the shadows. Beneath her poem Andrews inked small designs: a wolf's head for Woolpit, a Celtic cross, the ancient triple spiral of female power, and the Triquetra, adapted by early Christians as the Trinity knot from the pagan symbol of earth, air and water; life, death and rebirth.

Her doodles pick up the mood of a local story, dating from the twelfth century, telling how two green children came out of a pit at harvest time, speaking a language of their own and eating only raw beans, the food of the dead. The boy died but the girl, 'of wanton ways', slowly lost her green tinge, married and left the village. They came, the children claimed, from the twilight land of St Martin, deep underground.

In September 1932 Sybil and Cyril went back to Woolpit, joined again by Hal, who had spent the summer hiking in Devon, Yorkshire and the Lake District. In the early autumn warmth they walked and foraged, and Andrews stacked up jars of blackberry jam and elderberry jelly. One day, she and Hal took the bus to Snape and Aldeburgh on a house-hunting expedition, watching the calm sea and the small boats swinging on the tideway. House-hunting was a sporadic urge for Andrews in these days, not out of a desire to be alone, but perhaps spurred by the idea of replacing the Woolpit cottage with something larger, where she and Power could share a studio. They were working more closely together than ever, and both of them loved the East Anglian countryside. In the front of her diary for the following year she stuck clippings of newspaper advertisements: an eight-room house in Suffolk with two cottages; a farmhouse near Colchester with an acre of garden and 'numerous fruit trees'. Yet even while she looked, they all made much of Woolpit. Over the summer, they decorated the cottage. When the rain set in, Hal wrote, 'C. doing a great deal of painting & we all did some decoration of the cottage with wall paintings.'

The paintings, in chalk, pastel and watercolour, spoke of history and music. Beside the fireplace, where a black pot and kettle balanced on an old range, was the figure of St Edmund pierced with arrows. Above the mantelpiece they drew archers stretching their bows and above the sofa, between two tall beams, they painted the execution of Sir William Tyrell at the Tower in 1462. On the stairs they put 'the herd boys of the time, 15–16 century', taking their names from poems and carols and old plays. All the figures in this corner were musicians, including a drummer and 'Colin Clout' the shepherd with his bagpipes, his name harking back to the shepherds in Skelton's satires and Spenser's pastorals. Here too were the pipers, 'Joly Wat' and 'Tud, Tibbe's son' as well as 'Hal o' the Hall, Long Hal, Joly Hal, Hal the Piper', playing his flute among the sheep and goats, Sybil playing the pipe as the Chaucerian 'Joly Robin', and

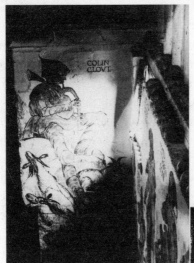

Wall paintings at Woolpit

Cyril as the jester, 'Joke Master', Master of the Revels. He earned the name of 'Jest Master', Sybil said, 'for his good wit and humour' and his 'lively and colourful personality'. (In her later diaries 'CEP' often became 'JM', while Cyril used his nickname for her, 'Sandra'.)

Their antiquarian fervour drew on the pre-war spirit of the Bury pageant and the collecting of folk songs, begun by Cecil Sharp in 1903 and now a national passion. Years later, when she pasted photos of the Woolpit murals into her scrapbook, Andrews labelled them 'The Herde-gromes Consort'. The name looked back to Chaucer's *House of Fame*, where the dreaming narrator sees a band of harpers – Orpheus, Orion and many others – and behind them a crowd of minstrels, playing all kinds of pipes, bagpipes, flutes and horns, and the green-corn pipes that shepherds play when they guard their sheep in the meadows:

> And pypes made of grene corne,
> As han thise litel herde-gromes
> That kepen bestes in the bromes.

In September 1933, as soon as she arrived for a month in Woolpit after a summer of work, the three of them tackled the wall painting again, concentrating on the stairs. Hal had just arrived back after a two-month trek through Egypt, Palestine and the Middle East. He was a great fan of T. E. Lawrence, hence his earlier learning of Arabic – by the time he reached Jerusalem he felt he could swear fluently. He came back to take up a new job as curator at the Bury St Edmunds museum, Moyse's Hall, where the finds of his grandfather Henry Trigg, donated by Beatrice, formed the core of the collection. Over a month, as mists and midday sun gave way to frost and sleet, they took up their music again: 'great sound of pipes', Sybil wrote. They graduated from the bamboo pipes that children then played in school to the newly introduced recorders, keeping up their roles from the wall paintings. 'Sybil (Joly Robin) and the Jest Master have been there,' Hal noted at the end of October: 'We have had great times on our pipes. Sybil & I can now play about 10 traditional carols in beautiful harmony & also "Cuckoo Song" as a round.' The interest in early music that began with the Herde-gromes Consort would soon become a passion for both Sybil and Cyril.

Back in London the medieval fantasy continued, with unself-conscious silliness. Looking ahead to December, Sybil cooked two Christmas cakes, salted almonds and made mincemeat. When Christmas week finally arrived Hal came to London (spending a day at the Zoo with Sybil, where, to their delight, they heard the wolves howl) and on Boxing Day they tried out their ideas for a medieval feast. Hal piped in the pudding to the Morris dance 'Lumps of Plum Pudding', Cyril arranged the 'Boar's Head Carol' for three recorders, and they all wore touches of medieval dress. On the menu they appeared as Sybil, 'the Ladye of the Feeste', Cyril, 'The Chief Musician, the Jest Master', Hal o' the Hall as 'The Pyper' and Geoff as 'Cellarer'. Woolpit had come to town.

22: FORMS OF FAITH

In the wake of her mother's death and her inheritance of the Woolpit cottage Andrews began to make religious prints. In London she had turned, but not with great intensity, to the Christian Science church that a friend had introduced her to when she was in Coventry during the war. This was one of many sects and religions that took root in Britain in the first two decades of the century, flourishing after the First World War as people searched for something transcendent, beyond the mass death and chaos of the conflict. Mary Baker Eddy's 1875 book *Science and Health with Key to the Scriptures* gained a wide readership from around 1900, and the faith it propounded appealed particularly to women (it was, after all, the first sect founded by a woman), fitting with a potent strand in feminist politics, the idea that social reformation could be propelled by a spiritual transformation.

Christian Science denied the dark material world, insisting that the true reality was spiritual rather than physical. In *Science and Health*, Eddy had answered the question 'What is God?' with a string of abstractions: 'God is incorporeal, divine, supreme, infinite Mind, Spirit, Soul, Principle, Life, Truth, Love.' Andrews never commented on the belief in healing by prayer, which caused such unnecessary suffering to Eddy's followers, but she was drawn to the sect's metaphysical teaching, seeing form in art as an expression of an 'essence' beyond external appearance. She was not alone in blending Christian Science teaching with art. Stanley Spencer's wife Hilda Carline and Paul Nash's wife Margaret were both devotees. Eddy's ideas of 'a transfiguring spirituality transforming the universe' had a powerful influence on Nash's mythic, abstracted landscapes and while Spencer was more sceptical, he admired Hilda's beliefs. In the

1950s, describing his visionary *Resurrection in Cookham Church-yard* (1924–6), he expressed the sense of immanence that pervades his work: 'Everything has a sort of double meaning for me . . . there's the ordinary everyday meaning of things, and the imaginary meaning about it all, and I wanted to bring these things together.' Elsewhere, Winifred Nicholson, who was converted in 1927 (apparently by Christine Nash) when she was badly injured in a fall while pregnant, drew in her husband Ben. In turn, he influenced Barbara Hepworth. Although Hepworth's stance fluctuated, in the *Christian Science Monitor* in 1965 she wrote that 'a sculpture should be an act of praise, an enduring expression of the divine spirit.'

A desire to express the divine could underlie the most realistic work. Evelyn Dunbar painted the countryside, the garden and ordinary people in the streets, and would become the only official woman war artist in the Second World War, recording the lives of land girls: her subjects were down-to-earth and poignant yet reflected her belief that 'all that is made is the work of God; and all is good.' The same attitude underpinned Winifred Nicholson's paintings of family life, light and flowers and her early abstract works. In 'Kit', a brief memoir of her close friend the artist Christopher Wood, who died in August 1930, she wrote: 'Besides the awful greatness of the universe, its solitude, its silence, its power, the vast deep unknown, there is only one thing as awe-inspiring, and that is the soul of a man who is inspired by a purpose that is to scale the high skies, to aspire to abstract beauty itself.'

The idea that the material world is vividly present yet unimportant hovers behind Andrews' prints, with their flat, brightly coloured two-dimensional forms and blank faces. The brilliant surface is there to convey the action, the idea, distilling the deep emotion felt in one's '*innermost* consciousness':

The emotion lies in our own Spirit – our own thought and consciousness.

St Paul put it very clearly:
'We look not at the things which are seen,
but at the things which are not seen.'
2 Corinthians 4 v. 18

If Andrews thought of a god, it was as a spirit of creativity. An artist, she wrote, 'cannot be confined within the bounds of one culture or another culture. He must work in eternity, in God, in Divine Mind, the one Creative Mind, which we reflect and express.' But this 'unconfined' concept was grounded by the Protestant ethic of her childhood, the trust in salvation through works rather than grace, and the duty to make use of 'God-given' talents. That conviction echoes through her book *Artist's Kitchen*, which she would put together in 1985 from notes written over the years. Throughout, she uses New Testament quotations to reinforce the idea that work, perpetual self-criticism, and striving for perfection are the keys to selfhood, to 'being':

Before you can BE
You must DO
'Faith, if it has not works, is dead'
'I will show you my faith by my works.'
St James 2, v. 17, 18

In essence, as one friend puts it, 'she was a curious mix of Christian Science and traditional Anglicanism, in that the Christian Science church have no religious art in their churches or reading rooms, but Sybil continued to work on the Stations of the Cross, and read the prayer book of the Church of England.' From childhood she had cherished the grand services in the cathedral at Bury, and had been profoundly moved when Power took her to the Tenebrae service in Westminster Cathedral for the first time, on Good Friday 1924. When she thought of the Passion and Crucifixion she was drawn, she said, not to the doctrinal significance of atonement on the cross but to the emotional drama, the violent action. Pressed on this in later life, she said that for her the Bible was full of human feeling, full of wars and love stories. Religious subjects 'hold the emotional side, and that gives you something to draw – a terrible accident, something terrible'. She began to work on the Stations of the Cross out of a furious impatience with the designs she saw in church after church, which seemed to her to miss this emotional depth. She didn't set out to do them all, but found she started one and then another over the years. It seemed to her a 'real-life story – very like today, when there was nothing but wars, invasion, revolution – all something to draw'. It was important to express emotion, to dig deep; if a work had no meaning 'you might just as well stop'.

Golgotha (PLATE 35), her first religious print, leaps straight to the central crisis, to Christ crucified. Its three crosses form a stern inverted triangle, with Christ in the centre against a panel of pale gold light. At the Redfern exhibition of 1931, *Golgotha* struck the critic for the *Connoisseur* as

> by far the most memorable feature of the exhibition, printed mainly in red, and suggesting pain, and grief, and breaking clouds by means of sweeping curves and jagged angles. If it is to achieve anything more than pattern, abstract art must be inspired by deep feeling and imagination. All these qualities were present in Miss Andrews' vision of the Crucifixion.

Golgotha is formally violent, with shards of light, brutal diagonals and sparse details – the nails, the crown of thorns. A receding line of crosses links Christ and the thieves who die with him to other outcasts who have perished here. The viewpoint is at ground level, as in the prints of pulsating energy, Power's *Merry-go-round* and Andrews' later *Windmill* (PLATE 31), as if the artist is a few steps further down the hill, slowly approaching the shadowy lamenting figures at the foot of the cross. A similar intensity marked the strange *Deposition* (PLATE 36), which appeared in the 1932 Redfern show with the title *The Darkest Hour*. The hour is not the darkest for Christ, but for his followers, for whom his death feels final, like the extinguishing of the candle in the Tenebrae service. This print, unlike the rest of her religious work, suggests the influence of Eric Gill, whom she greatly admired. Uncharacteristically, she made a land-scape-format print, marking a broad yellow line above the foot as if to emphasise the flat, arid ground on which the body lies. Her Christ, stretched out like a disjointed doll, seems supremely mortal: the bent thighs are a thin echo of the strained legs of working men in her other prints. Around his angular limbs, three women weep, the blue-robed Virgin holding his head, Mary Salome comforting her and Mary Magdalene embracing his feet, her long rippling hair tied back.

Andrews' prints of the Passion were imbued less with physical pain than with grief. In two scenes from 1932, *Mother and Son* and *Pieta*, the focus is on Mary. Reduced to elementals, in the former a sharply drawn figure stands beneath a downward triangle of crosses: in the second the triangle points up to the sky, with dark ladders sloping on each side. The balance is emotional as well as structural. In *Mother and Son*, Mary's face is a blank rectangle, tilted up to her son, and the composition is full of hard right angles and jagged edges. It has a powerful emotional charge. On one copy at least, Andrews drew on the early English poetry and music she loved, pencilling below the print the first line of the tender thirteenth-century dialogue between Mary and Christ, as he looks down from the cross to comfort his mother, explaining that he dies for all mankind: this is a time for joy, not for weeping – 'Stond wel Moder under Rode/Bihold thi child wyth glade mode.' The Mary of *Pieta*, by contrast, is a softly curv-ing figure, her bent head, beneath the harsh diagonals of the cross, embodying the despairing grief of any mother for her dead son.

Andrews returned to the Passion in 1935, with *Via Dolorosa*, a bold, angular print, combining three Stations of the Cross: Christ

Sybil Andrews, *Joseph and Nicodemus*, 1932

meeting his mother; falling under the weight of the cross; and Simon of Cyrene – or perhaps a Roman soldier – helping him to lift it again. Then she set the theme aside. A decade later, in the early 1950s, a time of hardship and loneliness, she would return to it again. But in her prints of the mid-1930s she carried the mood of mourning into another print, *Joseph and Nicodemus*, recording the moment when the council member Joseph of Arimathea and the rich Pharisee Nicodemus carry Christ's body for burial.

Outside the close circle of disciples, the two men demonstrate the bravery of those who risk all by defying the authorities. In the print book record for this work and on at least one trial proof, Andrews wrote a line from Shakespeare's *King John*, 'How easy dost thou take all England up!' She had seen Baliol Holloway in this play at the Old Vic in 1926, and it was staged again in 1931–2. Her quotation came from a speech made after the death of the rival claimant to the throne, Prince Arthur, addressed to his protector, Hubert de Burgh. It envisages a land laid waste:

> Go, bear him in thine arms.
> I am amaz'd, methinks, and lose my way
> Among the thorns and dangers of this world.
> How easy dost thou take all England up!
> From forth this morsel of dead royalty
> The life, the right, and truth of all this realm
> Is fled to heaven . . .

Behind Andrews' prints lingers something of the national grief of the First World War, in the woman weeping for her son and the old men carrying the young, the lost promise of a whole generation.

23: SAINTS AND MATRIARCHS

Power and Andrews, with their different religious allegiances, both thought intensely about faith, but Power, although steeped in the doctrine and ritual of the Catholic church, never turned in his art to the Passion, or to any gospel story. Instead his two religious works were prints of violent struggles, one of a historical saint, the other of Samson, the tortured giant of the Old Testament.

The first was *Monseigneur St Thomas* (PLATE 37), made in 1931. Astonishingly abstract at first glance, this dramatised the martyrdom of St Thomas à Becket at Canterbury in 1170, with the four knights wielding their swords, their curving blows bearing down on the tonsured priest. The subject fits with his interest in medieval history and in sainthood; in design and in colour it is a complex linocut of the type that he liked, printed in five blocks on buff tissue – light yellow ochre, transparent golden ochre, spectrum red, permanent blue and Chinese blue. He signed it and he probably printed it. But when Andrews looked through their print book in 1979, marking his prints as 'CEP' or 'Power', she wrote in red crayon across the page for *St Thomas*, 'signed by CE Power', and 'but my design, my print'. When she sent prints to London for sale, she wanted to keep this one, explaining that 'it was one that I had a great deal to do with, even the printing of it'. And it does look like hers: the composition is a variant of her favourite centripetal design – the men wielding their hammers on the central anvil, the hounds circling the otter's den. Andrews and Power are both there in this print. Every now and then their work elides.

It was hard, in the decades after the First World War, not to think of martyrdom in terms of that catastrophe. Four years after Power signed this print, T. S. Eliot wrote *Murder in the Cathedral*, with

Becket's powerful Christmas sermon: 'Now think for a moment about the meaning of this word "peace". Does it seem strange to you that the angels should have announced Peace, when ceaselessly the world has been stricken with War and the fear of War?' The angels' message, Becket says, was not, as people thought, peace as the world gives, but divine peace reached through suffering. When Becket falls, blinded by a rain of blood, he mourns – as in the speech from Shakespeare's *King John* that Andrews had quoted in relation to her *Joseph and Nicodemus*, for a lost England, now a land of barren boughs and dry stones: 'if I touch them they bleed./ How, how can I ever return, to the quiet seasons?'

———

Power drew many figures of saints in his sketchbooks, with notes on their attributes and symbols. Usually he showed them in archaic style, as they appeared in a reredos above the altar, in stained glass, or as sculptures in the niches on a church facade. He was drawn, too, to Russian and Greek Orthodox icons, with their still, hieratic figures, and sketched a company of Orthodox saints including St Nicholas and St Demetrios, St Basil, St Cyril of Beloozero, St John Chrysostom and St George.

His interest intensified when he read Josef Strzygowski's *Origin of Christian Church Art*. Startling at the time of its publication in 1901, this replaced the accepted idea of Rome as the birthplace of Christian art with that of Byzantium. The book was translated into English in 1923, and its powerful influence shows strongly, for example, in the images of death and rebirth in Yeats's 'Sailing to Byzantium', written in 1926:

> O sages standing in God's holy fire
> As in the gold mosaic of a wall,
> Come from the holy fire, perne in a gyre,

And be the singing-masters of my soul.
Consume my heart away; sick with desire
And fastened to a dying animal
It knows not what it is; and gather me
Into the artifice of eternity.

Strzygowski traced the evolution of architecture and painting in the West through a stylistic analysis of monuments from Greece and Asia Minor to Russia, including Coptic, Persian and Armenian art. As he read, Power jotted down odd details: how the Byzantine mosaics in the dome of the vestibule at St Mark's, Venice showed the cleft of Eve and the penis of Adam; how the renewal of life was celebrated in the inscription on the tympanum and dome of the twelfth-century Romanesque church at Corneilla-de-Conflent in southern France:

O You, who are in Life, come worship that
By which Life is given. That by which the
World is regenerated.

Where Andrews looked to the metaphysical teachings of Christian Science, to the belief that the material world is an illusion and the spiritual is 'real', Power sought the basis of creativity in human need, in contact with nature, in sex and procreation, death and rebirth, the regeneration of a fallen world. He saw religion as a personal, mystical experience, seeking its roots in different cultures across the world. The sense of a quest, of a rush towards oblivion that haunts his prints of speed, of the spinning roundabout and the devouring Underground, continues in his religious work. Reading a book on El Greco later in the decade he copied down a quote from Immanuel Hermann Fichte on ecstasy as 'Far sight with the overcoming of sensual perception in space and time'. The moment of absolute being could come, paradoxically, from the total loss of self, annihilating time in oneness with the universe, or with God.

At the end of that notebook he wrote a strange reading list, mixing studies of religion, the women's movement, sexuality and matriarchy. The book that caught his attention was *The Dominant Sex: A Study of Sexual Differentiation*. In this feminist polemic Mathilde and Mathias Vaerting argued that male and female characteristics are present in both sexes: the whole theory of a 'dominant' sex is a social construct that imparts a fatal bias to our understanding of history and culture. In their 1923 introduction, the translators Eden and Cedar Paul noted an article by Evelyn Sharp attacking the notion of the woman's sphere as 'a tendency that hinders the emancipation of women. For, after all, woman's emancipation simply means her emancipation as a human being.' Sharp's article was on Power's list as well as other works quoted by the Vaertings, including Johann Jakob Bachofen's influential theory of matriarchy in *Das Mutterecht* of 1861, Friedrich Engels' *Origin of the Family, Private Property and the State* (1884) and Charlotte Gilman's *Women and Economics* (1898). Above these notes he quoted Spinoza: 'Truth is the name we give to errors grown hoary with the centuries.'

Modifying Bachofen's argument, the Vaertings pointed out the reversal of roles in labour and courtship in ancient Egypt, India, Central Asia and elsewhere, the 'Mother-state', as they called it. Intrigued, Power jotted down the reference to an article on the love poetry of the ancient Egyptians, showing that women were the wooers. Much of his interest in comparative myth, religion and symbolism derived from Frazer's *Golden Bough*, which, as Eliot said in his notes to *The Waste Land*, 'has influenced our generation profoundly'. In different sketchbooks he copied Hindu designs of Shiva, ideographs of Peruvian symbolism, the stepped, zig-zag symbol of fecundity from Central Asia and figures from Jain rock statues, like the sainted scholar Chamunda Raya, noting the spiralled pattern of his hair, the rings round the nipple, the symbolic vine curled round his arms. His drawings often returned to spiral forms and 'the wheel of life'. In a small lined exercise book, he wrote careful notes on subjects ranging from Chinese Taoist symbolism to Christian saints, and noted a whole series of books on myth and legend – classic, Celtic and Teutonic, Egyptian, Indian, Babylonian and Assyrian, Cretan and pre-Hellenic – as well as Donald Mackenzie's *Migration of Symbols* (1926) and the fascinating *Book of Signs* (1930) by the German Rudolf Koch, illustrating nearly five hundred ancient symbols and runes.

In 1931, when Andrews made her first linocuts of the Stations of the Cross, Power was investigating the religions of Central and South America and making his print *Fire Dance* (PLATE 59), with archaic, Aztec-influenced patterning. While she was depicting Mary at the foot of the cross, he was working on his near-abstract *Matriarchy*. In this strange print, the crowned mother goddess holds human society in the circle of her arms – or her womb – while attendants with pointed breasts, Hellenic kilts and mock-Cretan hairstyles support her on each side. He printed this with two blocks, in ochre yellow and cobalt blue. The design is reversible: the print works either way up. One way up you see the queen in gold; turn it over and she is blue. To emphasise this balance of yin and yang, light and dark, good and evil, Power signed the prints both on the bottom and the top; and to bring it out still more starkly, he also printed it from a single block in black and white.

When he turned the following year to *Samson and the Lion* (PLATE 38), Power used zig-zag patterning to ornament the lion's flaring tail and to show the ripples of Samson's hair, like a crested helmet. Many artists had drawn, painted, sculpted and engraved this struggle, from Dürer and Cranach to Leighton, but Power made it his own, a ballet of physical force. His Samson is the traditional hero of supranatural strength, parallel to the Greek Hercules, but also a depiction of the union and struggle of humanity with our animal nature. In the story, Samson is on his way to marry the Philistine 'woman of Timnath' when he meets a lion and tears it apart with his bare hands: 'he rent him as he would have done a kid.' Returning later and finding that a

Cyril Power, *Matriarchy*, 1931

swarm of bees have nested in the lion's carcase, he collects their honey, and makes a riddle to test the Philistines: 'Out of the eater came forth meat, and out of the strong came forth sweetness' – the answer being a question, 'What is stronger than a lion? What is sweeter than honey?' In his print, beside the image of man and beast locked in their embrace, Power used the wild zig-zags of his matriarchal and fire-dance prints to decorate a tiny pattern of tilled fields, a glimpse of the soil itself.

30 Cyril Power, *The Merry-go-round*, 1930
31 Sybil Andrews, *Windmill*, 1933

ABOVE:
32 Cyril Power, *'Appy 'Ampstead*, 1933

OPPOSITE:
33 Cyril Power, *Speed Trial*, 1932
34 Sybil Andrews, *Speedway*, 1934

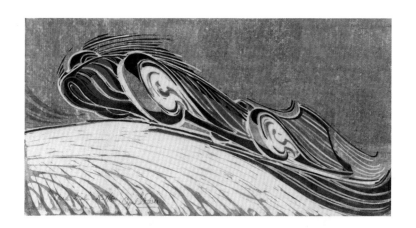

35 Sybil Andrews, *Golgotha*, 1931
36 Sybil Andrews, *Deposition*, 1932

37 Cyril Power, *Monseigneur St Thomas*, 1931
38 Cyril Power, *Samson and the Lion*, 1932

MONOTYPES

39 Cyril Power, *Battersea Power Station*, 1934

40 Sybil Andrews, *The Artist*, c.1932

41 Cyril Power, *Sybil Painting*, c.1932

42 Andrew Power, *Epsom Races*, poster, 1933
43 Cyril Power, *Lawn Tennis*, 1933
44 Andrew Power, *Football*, poster, 1933
45 Andrew Power, *Wimbledon*, poster, 1933

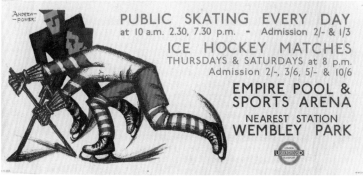

46 Cyril Power, *Skaters*, 1932
47 Andrew Power, *Public Skating at Wembley*, poster, 1934

48 Cyril Power, *The Tube Train*, 1934
49 Cyril Power, *The Sunshine Roof*, 1934

50 Cyril Power, *The Concerto*, 1935
51 Cyril Power, *The Trio*, 1936

52 Sybil Andrews, *Tillers of the Soil*, 1934
53 Sybil Andrews, *Haysel*, 1936

54 Sybil Andrews, *Day's End*, 1961

55 Sybil Andrews, *Self Portrait*, oil, c.1938

56 Sybil Andrews, *Cyril Power*, oil, c.1939

57 Sybil Andrews, *Little Ships*, oil, 1942
58 Sybil Andrews, *The Boat Yard*, oil, 1942

59 Cyril Power, *Fire Dance*, 1931

24: 'OUR SHOW'

The Brook Green studio was overflowing. The furniture from Phoenix Place was there: the plank table and carved chest, the Nigerian door and cloths and bowl. The walls were hung with their own prints but also with family miniatures, old plates and samplers from the Andrews' house in Northgate Street, and with Cyril's fiddles. The mantelpiece was piled with pottery and pewter, and old candlesticks stood on a small table next to a vase often full of tumbling flowers: daisies, roses and delphiniums from the market. At Christmas Andrews perched a small tree on another side table, swamping it in crackers, baubles and candles. A piano was jammed up against the grandfather clock from the Bury house, and in the corner was a flywheel etching press that they had bought to print their drypoints. Although there was more space to work than in Phoenix Place, usually every surface was covered. It did not help, as Andrews said, that Power was a famously untidy man, and she spent her time picking up after him.

Their linocuts were piling up: subjects from Tube trains and speed trials to skaters and ballet, racing and religion. Power's *Tube Staircase* was the first linocut to be bought for the nation and he had prints in the British Museum and the V&A, which also bought Andrews' *Steeplechasing* and *Golgotha*. In the early 1930s their work appeared in the United States, Australia and China. Canada would soon follow, and in most years they sent work to the Print Makers Society of California in Los Angeles. Writing about an exhibition in Shanghai in 1931, and picking out Flight, Andrews and Power for special praise, the critic F. Hindle wrote, 'No true enthusiast will miss this,' applauding a 'collection of linocuts by the world's leading masters in this phase of modern art'. Hindle especially admired Power, thinking that 'Perhaps, even among the modernists, he is most daring of all.' But for Andrews and Power all this was not enough: they wanted to move on, to show they were not limited to one form, to stand on their own rather than as members of a group.

These desires were fulfilled in 1933. In the previous year, Claude Flight had quarrelled with Rex Nan Kivell about the slow payment to artists from prints sold by the Redfern Gallery. Flight was right: Nan Kivell was slippery with money, always running things on a knife edge, and it took him three years to pay Power and Andrews what they were owed for sales in 1931. Infuriated, Flight moved the annual linocut exhibition from the Redfern to the Ward Gallery. Power and Andrews, however, decided to stay. They had already had their own rows with Flight, who could be high-handed with his demands as well as slipping out of obligations. 'End justified by means,' Andrews wrote angrily, but cryptically, at the end of her diary for 1931. 'Flight makes me feel sick. If he *had* been sick he would have achieved his ends.'

In September 1932, before they escaped for their month in Woolpit, Power went to see Nan Kivell, who came round to the studio a week later for a long discussion and offered them an exhibition of their own. 'Joyful news', wrote Andrews. Nan Kivell was a rogue but he was good to them; in 1976, when he was knighted, she told the gallery owner Michael Parkin, 'I rejoice in Rex's honour. He deserved it.' In Woolpit they thought over what they wanted to show and when they came back to London in late October they signed the agreement. 'Our show', as Sybil called it, would run from 5 to 28 January 1933. The second part of the show would feature the linocuts for which they were known, but the first, and largest, section would include a new and different body of work – monotypes.

———

A monotype, or monoprint, is a curious creature – not a print, as it can't be produced in multiples, and not a painting, as it is 'printed'. In a way it is a reverse painting. Using printer's ink or oils straight from the tube, Andrews and Power painted directly onto a metal plate to get the tones and lights they wanted. Since the plate's smooth surface did not absorb the paint, it kept the marks of brush or roller so that the layers and swirls gave the print a distinctive texture. Also, because the ink stayed wet for longer on the hard plate, they could manipulate it more easily, dabbing and wiping, adding line and detail. Once satisfied, they placed their paper – slightly dampened to give a greater range of tones – over the metal. Then, although they could get a print in the way they did with lino by rubbing with the back of a spoon, they preferred to put it through the Brook Green hand press. When they rolled back the paper the image appeared, vivid and dense, its softness a contrast to the hard, geometrical blocks of their linocuts.

Sometimes, to get density or definition, they added another colour to the plate and ran it through again; sometimes they drew extra outlines while the paint was still wet, or added details in pastel or watercolour. Sometimes, too, the result was close to an original drawing or drypoint (or an eerie reversal) because they traced the image first, perhaps outlining it with fine chalk before they began to paint. As Andrews explained to one reviewer, the paint looked entirely different on the paper, 'and unhampered by any tradition, and in the spirit of explorers, she and Mr Power carried out innumerable experiments before they were satisfied as to the colours to use on the metal.' Some colours worked better than others and each subject, she said, 'seemed an adventure'. The first print was as immediate and unique as a painted sketch or a drawing, with the added thrill that you never quite knew what you would get until you rolled back the paper. Monotypes were always surprising, and that was part of their joy – the colours weren't quite under control, accidents happened, the paint could squeeze or clump in unpredictable ways – so taking the paper from the press was a moment of real excitement.

Most of the ink or paint came off the plate in the first printing, but if they ran the plate through the press again they got paler effects, 'ghost prints' or 'maculatures', something they quite liked. 'Each individual print is unique,' they noted in their catalogue, 'inasmuch as the first print shows all the strength and vigour of the pigment, but any further proof is necessarily reduced to the underlying paint and produces a delicate and sometimes subtle impression.' In Andrews' second and third pulls of scenes of 'Le Petit Bay' in St Malo or the Rue du Hallage in Rouen, the fading paint gave a dusty effect, and pale blue shadows and small touches of red were unusually delicate, as if the scenes, like the holidays themselves in the late 1920s and in the hot June and July of 1931, were vanishing into memory.

Monotypes had seen spurts and lapses in popularity. The term was not used until the 1890s, although one artist, Benedetto Castiglione, was known to have worked in this way in the seventeenth century. Then came a blank, until Blake produced his extraordinary twelve 'Large Colour Drawings' in 1795, painting with oil and egg tempera, pulling off the print and retouching with ink and watercolour. After that the monotype disappeared again, until the Impressionists, interested in experiments with etching, inking and reusing plates, and with the effects of photography, began to make 'printed drawings'. The most avid practitioner was Degas, who made over four hundred monotypes: in his 'dark field manner', he coated the plate with dark ink then removed it in places with rags, his finger or a brush, to print a black-and-white image; in the 'light field manner' he painted the design in colour straight onto the plate. His prints inspired others, including Gauguin, who developed his own method of traced monotype, later modified by Paul Klee in his eerie 'transfer printing' in the early 1920s. In 1930s London, however, Andrews and Power were on their own. No one else was exhibiting monotypes, although following them, more Redfern artists would try their hand. In the next decade a separate movement would grow, inspired by the

Polish painter and print-maker Jankel Adler, who had known Klee's work. A member of the Polish army, evacuated after Dunkirk, Adler shared a house in London with the artists Robert MacBryde, Robert Colquhoun and John Minton, and from here the vogue spread. By the late 1940s, it seemed, everyone was doing monotypes – 'it was in the air.'

Lacking such company, Andrews and Power knew that they would have to explain what they were up to. At the start of their catalogue they declared that their monotypes were perhaps 'most characteristic and typical of their methods of work, deriving from, and combining the methods they use in water colour, oil colour and linocut'. The Foreword went on to describe how these were made, adding:

> In the past Monotypes have hardly been regarded seriously and have been looked on more in the light of a *jeu d'esprit*, yet they are worthy of serious consideration . . .
>
> Monotypes call for intense concentration in execution, and directness and certainty in handling.
>
> It is very difficult to judge of the final effect until the print has been taken.

Andrews showed twenty-one monotypes, Power twenty-four. It was a lot to get ready but they had been working on these for some months. The previous August, in a flaring summer heatwave, ninety-seven degrees in the shade, they had gone through a burst of printing linocuts for the Redfern travelling exhibition: '6 Tube stations', '6 skaters, 8 steeplechases'; and then of drypoints, still a staple of their income. Then, in a rapid change of direction, Andrews wrote abruptly: 'started monotypes'. Every day from then on they worked on these, and they already had a stock of prints when they signed their agreement with Rex Nan Kivell in September.

Their first monotypes were of the London scenes that filled Power's sketchbooks: King's Cross station, Tower Bridge, Chelsea Bridge, the Grand Junction canal and Battersea power station (PLATE 39). Ransacking sketchbooks for subjects, they turned to their early dry-points of Wapping and Pickle Herring Street as well as drawings from France. Other subjects came from walks round Woolpit, especially the deserted brick fields outside the village, with their crumbling kilns and old drying sheds. They made portraits of each other too, almost post-Impressionist in colour and effect, Power's *Sybil Painting* (PLATE 41), sitting in the sun, her head bent, Andrews' of Power as *The Artist* (PLATE 40), glancing sideways from under his hat.

In late October 1932, after the Redfern agreement was signed, they plunged into a further month of printing. Anxious that they might not have enough to show, Power made startling prints of domestic objects like a spice jar and his own collection of fiddles, while Andrews walked up the river, 'looking for subjects', and dashed out to buy more paper – they used Whatman wove paper for these as it held the impression better than the Japanese tissue of the linocuts. By early November she calculated they had thirty-six monotypes, jotted down with hasty titles: 'C. gasworks, Silver Tower, The Brook. – S. St Malo, Storm, Mud, Timber yard'. Occasionally they escaped for walks up the towpath, and across to Barnes or down to Chiswick. But they kept on working, side by side, and by the end of November, Sybil was exhausted: 'Feeling like cold boiled mud.' A week later they both collapsed, spending days in bed. But they had done the work they needed. On 15 December Nan Kivell and his Australian assistant Richard Smart came down to see their prints and the next day Power took them to the gallery in Old Bond Street for framing. Two days later it was his birthday; 'CEP Fête', wrote Andrews. He was sixty this year, and she was thirty-four – but the age difference meant very little, as yet. Briefly they could relax, buy books, ice the Christmas cake, salt the almonds and walk to Putney in the pale winter sun.

On 5 January, when the show opened, they had a private view, hosted by Nan Kivell and his co-director Lord Alington, and three days later they held their own party for friends: 'Festivity', wrote Andrews.

Within a couple of days, while Andrews went to New Bond Street to have her photograph taken by the society photographer Frank Swaine (who also took portraits of Benjamin Britten and Margaret Epstein), Power was ill again, with flu or exhaustion. Was all their effort worth it? It is hard to tell in Andrews' case, since almost all her monotypes were lost in a fire at an Ottawa gallery warehouse in 1959, but Power's work survives in stray examples, showing that monotypes released him back into a painterly mode that he had missed. Some of his prints were vibrantly successful, like one of Cattawade Bridge, with the swell of the old bridge solid and thick in green and gold, or *Gasometers*, where dark iron fretwork looms against the clouds, and *Power House at Dusk*, the 'Silver Tower' as Andrews called it, set against the tumbling brushstrokes of a greeny-grey sky. There were failures too, especially when he worked over a print later, but his London scenes were all mysterious and atmospheric.

Their show put them in striking company: the next exhibition at the Redfern included works by John and Paul Nash, Epstein and Gill. In their catalogue, they made a point of insisting that they were not merely two artists sharing gallery space: this was a joint show in a real way. 'These two artists', their Foreword began, 'have been collaborating since 1918 and this exhibition shows the results of their association.' Emphasising this, instead of separating their monotypes they hung them in small groups, mixing their prints in each. When it came to the linocuts, they chose the opposite route, with Power's prints all grouped together first and Andrews' second. In a way the stress on collaboration backfired, as reviewers noted how similar their works were, particularly the linocuts. 'The prints are so much alike that it is often difficult to distinguish the authors,' the reviewer in *Apollo* decided, noting that Andrews had, on the whole, 'a suaver curve'.

Reviewers liked the immediacy, brilliant colour and force of the monotypes, often commenting on their focus on industrial or urban subjects – they were still 'artists of today'. *The Times* commended them too on their clear distinction of form, and their boldness in using 'two artistic "languages" as different in capacity as suggestive English and precise French – or modelling and carving in sculpture'. But some reviews, like that in *Apollo*, were patronising:

> I once observed a water-colour painter rocking a drawing of his to and fro as if he were developing a negative. Enquiry brought forth the explanation that by rocking the very wet colour about in this manner he obtained 'lovely effects' and 'beautiful accidents'. That, although I am sure it would be fiercely contested by Miss Andrews and Mr Cyril Power, is also part of the main attraction of 'monotypes'.

So, skill had little to do with it? Well, the reviewer admitted, 'some pleasurable effects can be got' from monotypes, and Power, he thought, had 'got them', especially in *Liverpool Street Station*, *My Fiddles*, *The Power House at Dusk* and *Gasometers*. (*The Times* agreed that Power had greater command of colour.) But perhaps to their disappointment, the linocuts were still admired more and if the critics were lukewarm so was the buying public. Nan Kivell had set the price of the monotypes at five to seven guineas, more than double that of the linocuts. Very few of them sold. And that has been the case ever since, compared to the linos, which are always in demand. The form itself was part of the problem, as Power noted in a wry poem. Was a monotype an original or a multiple, a painting or a print?

> They call it a print
> But it's really a painting
> It gives critics no clue
> So they look merely blue
> and stutter & squint
> and call it a print.

———

When they took down the show there were still sheets to wash, marmalade to make, books to change at the library. List of prints made – '4 Bringing in the Boat, 6 Giant Racers' – shared a diary page with a shopping list: 'sevilles, bacon, butter, cheese, lux, paper, milk, coal'. Nan Kivell was planning to send another travelling exhibition of linocuts to the States (this was shown in Brooklyn in September but seems to have travelled no further), so in the spring of 1933 they worked on the prints for this: '144 all told'. Then they started on the cuts for the Redfern's summer exhibition, *Colour Prints and Contemporary Oils*. For this Power printed *Acrobats*, *'Appy 'Ampstead*, *The High Swing* and *Lawn Tennis* (PLATE 43), while Andrews worked on *Otter Hunt* and *Sledgehammers*. She also made a new print, *Windmill*, a colour version of Power's black-and-white linocut of Elmer's Mill, simplifying it radically, so that the sails of the mill and the fantail balance each other, mirrored by the shadows on the hillside below.

Day by day, the prints mounted up, with Power taking batches to the gallery, their work broken by walks and the odd lazy Sunday by the river. The weeks of cutting and proofing and printing multiples in April and May came to an end, and in June it was time for the exhibition. It was a big show, with over seventy prints and twenty oils, including paintings by Matthew Smith, Augustus John, Cedric Morris and Paul Nash, as well as linocuts, lithographs such as Edna Clarke Hall's bold, Blake-inspired 'Poem Picture', colour drypoints, woodcuts and aquatints. Despite Flight's move to the Ward Gallery, many Grosvenor artists were there, with lithographs from Macnab of the French Alps and wine casks, linocuts from Tschudi, Greengrass, Mayo and the glamorous Ethel Spowers, as well as from Flight himself and his partner Edith Lawrence.

Although they showed only two monotypes and seven linos, one review declared that 'two artists, Miss Sybil Andrews and Mr Cyril E. Power, take the honours of the exhibition. Nearly all their works reveal an extraordinary mastery of media . . . in linocuts and monotypes they sometimes achieve perfection, – or, rather, it is hard to conceive more satisfying things.' Letters flooded in, and there were more and more sales: the profits were not much at £3 or £4 a print, but they padded out their meagre incomes. In a fit of glee Andrews bought a green hat to match her new skirt. But she was tired, and the idea of mixing with all the other artists and chatting at a grand launch party was too much for her; she preferred being on her own, or with Cyril and Hal, or in a small group of friends. 'Private View Colour Print Show', she wrote on 1 June. 'Did not go, went to Kew and sat in sun, lovely day.' In the hot Whitsun weather her relief was intense.

As the summer rolled on she took to jam-making again – Morello cherry, raspberry, blackcurrant, damson – and the studio was rich with the sweetness of fruit and sugar. They had time to shift cupboards, sort out their prints and go to the theatre, concerts and the Russian ballet, and to spend more time on their own music making. In early September they left town for a few days in lodgings in Folkestone. In a windy, end-of-season week Andrews swam every day, Power less often. They explored the castle, took a day trip to Canterbury, walked along the cliffs and sunbathed in the shelter of Shakespeare Cliff, watching the waves tumble in the grey English Channel. Then at last, as October rain began to fall, they went back to Woolpit.

25: THE SPORTING LIFE

Work for the *Colour Prints* show was interrupted – and the pressure intensified – for Andrews in particular, by a different task, designing posters for London Transport. Edward McKnight Kauffer, who had spearheaded the poster drive, held a hugely successful solo show in 1933 and continued to produce striking new designs, but he and other artists of the 1920s were joined in this decade by many newcomers. Some were well known, like Jacob Epstein and Laura Knight, while younger artists emerged from different groups at the Central School of Art and Goldsmith's and from Paul Nash's students at the Royal College of Art: a stellar bunch including Graham Sutherland, Barnett Freedman, Enid Marx, Clare Leighton, John Banting, Edward Bawden and Eric Ravilious. In turn Andrews and Power brought the dashing style of the Grosvenor School.

There was no 'London Transport style', apart from Edward Johnston's bar-and-circle logo and the typeface Johnston Sans, chosen by Pick in 1915 and modified by Johnston and Gill. The range of approaches and techniques for the posters was astonishing, from bold graphics to whimsical cartoons, from black-and-white photomontage to idyllic watercolours advertising the city fringes (1932 saw four of these by Anthony Blunt for Staines, Virginia Water, Windsor and Sunningdale). Abstraction and Surrealism also found a place: Man Ray turned the Tube logo into Saturn with its ring; László Moholy-Nagy wove words and images together. Pick held true to the generous ideal he had expressed in 1927: 'There is room in posters for all styles, they are the most eclectic form of art. It is possible to move from literal representation to the wildest impressionism so long as the subject remains understandable to the man in the street.'

Pick was still in charge. After the Underground and the bus and tram companies joined forces in 1933, he was appointed Chief Executive of the new London Passenger Transport Board. The following year he became chair of the new Council for Art and Industry, another step in his promotion of 'useful art', educating the public and forwarding what he called 'the English tradition in design'. Nikolaus Pevsner would call him a 'modern Medici', a patron of the finest public art and design, who made London Transport a centre of art education and 'a hub of civilised urbanity and modern sense'. To the modern artist, according to an editorial in *The Listener* in 1932, 'art' no longer meant a painted canvas to be hung on a wall, 'but an impulse which can equally well be expressed in a bowl, a table, a finely printed book, a theatrical curtain. We have artists of the stature of Henry Moore, Vanessa Bell and John Nash turning quite naturally from painting a picture or carving a statue to designing a lampstand or a wall paper or a book cover.'

Although Power did design a book cover in 1931, a stark geometric pattern in black and white for the long Catholic poem *The Seven Niches* by Toby's friend Egerton Clarke (a Cambridge friend of Dorothy Sayers), posters were their main foray into commercial art. All London Transport posters were printed commercially, by colour lithography, but Andrews and Power still created their designs in their usual way as linocuts. Power took up a suggestion that they should send in roughs, after which he met Pick and obtained the contract, but as he was busy at RIBA Andrews took over, more than faintly resentful that the posters appeared under the combined name of 'Andrew Power'. She felt that 'the Andrew Power mess up' had left her in an awkward position: 'Power got the order, I did all the work, except the one that was done from his "Giant racer" – I should have taken them, all that were mine, in my own name.' (The 'Giant Racer' rough, apparently never completed, she thought was 'a beauty'.) He gave her the cheque, but she wanted the credit. Her crossness suggests that despite their closeness, collaboration was not always to her advantage. Like most women artists of the time she was made to feel overshadowed, marginal – aware that, however close the partnership, the balance of power lay with the man. You had to fight for a place of your own.

The simplified form of linocuts, with their geometric designs and use of three or four flat, specified colours, made them relatively easy for the lithographer to copy and for the press to work with: the printers took the coloured image and broke it down into four 'workings', overlaid as in a linocut. Andrews aimed to produce bold designs, as clear as could be, with room for any text that was required. Yet however simple the design appeared, the task was far from easy: digging out some posters years later, she remembered how much time and trouble she had taken with them.

Posters were a valued source of income for many women artists, and some made it almost their career: Dora Batty, who taught textile design at the Central School, and the wood-engraver and book illustrator Herry (Heather) Perry made a hundred between them in the 1920s and 30s. Andrews and Power's friend Adolphine Ryland, 'Delilah', made two, 'Home from the Office' and 'Into the Sunshine, out of the Fog'. But while most women artists were commissioned to design posters for fashion, shopping or the delights of the suburbs, the Andrew Power posters were for sporting fixtures, apart from the straightforward 'To Hire a Bus or Coach', a witty design with the red London Transport bus on one side and the private Green Line coach with its sun roof, full of faceless, square-headed figures, on the other.

Conversations with the redoubtable Walter Patmore (who worked on posters for the LPTB for thirty-four years) had begun in February 1933, when they were recovering from the excitement of their monotype show. A month later Andrews devoted a whole fortnight to a poster for Epsom races (PLATE 42), working out a design, drawing roughs, cutting and printing and sending in the finished proof, and then waiting anxiously for approval. The Board commissioned about twice as many posters as they used, and some of those mentioned by Andrews in her diary – on greyhound racing, the Trooping of the Colour, Richmond Horse Show and the Lord Mayor's Show, never saw the light of day. For the Epsom meeting, which included the Derby, she let her imagination run free, taking a bird's eye view, showing the race track as a pale green curve, a ribbon swinging up to encircle and highlight the text, and catching the horses' speed by elongating their forms. Her poster evoked the race track excitement by signalling crowds clinging like iron filings to the track, backed up by cars and trucks and buses. Epsom is the place to go to – buzzing, unmissable, alive.

When the LPTB Publicity Committee had considered the design at their fortnightly meeting, she dashed to the Underground office to collect the rough, sent Power out to buy paper and printed the final version on their press in the studio. On 1 April she wrote wearily, 'finished poster': a week later, to her relief, a letter arrived approving her ideas. The intense work continued, mixed with printing linocuts for the Redfern travelling show: 'Proof from Undergrd. Bed *3.15*', she wrote with amazement on 20 April. In early May, coinciding with a flurry of lino printing for the *Colour Prints* exhibition, an order came for a poster for Wimbledon (PLATE 45): this was delivered in early May, bringing a welcome cheque for £26 10s.

Soon another request came, this time for a football poster (PLATE 44). This was a daunting task, packing in the ten London football fixtures on 7 October 1933, from Spurs v. Sunderland to Arsenal v. Fulham. 'I was tearing my hair out, there was not an inch of space left for my design & then I had a brainwave,' she remembered, deciding 'to design a large "footballer" in colour to add action, & print the whole sheet of fixtures on top in black – & they looked good, all in a row in different colours'. It looked daringly modern with the huge outline of a player kicking behind the list of fixtures, like a square-headed, faceless 'robot man' of avant-garde science fiction. The player could be printed in different colours – orange, yellow, blue, green and red – and he could also appear behind different kinds of text. In one version, for the Tramways rather than the Underground, a red player kicks off behind a message in huge capitals: 'TAKE A CHEAP RETURN TICKET – FOOTBALL'. There was no need for more.

As the summer heat rose, work on the football poster was competing with printing linocuts, and with her jam-making:

7 July: Very hot. 12 lbs Morello . . . prints of Tennis
13 July: 13 lb Raspberry jam, 9 lb Redcurrant and rasp.
21 July: Patmore rang up for Football Poster.
24 July: 4 Appy Ampstead. Football Poster
25 July: Music group in evening. Poster all day
26 July: Football poster
27 July: Rough for poster finished.
28 July: To Russian ballet with Gwen. To see Patmore, left 3 large and 5 small. 7 lb blackcurrant jam.

And so it went on, with more trips to discuss the poster with Patmore, more roughs, more prints, more jam: '11 August: Poster & 14 lb Damson jam. Rained today'.

The placement of image and text was always a challenge, demanding many preliminary drawings, juggling of composition, ironing out of detail. But Andrews seemed to visualise the message from the start, seizing on a key action that summed up the whole sport: a tennis volley, a football kick, a hockey tackle. Although she did the hard work the designs often blended her ideas with Power's. His 1933 linocut *Lawn Tennis* drew on the flamboyant style of Jean Borotra, 'the Bounding Basque', who won Grand Slam singles five times from 1924 to 1931 and the doubles at Wimbledon in 1932 and 1933. Andrews always remembered the dramas of Centre Court in the early 1930s, with Borotra and Henri Cochet, two of the 'Four Musketeers' of French tennis, and Bunny Austin, the British hero defeated in the final by the American Ellsworth Vine. (Austin was the first player to wear shorts, pushing the trouser-clad players into the past.) Borotra, she thought, 'must have been a wonderful dancer – wonderful lines – he was a marvellous person to draw.' And as with the men pulling the cable, as she made her quick five-minute sketches, watching him made her ask questions about the detail of the physical effort: 'How do you hold the racket?' and 'How do you really, really go for that ball?'

Power caught the rapid exchange of a battle at the net with cartoon-like enjoyment, making the volley seem to flash so fast before the eyes that the speed eerily distorts the shape of the players' limbs and their rackets. For her Wimbledon poster, Andrews borrowed this style, turning the name 'Wimbledon' into a net, with leaping singles players volleying across it and the racket cracking down on the central 'B'. The curt transport details fitted low in the corner beneath the players' feet: 'By Underground to Southfields Stn. Thence special bus to Ground'. London Transport chose her for this poster because of her stylish, unconventional approach, but at the same time they commissioned another Wimbledon poster, by the Parisian illustrator André Edouard Marty, a far more traditional image with two players on a deep green court politely shaking hands over the net. The contrast was a shrewd commercial gamble, two styles to attract two different audiences.

Each time, Andrews thought hard about the atmosphere of the event. Thus her poster for the Aldershot Tattoo of 1934 was firmly regimented, the soldiers in their red coats and beaver hats, the dark lettering shouting out the title like a sergeant major's bark. The Andrew Power posters promoted big events and big venues, like the Empire Pool at Wembley, opened in early 1934. The pool was a marvel, 'more like a sea than a pool', wrote the *Guardian*, with a shelving beach at the shallow end and a deep end where 'the clumsiest diver from the 10-metre board can come to no harm'. Great pistons below the pool created waves, and the terraces on each side, with cafes and restaurants and galleries, could hold up to five thousand spectators. Every year in mid-October the pool was drained

The Brook Green studio, with posters and flywheel press
Sybil Andrews, *Racing*, 1934

and decked, then given over to skating until the spring; Andrews' poster advertises 'Public Skating Every Day' (PLATE 47), with ice hockey matches on Thursdays and Saturdays.

A couple of years earlier, inspired by a hockey match across the river on Duke's Meadow near Barnes, Power had dramatised team-work in *Hockey*, a near-abstract linocut in blue and brown, with the players brandishing their sticks, head down, grappling for the ball in swooping curves. For her Wembley poster Andrews set aside curves in favour of more aggressive angles, using a long horizontal frame – she called it her 'ice hockey panel' – with the players battling on one side, leaving space for the long text on the other. She caught the explosive movement, the dark opponent behind, the smash of the sticks on the ice. In the foreground she placed a determined player from the Wembley Lions, his skates swishing round beside the name 'Empire Pool', making the most of the team's red shorts, and the red and white stripes of their long stockings and bands on their arms. This was a clever move as the Lions were a new team, specially cre-ated for the venue, their name a tribute to an earlier 'London Lions': they joined the English National League, and became champions straight away in the 1935–6 season.

In 1934, the same year as she made her Wembley poster, Andrews created one for the two London cricket grounds, Lord's and the Oval. This was a model of crisp design, ruthlessly arranged into four rec-tangles, with the players on green backgrounds. In the lower right-hand corner the batsman stands with bat raised, and as the fielder high in the upper left-hand corner stretches to catch, the imagined arc of the ball soars in a cracking diagonal, leaving space on each side for details of routes and fixtures. Yet Andrews herself disliked this, to put it mildly. 'I hate & detest the Cricket poster', she fumed, angry that someone at the printers had added meaningless black touches, tracing creases in a shirt, the lines in the batsman's pads and the outline of the bat: 'It makes me mad every time I look at it.'

In her linocuts of this year, Andrews turned to different sporting subjects, free from all constraints and maddening printers. In the powerful, charging *Speedway* (PLATE 34), the sport was dirt-track racing, where riders on bikes with no brakes careered on loose trackways, leaning, skidding and 'broadsiding' round corners. Speedway had only been brought over from Australia in the late 1920s, taken up first by motorcycle clubs and instantly soaring in popularity: in February 1928 a meeting on the cinder track behind the King's Oak pub at High Beech in Epping Forest drew a crowd of thirty thousand. New tracks followed, including one not far from Brook Green on the cinder track round Chelsea's football pitch at Stamford Bridge; you could collect cigarette cards of 'The Chelsea Pensioners'. Andrews remembered the excitement of 'seeing these boys come sweeping round the corner in line, looking like a lot of goblins . . . it's the action I'm always looking for.' In her print, Andrews' three bikers wheel round, like triangular arrows, their bikes slanting up from the narrow front wheel to the symmetrically placed feet and knees in their dusty leathers and the curved handlebars. In their identical goggles and helmets, like cartoon symbols, the riders are almost part of their machines. As the bikes slice diagonally across the print, radiating lines convey the speed, while a stipple of red and yellow dots in the top left corner evokes the roaring crowd. We are slap in front of the action, as if we had to jump out of the way.

A linocut of horse racing felt even faster, a supreme illustration of her instruction to her students: 'Find the lines, curves, masses and rhythms and their balance, which will give you the Spirit of your idea.' *Racing* was based, she said, on Tattenham Corner at Epsom. As in her Epsom poster, she showed the horses as near-abstract arching forms, legs outstretched, nose forward, ears back. The jockeys' elongated arms follow the pull of the horse, the riders distinguished only by the colours of shirts and hats, bright yellow, orange, red, blue and black. They rush towards the stylised fence, propelled by arcs of speed. Betting on the horses was the biggest form of gambling in Britain between the wars; London newsstands sold over half a million copies of the racing editions of the evening papers every day, and although racing was riddled with snobbery it pulled in millions of middle-class and working-class punters, following form, taking packed trains to race meetings, laying bets with the bookies. While some critics linked it to the mob, 'given to greed, rapacity and depravity, involved in clearly illegal acts', others cheered it as the national sport, the sport of kings. But in the posters and linocuts of Andrews and Power all these sports, from skating to speedway, tennis to racing, became ballets of adrenaline-spiked speed and skill, linking classes across the nation.

26: PIPES AND VIOLS

In March 1933, a month after their joint show of monotypes and linocuts finished, Andrews and Power went to a concert at the Art Workers' Guild in Queen Square. It was given by the Dolmetsch family, the leading spirits in the movement to perform early music as it was originally played – or so it was believed – using carefully 'reconstructed' instruments. 'The first Dolmetsch Concert I heard – with CEP', Andrews wrote on the programme. 'Heaven!'

In their Herde-gromes Consort at Woolpit, Andrews and Power had played folk songs and medieval carols, seeing these as the music of shepherds and herders, tanners and brewers, the people who had made a pilgrimage to the Ladye's Well in the thirteenth century, the folk of *Piers Plowman* and the *Canterbury Tales*. But the music at the Dolmetsch concert was different, more European, its spread reaching from songs of the middle ages to Renaissance and Baroque trios and quartets. The programme included a consort for four recorders, playing the folk songs 'Go from My Window' and 'Bonny Sweet Robin'; a thirteenth-century Portuguese air for lute and viol; a suite of dances for four viols from the 1650s by Matthew Locke and another for six viols by William Lawes. Then came a fourteenth-century lullaby ('Lovely', Andrews pencilled in her programme), Handel's 'Chaconne in G major' and a sonata for violin, viola da gamba and harpsichord by Veracini, from the 1720s.

In the 1920s a revival of courtly lute music overlapped with the well-established cult of carols and folk songs. Anthologies began to appear: Andrews pencilled a reminder to buy Percy Buck's 1929 *Oxford Song Book* on the first page of her Dolmetsch programme. (Auden would include a host of early songs and rhymes in his *Oxford*

Book of Light Verse in 1937.) After the First World War, the hunt for early music gained a nostalgic nationalist tone, a distinct form of 'Englishness'. If music from the English Renaissance was widely played, argued T. H. Yorke Trotter in *Music and Mind* in 1924, 'the feebleness and mechanility of the nineteenth century would give place to the freedom and spontaneity of the Elizabethan age. Music would take its place as a civilizing and ennobling influence.' The focus on Tudor music was both religious and secular. In the 1920s Edmund Fellowes, a canon at St George's Chapel, Windsor, edited the ten-volume *Tudor Church Music*, with Percy Buck and the novelist Sylvia Townsend Warner (prompting criticism from purists for introducing modern choral clefs). But Fellowes also published a collection of English lute songs and madrigals, and went on to record these with the Gramophone Company (His Master's Voice), sung by the English Singers. Gradually, concert-goers, radio listeners and record-buyers became familiar with composers like Henry Lawes, Thomas Tallis, William Byrd and Orlando Gibbons, and Thomas Morley.

In the middle of the decade, the composer Peter Warlock (a friend and biographer of Delius, who with Elgar was credited with the revival of English music), published *The English Ayre*. This retrieved a whole range of works, 'a body of English song of which any country, at any period of history might well be proud'. Warlock showed, too, how 'new' this could feel, opening his introduction with a passage from James Joyce's *Ulysses* – a book still regarded as shocking, and not legally published in Britain – where Stephen Dedalus responds to Bloom waxing lyrical over 'Mercadante and Meyerbeer' by launching into praise of Shakespeare's songs, of the lutenist Dowland and of Byrd, 'who played the virginals in the Queen's Chapel, he said, or anywhere else he found them and one Tomkins who made toys or airs and John Bull'. Joyce himself admired and played Dowland's pieces, copying them from manuscripts in the National Library in Dublin.

The reaffirmation of a lost heritage, catching the attention of modernist artists, musicians and writers (one literary parallel would be Ezra Pound's fascination with the troubadour tradition), ran alongside a concern for 'authentic' performance and instruments. At the concert that Andrews and Power heard in the spring of 1933 Arnold Dolmetsch announced that, having successfully built a medieval harp, he was now 'introducing a combination of instruments seen in early pictures' – lute, harp, rebec, recorder and viol. Andrews herself collected reproductions of such pictures, sticking them in her scrapbook: Vermeer's *Girl with a Guitar*, Orazio Gentileschi's *Lute Player*, Frans Hals' *Boy with a Lute*, Hendrick ter Brugghen's *Boy Playing the Violin*. She followed Dolmetsch too in believing that the insistence on correct instruments affected singing as well as playing. As she put it, Dolmetsch insisted that 'the singing in any period is based on the musical instruments in use at the time. Witness the Elizabethan musical instruments and the swing and jazz music of today in relation to the saxophone and the electric guitar.'

Scholarship and performance also threw a new light on the recovery of folk song and folk dance. While the passion for old songs faded slightly in the twenties, the interest in dance soared. Cecil Sharp's *Country Dance Book*, which appeared in six volumes between 1907 and 1922, had published the tunes of many dances, including those in Playford's mid-seventeenth-century manual, encouraging enthusiasts across the country to revive different forms, including Morris dancing, clog dancing and sword dancing. In 1932, when Power made his print *Folk Dancing*, the first new collection of English country dances since the 1820s was published under the title *Maggot Pie*, and the English Folk Song and Dance Society was formed from a merger of smaller groups, with Vaughan Williams as president. The vogue for folk dancing could be easily mocked as a fad of cranks, sandal-wearing vegetarians. Dora Carrington, for example, dismissed John Nash's wife Christine as tiresome, although she had adored her when they were students at the Slade: 'She is German,

& does Folk Dancing, & walks with a Bouncing movement, & has expectant shining eyes & spectacles. But now I see she is just like all other young ladies who teach Eurythmics in the Chilterns.'

Andrews and Power felt no such scorn. In a programme from the Festival of English Folk Dance and Song at the Albert Hall in 1931, Andrews put firm crosses against Morris dances from Lancashire and Essex and 'The Fool's Dance' from Bampton in Oxfordshire: '*good*', she wrote. She filled her scrapbooks with music for folk songs and dances, often arranged by Power, including old favourites like 'Westron Wynde', 'Sumer is icumen in', Morley's madrigal 'Now is the month of Maying' and Shakespeare's 'Lover and his lass', with its cornfields and rye and message of the transience of youth and love.

> It was a lover and his lass,
> With a hey, and a ho, and a hey nonino,
> That o'er the green cornfield did pass,
> *In springtime, the only pretty ring time,*
> *When birds do sing, hey ding a ding, ding;*
> *Sweet lovers love the spring.*

As well as English songs and carols and medieval poems, carefully written out by Power, in this scrapbook Andrews copied Basque songs, Breton lullabies, Hebridean laments, folk songs from Russia and Romania. Among these, underlining mentions of particular dance tunes like 'The Bonny Broom', 'Newcastle' and 'Dargason', she pasted in an article from *Country Life*, linking the 1934 festival of the English Dance Society at the Albert Hall to a new biography of Cecil Sharp. Describing the mockery that assailed early enthusiasts as 'the cult of the village pump', the article wittily tied folk dance to British institutions: 'Those who cried "faddist" were not silenced until one year when the Oxford City police sent their Morris team to the London Festival. Then it had to be dropped, for after all, policemen cannot be faddists . . .' Noting the use of folk tunes by Holst and Vaughan Williams, the writer argued that England had needed the Cecil Sharp movement just as it needed the revival of Tudor music: both embodied a fruitful form of nationalism, as opposed to a rasping jingoism, offering a counter to 'showy, hard and soulless' cosmopolitanism: 'The discovery of the folk music, the unearthing of the Elizabethans, meant the opening of new vistas, springs of poetry unsealed. The native soil was proved richer than had commonly been thought. Those whose job it was to grow things rather than trade saw an opportunity, and grasped it.'

—

At the Dolmetsch concert in 1933, the revivalist streams overlapped. The annual concerts were held at the Art Workers' Guild in Queen Square, and the very place, with its wood panelling, beaten brass lamps and portraits of founders, linked them to the great days of the Arts and Crafts movement. William Morris had been the Guild's first president and Arnold Dolmetsch had played the virginals to Morris on his deathbed. Dolmetsch was now nearly eighty – craggy, beetle-browed and difficult – but although he had handed over the recorder business to his son Carl in 1925 he still dominated the family ensemble. He had trained in his parents' piano and organ business in Le Mans, and after studying at the Conservatoire in Brussels and the Royal College in London, had begun collecting viols, lutes and early keyboard instruments, playing them at concerts with friends and family, often in Tudor dress. In the years before the First World War his fame spread, his admirers including Pound, Shaw and Yeats, and his *Interpretation of the Music of the Seventeenth and Eighteenth Centuries*, published in 1915, became a key text. Since 1917, when he opened a workshop in Haslemere in Surrey, he had been making and selling period instruments (often 'improving' them in ways that cast more than a little doubt on any authenticity) and from 1925 had been running a summer festival at Haslemere; at the

1930 festival Sir Henry Wood and the composers Constant Lambert and Percy Grainger were in the audience.

Broadcasts by the Dolmetsch family and players like the lutenist Diana Poulton reached out to a public beyond the concert hall. Poulton had been a student at the Slade before she became Dolmetsch's first student in the early 1920s – not a happy experience, as he often reduced her to tears – but encouraged by his elder son, Rudolph, she played her first concert for the BBC in 1926 (live from Battersea Baths, recorded in the humid atmosphere of the covered-over swimming pool). After Peter Warlock gave her a trove of transcripts of Dowland's tablature that he had copied in the British Museum, she began to record Dowland's songs and English Renaissance music generally, winning many new devotees. To most listeners, however, early music still seemed far outside the mainstream: Bach's Brandenburg concertos, for example, sounded hard, crisp and jangly when played on early instruments, compared to the usual lush orchestral settings.

At the Haslemere Festival in 1926, Dolmetsch controversially replaced the flutes in Bach's Brandenburg Concerto IV in G major with two recorders. The sound seemed as strange as Stravinsky or Schoenberg, startlingly new. The instruments appeared strange too, striking players at Haslemere by their 'newness' rather than their antiquity. Andrews and Power, naturally, welcomed both the link to the past and the sense of the modern. Early music was the sound of their own age, and the paring down and preoccupation with pattern seemed akin to their own craft. The blocks of their linocuts overlapped like voices, working together, overlapping in harmony and counterpoint, containing all their skill and experience. 'All I have learnt of drawing, form, colour, pattern & design', wrote Andrews, 'is needed for a good print. It is all there, or it should be. The Block sums it all up . . . A colour block is like a Madrigal in music. Soprano, treble, tenor (trio) or Soprano, Treble, Tenor, Bass (Quartet)'. She kept a card on which Power had written the first verse of a hymn by the Scots poet Horatius Bonar, which they had quoted in 1924 in 'Aims of the Art of To-day':

> In the still air the music lies unheard;
> In the rough marble beauty hides unseen.
> To make the music and the beauty needs
> The Master's touch, the Sculptor's chisel keen.

Amid the hurry of cutting, proofing and printing, their interest was intensified by Dolmetsch's reintroduction of the recorder, ignored in Britain since the eighteenth century. In 1918 Ezra Pound, linking this 'bewildering and pervasive music' to the contemporary cult of Pan and the spirit of art in nature, was astonished, he claimed, to be shown a tube of wood with ivory rings: 'it was a "recorder", whatever that is'. For years it remained a quaint, exotic instrument, the plaything of a few intellectuals: in 1925 the poet and socialist Miles Tomalin noted with amazement, 'Here was an instrument which perhaps a score of people in the world were playing, and the Dolmetsch family accounted for half a dozen of those.'

Year by year, however, recorder sales grew, reaching over five hundred in 1932, when Andrews and Power daringly splashed out on a set of Dolmetsch recorders: a sopranino, descant, treble and tenor in Tulip Wood, and a separate descant recorder for Hal, in African Blackwood. With these, their most extravagant purchase was a Great Bass viol, costing around £20. One Saturday in the following May they drove out to Haslemere with their friends Cuthbert Greig and Doris Holmes to tea at the Dolmetsch workshop. A few weeks later, on a hot July Friday, when the *Colour Prints* show for 1933 had opened at the Redfern and the rush of printing had passed, Andrews headed across town to Belsize Park Gardens to discuss recorders with Miles Tomalin, who had played at the Haslemere Festival since 1925. For Tomalin, as for Diana Poulton, music and politics were mixed: both were committed communists. Tomalin took his recorder with him when he fought in the Spanish Civil War, and was photographed playing it with his anti-tank brigade.

Andrews had no political zeal, but when she alighted on a new project – whether it be linocuts, monotypes or music – her drive was ferocious. Having talked to the charming Tomalin (friends called him 'Apolla', a cockney Apollo), next day she went to meet the oboist Sylvia Spencer, a fellow student of Benjamin Britten at the Royal College – two years later Britten composed two *Insect Pieces* for her, 'The Grasshopper' and 'The Wasp'. Sensing another useful musical contact Andrews carefully wrote down Spencer's Kensington address, but the other people she met that day, Doris ('Dot') and John Bickerdike, would be even more significant. Both were in their early thirties, living with their seven-year-old son in Earls Court, not far from Brook Green, and had just started a company, Omnibus Puppets. Bickerdike was a sculptor, with work already in the V&A. He was a superb woodcarver, specialising in cherubs, angels and saints for cathedrals and churches, but also making smoothly beautiful modernist pieces: his puppets were works of art, dressed in period costumes made by Dot, who was a brilliant puppeteer. In 1934, when the company staged Purcell's *Dido and Aeneas*, it was renamed, becoming famous as the Ebor Marionettes.

The Bickerdikes were early music fans, as many artists were. John Bickerdike's lifelong friend, the painter Richard Eurich, had produced exquisite drawings of a woman at the virginals and a man playing the bass viol in the mid-1920s, while a photo of Barbara Hepworth with her first husband John Skeaping in 1927 shows her holding a cittern, its broad, stringed form a surprising anticipation of her hollowed, stringed sculptures of the 1940s. Within a week of first meeting Andrews, the Bickerdikes came round to Brook Green, playing the lute until midnight; next day Andrews and Power returned the visit and the day after that they all went together to Morleys piano shop in Lewisham, which specialised in early keyboard instruments, to hear John Bickerdike play on the clavichord and virginals. Soon they formed their own weekly music group at Brook Green, and John Bickerdike became plain 'Bicks'. 'Very hot', sighed Sybil on 6 August 1933, 'to V&A to see Viols . . . To Bicks in evening'.

As Power already played the violin and viola their interest grew in viols and other stringed instruments. Alec Hodson from Lavenham, an instrument maker who specialised in harpsichords, spinets and lutes, had lent them pipes and viols to try when they were in Woolpit. This too was the start of a friendship. Andrews kept a photo of Margaret Hodson, known for harpsichord recitals at concerts and on the radio, playing Italian virginals in Elizabethan dress; another showed the Hodsons and friends playing viols outside their house and on the back of this Andrews pencilled a note, 'got my first recorder from Alec Hodson'. Hodson came to see them when he was in London, and they copied early tablature for him from old books and manuscripts in the British Museum. 'S copying lute MS for Hodson, C viol music'. At the same time, Power was cutting and printing his *Folk Dance*.

By the start of 1934 music evenings were a part of life, if not always successful – 'No lute, awful singing', Andrews wrote crossly. 'No lute' was a problem, and to solve it they set out on a shopping trip, first to the Army and Navy stores to see a viola da gamba, and then to the long-established instrument shop of Barnes and Mullins in Rathbone Place. The next day Power bought a modern viola da gamba made by Hans Jordan of Markneukirchen in Germany, a famous instrument-making region.

Soon Dot and Bicks were coming over regularly to try lute songs. Other friends joined them, bringing new music with them, including the funny, unassuming, immensely knowledgeable Edgar Hunt. At twenty-five, the youngest of the group, Hunt played the recorder, flute, clarinet, piano, viola and harpsichord and had played an eighteenth-century ivory flute at the Haslemere Festival in 1931. A graduate of Trinity College of Music, where he would soon give the first recorder classes and found the first early music department, he had grown up surrounded by Tudor music; his father Hubert was Master of the Bristol Cathedral Choristers and Conductor of the Bristol Madrigal Society, as well as a fine violinist and lover of chamber music, and a friend of Edmund Fellowes and other early music fans. Hunt was also passionate about the importance of everyone playing music, especially children, and was beginning his extremely successful campaign for teaching the recorder in schools, thinking it not only an unusual historical instrument with a lovely tone, but one that all ages and abilities could master.

When he joined the music-makers at Brook Green, Hunt was working with the German Emil Brauer, who taught him about German recorder traditions and instrument makers. He quickly asked Power and Andrews to lunch to meet Brauer, 'after which we could probably have some music together . . . if it is not too hot & you feel energetic enough to bring Hans Jordan also (with bow).' He had his own viol, he said, 'longer than "Hans", and I have guitars, lute & umpteen recorders & music to make up a pleasant "broken consort". If you could come I would arrange some special music which we could play & which I could send you beforehand to look over.' They met Brauer again on his next visit the following spring and Andrews pasted a photograph of him in her scrapbook, playing the German *Dudelsackpfeifer*, an enormous set of bagpipes, next to a contrastingly elegant photo of Hunt on the treble recorder. By late 1934 Hunt was commissioning cheap recorders, specially designed with easier 'English' fingering, from Wilhelm Herwig in Markneukirchen. Always in debt, he acted as Herwig's agent until the growing demand left his flat overflowing with recorders, when he found an agent in Schott & Co., who would handle this for him. He also wrote instruction books for amateur ensembles and schools: in January 1935 Andrews drew his hands for the fingering diagrams. Slowly the school recorder movement took off and generations of children would tootle away to the end of the twentieth century and beyond.

———

Music meant friendship. Andrews' energetic enthusiasm always won friends and Power's kindness and gruff wit, as well as his musical knowledge and skill, impressed the whole group, who viewed him with great affection. In November 1934 they formed an ensemble, calling themselves the Brook Green Consort. They had the treble, tenor and bass recorders needed for a recorder consort, as well as a descant and sopranino, but they also wanted to have a consort of viols. For this Power had his Hans Jordan viol and John Bickerdike had a bass lute, or theorbo, with eleven strings. Bickerdike was also restoring a seventeenth-century viol made by Henry Jaye of South-wark, one of the most famous of all British viol-makers. This had been converted into a 'violin' and he was slowly bringing it back to its original form, inspiring typical Power doggerel:

> It's certain that we'll
> Unsatisfied feel,
> Till you alter that viol
> And as we kneel
> & pray & squeal
> To excite your zeal
> To finish the deal,
> Repair & heal.

The group met every Sunday, sometimes spending the whole afternoon and evening together at the studio or at the Bickerdikes'. The core was made up of Andrews and Power, Hunt and Bickerdike, and Hunt's close friends, Max Champion and his wife Stephanie, who played both the violin and recorder. When Andrews made leather covers for their recorders she decorated them with paintings of 'The Brook Green Consort', Power and herself, Hunt and the Bickerdikes and their instruments.

Other friends came and joined them, including some of the Dol-metsch group, as the young Irish artist Medora Heather, who had just finished at the Slade, remembered:

Sybil Andrews, designs for decorated recorder cases

In the winter I used to go to their studio in Hammersmith on Sunday mornings and listen to the Dolmetschs and others playing violas da gamba and other ancient instruments. One man made and repaired violins, and he told me that inside some German ones were engravings and poems where no one would ever see them. Some words he had found in one remained with me: 'When I was alive I was silent, now I am dead I sing sweetly.'

The man repairing violins must have been John Bickerdike, but for all of them music had a touch of magic. The passion deepened. Andrews went to a recorder club in New Malden with the Champions while Power joined the Madrigal Society, and hunted for a guitar to add to his violins and viola. Odd though it seems now, guitars were rarely played at the time. Despite the popularity of Segovia's concerts on the radio it was hard to find one to buy, although Italian luthiers, known for mandolins and violins, were just beginning to produce fine Gypsy Jazz guitars. Instead, in January 1935, Power found a large cittern in Morleys, a lovely instrument with its flat back and metal strings, made around 1725 and still in the original stamped leather case. They also strung Hunt's viola d'amore (played under the chin) as a treble gamba. At that point all these could be picked up astonishingly cheaply, and they spent what little money they had on building a collection. Within a couple of years the studio was full of instruments: an English ten-string baroque guitar, a smaller treble cittern, a Moorish-influenced Spanish guitar, a beautiful mandolin made by the Vinaccia family in Naples in 1779 and a French five-course guitar of 1722.

Power and Andrews, though engrossed in early music, still went to large orchestral concerts and in 1935 Power made a vivid linocut of a piano concerto at the Albert Hall. In *The Concerto* (PLATE 50) we see the orchestra from above and to the side, looking down on the excited conductor with his quiff of black hair and his coat tails swaying like the tail of a cat, echoing the waving baton. In front of him the pianist spreads his arms wide, his whole body seeming to shake as he plays, and the ranks of the orchestra rise up around him. The gaze is that of a music lover, leaning over from his box, almost on top of the stage. Below him two scores flutter like birds about to fly.

Music had always been his great love, and now Andrews joined him. In one photograph, leaning against a table was a new viola da gamba – 'Sybil's bass'. She began collecting books, including Gerald Hayes's *Musical Instruments and Their Music* (1930), Francis Galpin's study of old English instruments, and Robert Donington's account of Dolmetsch's work and theories. Bicks lent her his copy of Christopher Simpson's 1714 work, *Compendium or Introduction to Practical Music*, and she copied out the final paragraph:

> Now I have delivered (although briefly) all such instructions as I thought necessary for your learning of practical Music.
> But it rests on your part to put them in Practice, without which nothing can be effected.
> For by Singing a man is made a Singer; and by Composing, he becomes a Composer. 'Tis practice that brings experience & experience begets that knowledge which improves all Arts & Sciences.

She began to practise her viola da gamba intensely. It was hard work, a real physical strain, as Power noted with amusement:

> *On learning to play the viol*
> When I play on the viol
> Lord! It's a bit of a trial, –
> My legs go all wibbly-wobbly.
> My back! How it aches
> This instrument takes
> Some practice to play it properly
> There was a gambist of West Ken

Some of the Brook Green instruments, around 1937

Who practised from midday till ten.
But her legs started swaying
So she gave up viol playing
And peace once more reigned in her den.

He may have longed for peace, but she was not one to give up. By February 1935 she was good enough to play in an informal concert, which Power celebrated in another of his verses.

Now when I play on the viol,
It's no longer a trial
Why – see how I smile
Sweet sounds I beguile
Though the neighbours revile
I practise meanwhile
In professional style.

The evening of the concert is also the subject of Power's only portrait linocut, *The Trio* (PLATE 51). The viewpoint, unlike that of *The Concerto*, is close up and intimate. The open lid of the harpsichord stretches beyond the frame as Edgar Hunt (rather than Power himself) leans forward intently. In the foreground John Bickerdike sits back, fingering his recorder, and opposite them, in the centre, sits Andrews with her characteristic bob, her fringe flopping forward as she plays. Her bare arms catch the light. She has taken off the jacket of the green silk dress that she made for the occasion (she kept it, wrapped in tissue paper, all her life). Her skirt pools around her feet, soft as water. In the heart of the picture the score shines like a lamp, the rough lines of the staves echoing the radiating lines of light in the background, a waterfall of sound.

27: 'PEOPLE AND FREEDOM'

In the mid-1930s Power made more attempts to get to know his children, whom he had neglected for more than a decade. Now that his work was successful – he knew they were proud of his prints – he seemed more at ease. By 1934 his second son, Cyril, had worked his way back from Australia and was driving buses for the Green Line Company: a trip to Hertford with him inspired Power's *The Sunshine Roof* (PLATE 49), where the hatted passengers gaze ahead in the tilting bus, their backs to the artist. It's a happy print, the patterns on the seats a dazzle of light and dark, reflecting the angular shadows as the bus lurches on. He was also more in touch with his youngest son Kit, fourteen in December 1935, who came up to London to see him at weekends. Kit remembered how interesting 'as well as exhausting' it was, as a teenager, to walk round London with his father, when a sudden turn into an alleyway 'would bring one face to face with an off-the-beaten track gem of Georgian architecture, the quiet corner of a tree-lined square, where time seemed to have stood still, or perhaps an unusual vignette of the Thames waterfront'. He remembered the linocutting too, the long hours of printing and the crumpled proofs.

Power saw his eldest son Toby even more. Deprived of his place at Cambridge, Toby had taken a correspondence course while working at the bank, and gained a BSc in economics, specialising in anthropology, sociology and political theory (he always felt that his banking career was hampered by a reputation as an 'academic'). He then embarked on a doctorate on Hertford's local history, coming up several times a week to the LSE or the British Museum, meeting his father, who was immensely proud of Toby's academic achievement, on odd evenings. In Hertford Toby was part of a network of Catholic artists, poets and intellectuals, connected to the Meynell family and to the anti-fascist 'People and Freedom Group', started by Don Luigi Sturzo, founder of the Christian democrat Partito Popolare Italiano, forced into exile when Mussolini came to power.

They were not the only exiles. From 1933, when Hitler became chancellor, refugees began to arrive in Britain from Germany and Austria. Yet in Britain, too, Hitler had his admirers. On 21 January 1934 ten thousand people turned up to a rally of the British Union of Fascists in Birmingham, organised by Oswald Mosley; a few months later, after several meetings at the Albert Hall, Mosley held a huge rally on 7 June at Olympia in West London, where his black-shirts brutally attacked Jewish and left-wing hecklers in the crowd. A month later, in Germany, came the Nazi killings and arrests of political opponents in the Night of the Long Knives and after a referendum on 19 August Hitler added the title of president to his role as chancellor, becoming the supreme head of state, the Führer.

Yet in Britain that summer, among the elite the Season skipped on as usual, with the Boat Race, Ascot, Henley, Wimbledon and the Test Match at Lord's, and now a new addition, the first Glyndebourne Festival. Stockbrokers set off with their golf clubs, debutantes donned muslin dresses, artists produced new work and galleries put on new shows. The posters Sybil Andrews and other artists were producing evoked a world of sport and pleasure. For many people, however, although prices were low and living standards were gradually rising, life was hard. The Depression continued: the families of coal miners, steelworkers, shipbuilders and textile workers often went without bread.

What did this mean to Power? His prints have no political reference but in these years their mood became both more uneasy and more immediate, acknowledging people as individuals in the crowd, rather than elements in a pattern. In *The Exam Room*, based on his time invigilating for RIBA, the students sit in ranked desks between

Cyril Power, *The Exam Room*, 1934

the pacing invigilators. In contrast to the bus passengers escaping to the country, the candidates are surrounded by walls gleaming with intimidating eyes, a conceit that Power developed from an optical illusion that he had drawn in his sketchbook during one session, where the skylight in the ceiling of the exam room at Conduit Street, seen at an angle, looked down like a lidded eye. The room seethes with sweaty anxiety. Yet all the students, with one woman among the ranks of men, are distinct individuals. They twist their legs or spread them wide, they hunch to the left or lean to the right, they yawn or grimace, hold their heads in gloom, or look smugly at the sufferer on the next desk. Lino does not take kindly to realistic detail. The cutting hand demands wide sweeps, curling lines and bold angles. The faces of these examinees are near caricatures, with something of the grotesquerie of German Expressionist art, the sinister expressions of George Grosz, but, paradoxically, the technique works to add to the disquiet.

The same is true of the passengers in *The Tube Train* (PLATE 48), another print made at this time. The London Underground had long been Power's theme, but this time he moved inside the train, away from the plunging escalators, the swerving tunnels and long platforms. One can almost feel the fug of the carriage as the Tube lurches round a corner, rocking them all sideways. The passengers are crowded together yet separate: like the exam candidates, they are each in their own world. Patterning controls the print, carrying your eyes upwards from the zig-zag lines of floor space, shoes, knees and newspapers, noses and hats, to the glaring lights of the ceiling above. At the back, a group of swaying straphangers breaks the even line.

The faces of the seated figures are schematic, almost cartoon-like, but we know them all: the bored city gent in his hat; the woman with bobbed hair pretending to sleep on her way to the office; the man next to her with his sly sideways glance; the girl at the end in her red dress and high heels. On the right, breaking the row of profiles, a girl with a pale oval face, highlighted with red lipstick and rouge, stares towards us. She is like the drummer girl in Hogarth's *Southwark Fair*, the haunting face in the crowd. Power's print is sardonic yet full of compassion. He took immense care in carving the detail, from the lines of newspaper print and the different types of shoes to the pattern on the upholstery. Andrews told him to cut the detail in his prints and to emphasise the design but for once he ignored her, evoking the packed interior, the human sway and rush beneath the city streets.

In the students at their desks and the workers on the Tube Power caught the disturbing pressure and unease of city life. But in one new print he made in 1935 the people are missing, invisible. *Air Raid*, which Andrews called 'Dog Fight', looked back to the biplanes of the First World War, whirling and diving, crashing in flames. But like the bombed city centres of Alexander Korda's 1936 film *Things to Come*, Power's roaring, circling planes also looked forward, harbingers of carnage ahead. Soon German planes would be bombing and strafing civilians in Spain, and Italian aircraft dropping bombs and gas on villages in Abyssinia.

28: OUT OF LONDON

Although the anxieties of the time seem to seethe behind Power's prints of the mid-1930s, on the whole he and Andrews held back from politics. Her scribbled diary jottings were close-ups of daily life, shopping lists and dentist appointments and printing dates, rather than comments on a wider world. She pencilled in the death of George V in January 1936, but eleven months later, when the papers were full of Wallis Simpson, her priorities were clear: 'December 11. King Edward VIII abdicated the throne. King George VI succeeds. Worked very hard. Got ready puff paste. Decorated Christmas & CEP birthday cake.' She was more excited about the coronation the following year, joining the crowds the night before and watching the procession from Buckingham Gate. But as to what was happening abroad – Germany's invasion of the Rhineland, Stalin's show trials in Moscow, Roosevelt's landslide second-term victory, the coming of the Spanish Civil War – she was silent.

While Power was exploring the crowded spaces of the city – the exam room, the concert hall, the packed carriage on the Underground – her work was taking a different direction, moving out of the city and into the country. Her mood reflected the revival of interest in country crafts and traditions and the rosy ideal of the village, but it was also intensely personal. On the long stays in Woolpit when they painted the walls and explored the village and the well, she had come to see the Suffolk countryside afresh. With its copses and lanes and undulating fields of barley and corn, this was a landscape she had known since childhood, and she cherished its old ways, slowly disappearing like the wild green girl of the Woolpit legend.

In the winter of 1934 she had begun working on a series of country linocuts, in complete contrast to the tense, complex, urban interiors of Power's *Exam Room* and *Tube Train*. Six years later, looking back on twenty years '*entre deux guerres*', T. S. Eliot seized on similar contrasts in *East Coker*, the poem of his own ancestral village. In one realm are the city commuters, stuck in the Underground train when it stops between stations,

> And the conversation rises and slowly fades into silence
> And you see behind every face the mental emptiness deepen
> Leaving only the growing terror of nothing to think about.

In another realm are the deep lanes and open field. Here,

> On a summer midnight, you can hear the music
> Of the weak pipe and the little drum
> And see them dancing around the bonfire . . .
>
> Leaping through the flames, or joined in circles,
> Rustically solemn or in rustic laughter
> Lifting heavy feet in clumsy shoes,
> Earth feet, loam feet, lifted in country mirth
> Mirth of those long since under earth
> Nourishing the corn.

Those dancers, as Eliot said, had all gone under the hill. Something of that ancient life is felt in Andrews' *Fall of the Leaf*, where the trees rise above a billowing hill, forming fans against the white paper of the sky. Below them a team of horses follows the sweep of the ploughed fields. Simple in conception and design, the glowing autumn scene was in fact an elaborate work, printed in five colours – chrome yellow, 'transparent golden ochre', crimson, viridian and Chinese blue – and made almost three-dimensional by her cross-hatching on the blocks to get texture and depth, so that branches, grasses and stubble seem to rise and sway in the wind.

In *Fall of the Leaf* the ploughman and his team are dwarfed by the immensity of fields and trees, but in *Tillers of the Soil* (PLATE 52), made around the same time, the horses are huge. They surge towards us in their heavy collars, over the top of the hill, with the clouds and swooping gulls behind. She had, she said, made many sketches on her walks through the deep hollow lanes around the village, stopping at the corner of a field and seeing the horses bearing down. The breezy day is light and alive, while the horses' bent heads and knees show the effort needed to pull the iron plough, turning the sticky soil into furrows as sharp as small cliffs. Behind the horses, the ploughman's strength is clear too, from his stance and firm grasp of the arms of the plough. A quarter of a century later, halfway across the globe, Andrews would make a linocut she called *Day's End* (PLATE 54), almost a dark, reversed image of *Tillers of the Soil*. Living in Wool-pit, she said, she 'used to see the team of 3 very often, at all times of day. Thus came "Day's End". I met them at dusk, day's work over, a catch of frost in the air – the plowman has hoisted himself up across the horses' withers as was the custom, not astride, & has thus come jingling.' *Day's End* was one of her favourite prints.

In 1935 another Suffolk print, *Michaelmas*, used a bold, dramatic, angular view from above, as if a crow was flying over an autumn field, looking down on farm carts and horses as men spread muck on the fields. 'Get the horses dark', she wrote in her print book. Explaining *Michaelmas* to the New York gallery owner Mary Ryan and her sister Catherine, Andrews told them that this date in late September, the old church festival of St Michael and All Angels, is 'the end & the beginning of a farmer's year'. With the harvest safely housed,

the barns, byres & farm-yards & muck heaps were all taken out & all piled in regular piles in the fields, all ready for the farmer to plough in, giving back to the soil what was taken out of it . . . soil

Sybil Andrews, *Fall of the Leaf*, 1934

to soil . . . and so you see in my print the men all busy tramping the heap of muck, nice black, steaming, stinking muck, into tumbrils to convey to the fields, ready for the plough. It was nature's way . . . I wanted to call my print 'Muck Spreading' but thought it might offend sensitive ears . . .

Soil to soil. The following year, she returned to the fields in a print named *Haysel* (PLATE 53), the East Anglian term for haymaking season, showing two men working in harmony, their bent legs and curving scythes forming a counterpoint to the straight ridges of stubble. The men reappeared in another print, *Mowers*, a jagged trio wearing straw hats as they sharpen their scythes.

———

Andrews showed *Fall of the Leaf* and *Tillers of the Soil* in the Redfern *Colour Prints* exhibition of 1934. But while she was depicting Suffolk scenes in her work, she was also exploring new landscapes in person. A week after the show opened, while Power was invigilating at RIBA, stuck in that exam room from nine in the morning until nine at night – '*en loge*', as Sybil put it, as if he were in a concierge's cubby-hole – she was off and away, camping with Hal in the New Forest.

Hal was in high spirits. In March he had become engaged to a nurse called Norah, whom he had met by chance a month before in the Bury Museum. He taught her to ride (she looked lovely in jodhpurs, he thought), bought her a ring of carved jade and took her for a weekend in London, going to the theatre and visiting the Zoo and on to see Sybil at the Brook Green studio. Finally – at least for a while – his life looked settled.

In the four years that Hal had spent his holidays camping in the Forest Sybil had only been down twice, for short weekends. This was her first long visit. On 17 July Power took over her diary for the day, starting with a reminder: 'Meet Hal am 8 o/c Waterloo. Very

Hot all day. Thunderstorm in evening'. Then she continued herself, her pencil running on to the next day: 'leave here 8 o'clock get up 7 o'clock at latest take Ryvita. Bring food. Be there.' On a baking hot morning she met Hal and they took the train to Brockenhurst. Then they tramped three miles with their packs to Dilton in the heart of the Forest, pitching their tents in a glade above a pool, swimming in the water – very cold despite the heat – cooking bacon over the fire and wandering through the woods in the falling dark, hearing the owls hoot. On windy days with great cumulus piled high in the sky they walked through the trees in a cloud of butterflies – Red Admirals, Painted Ladies and Great Whites – and spent idle afternoons writing letters and splashing in the pool. They watched a kingfisher catch minnows, a lizard dart between the stones, a fox slipping through the bushes. Before breakfast, Sybil drew and painted. In the early morning cool, they wore long cloaks; with his green jerkin, hooded cloak and sandals, wrote Hal, 'I look and feel medieval.'

After a week, interrupted only once by thunder and showers, they took a train to Lymington and walked down to the Solent, camping at a little bay called Pitts Deep, where the forest oaks met the mudflats and salt marshes. This was their Crusoe moment, their 'Castaway Camp' – not wholly idyllic as a huge spring tide rushed up fast and flooded their camp in the middle of the night. 'Most marvellously', said Hal, the edges of their groundsheets floated up, leaving them dry with water ankle deep around them. Stumbling in the dark they moved camp to a bank of gorse, waking at dawn to heavy clouds and quitting at six in the morning, before wandering and camping for another few days.

Soon she was back in Brook Green, with friends coming in to play music, the laundry to do, the kitchen to scrub. Yet she was not in town for long. A fortnight later she and Power set off for Sark in the Channel Islands. This was both a holiday and a plunge into another artistic circle. The teacher Eric Drake and his rich American wife Eloise, 'Lisel', an ex-Slade student, had started the Sark Art Group a few years earlier, hoping to imitate the artists' colony in St Ives in Cornwall, and had built a studio and a gallery with a distinctive curved roof, opened in 1933 by the young Sybil Hathaway, Dame of Sark, already a fiercely autocratic figure. For a few brief years, until Drake ran off with the gallery's receptionist and Lisel left, taking her money with her, the gallery became a social centre, and a haunt of art students, including Drake's former pupil Mervyn Peake.

In 1933 Iain Macnab sent woodcuts for the group's opening exhibition. Other Grosvenor artists then joined in, including the wood-engravers Tom Chadwick and Gwenda Morgan. For a month's show in June and July 1934 Andrews sent her monotypes *Rue du Hallage, Rouen* and *Le Petit Bay, St Malo*, and Power his *St Malo* and *Riverside*. Now they were bringing linocuts for a different show in September: Andrews' *Haulers* and *The Gale* and Power's *High Swing, Giant Racer* and *Folk Dancing*. But their trip to Sark began badly: a slow train to Southampton, an 'awful trippy crowd', many of them drunk, on a crammed overnight ferry to Guernsey, then a boat across rough seas to Sark. The arrangements had all been made, or so they thought, by Ala Story, who had worked both at the Redfern and in Sark and was now running her own gallery, the Storran, next to the Royal Academy. But Ala's promised friend did not turn up, they could not get into the harbour through the narrow channel and had to be taken off in fishing boats and then 'Ala mucked everything – no rooms – only temporary. Left us after 5 mins & went off in a boat. Mercy that we brought grub.' The rain set in. Power sent a postcard to Edgar Hunt, and Andrews wrote too. 'So sorry to hear you have been disappointed in the islanders and the weather,' wrote Hunt, replying to them jointly. 'Hope things have improved. I enjoyed reading your words of venom! So nice to feel you "letting yourselves go!" In pencil – hope it has inspired the paint brushes into something vigorous.'

Things did improve. They made no attempt to see the island's other artists: as so often, they were outliers to the main group, and they liked being together, by themselves. There were no cars on Sark (and there are still none today) but the island is only three miles long and a mile and a half wide, and they explored slowly on foot, staying in different cottages overnight. Even on wild days they managed to sketch. Taking it in turns, they jotted brief notes in Andrews' diary, a loop of names: La Ville, Dixcart Bay, Havre Grosselin, La Grève with its sand at low tide, Port du Moulin, the sea rushing through the narrow channel between the small isle of Brecqhou and the Gouliot caves, whose walls and floor were covered with sea anemones, scarlet, deep pink, pale and dark green, gleaming in shafts of light from above. They walked to Little Sark over the narrow isthmus of La Coupée, with a dizzying drop on each side, and looked back past the headlands towards Jersey and the distant coast of France. At Pointe Derrible and Dixcart Bay they watched the tides swirl through the rock arch, and the great surf break and spread.

They picnicked on the cliffs, Power in his short-sleeved shirt, rolling up his trousers, Andrews in her favourite sandals and the long skirt she had made herself over the winter, tying a handkerchief over her head to act as a sunhat. They scrambled down to pebbly bays and when the gales gave way to sea mist and sun, they sunbathed and swam in the clear water. Andrews' crossness disappeared: 'lovely day', 'beautiful day', 'very hot day', 'gorgeous day'. Power filled a whole sketchbook with drawings of the castle on the hill, the jagged strata and sloping grass of the cliffs, green on grey, the bracken-covered headlands, the little town with its roofs of slate, red tiles and rusty corrugated iron, the winding paths and overhanging trees. Both would use these sketches in a new run of monotypes.

On a stormy day towards the end of their time on the island they took refuge with the artist Medora Heather, who had fallen in love with Sark and came out to the island every autumn and spring, living in a cottage high above the Gouliot caves belonging to Elie and Hannah Carteret, from an old island family. 'Sybil Andrews and Cyril Power came in the afternoon,' Medora wrote, 'dripping from head to foot and cold. We had tea round the fire and good interesting talk.'

Being with her, talking round the fire, as they did in the studio at Brook Green, was a step back into normal life. Early on the morning of 15 September they crossed to Guernsey and took the mail boat home. Sark had been a breathing space. It gave them time to enjoy each other's company, reaffirming their close bond, exploring and sketching and discussing their plans, in the way that they had done on the earlier French holidays, free from the pressure of London life.

———

Power had bought a new camera and several photographs from 1934 to 1937 recorded the different aspects of their life: the murals at Woolpit; the studio at Brook Green, with the printing press and the poster of Football hanging up to dry; the collection of recorders, viols and guitars. In Sark they photographed each other sitting on the cliff tops at Pointe Derrible, looking out to sea, Cyril in shirt-sleeves and Sybil walking through the heather in her long home-made skirt. At Dixcart Bay Cyril snapped her in her swimming costume, leaning against the rocks. Later she pasted these into her large scrapbook, 'Sybil's Delight', beneath transcriptions of island folk songs, not from Sark but from the Hebrides, songs like '*Tir-nan-og*', ballad of the sunset country in the western seas. 'land of the ever-young'. Other photographs recorded New Forest days: Hal in front of a tent, bare-chested with a bandana round his head; Power playing his pipe beneath the trees. The music that surrounds these is lighter, with songs such as 'A roving', 'Rio Grande', 'Waltzing Matilda', and arrangements of Kipling poems like 'Merrow Down' and 'Lukannon'.

Memories of Woolpit, Sark and the Forest were a solace in the winter city. In the cold February of 1935, when Power was working on monotypes of Port du Moulin and the Gouliot rocks, Andrews was painting watercolours of the New Forest: 'Root Rampant', 'Forest Stream', 'Trees by the Pool', 'Early Morning in the Forest', 'Beech Glade'. She found time to paint, even though their days were full.

Sybil and Cyril on Sark, 1934

Cyril at Castaway Camp,
New Forest, 1935

There were new instruments and more meetings of the consort; the publishers Eyre and Spottiswood ordered drypoint illustrations of Ely and Norwich; the Redfern wanted linocuts for Los Angeles; the London Transport Board was waiting for the posters for ice hockey and cricket. Add to all this activity Andrews' new passion for shopping, spending her London Transport fees: Chinese beads from the Army and Navy store; green Palestine sandals from Jaeger; material for a kilt; a belt and buckle from the 'Russian shop'; a green Dunlop mac; suede shoes from Lillywhites, a hat from Baldwins.

Power was still invigilating at RIBA, but in March he gathered together his architectural drawings, asked his reliable old friend Cuthbert Greig for a reference and applied for a full-time job with the London County Council. He was a well-known artist now, but like many artists, who often took jobs as teachers, the sales of his work would never bring in enough to contribute properly to the family in Hertford, or to pay for his instruments, his trip to Sark, his lino and paints, his share of the expenses at Brook Green. Ralph Wilson, a student of his at Goldsmith's many years ago, was now in charge of the Architects' Department at the LCC: the job was offered, due to begin at County Hall in May.

The bustle at Brook Green was accompanied by incessant noise from gymnastics and dance classes upstairs. This had begun the previous autumn, with 'awful banging upstairs in evening. Dancing & lumping about', and seemed likely never to end. They both wrote irate notes in the diary: 'Musical Drill in morning frightful racket, bumping & jumping in pm. We both had to complain (twice)'; 'Hell's delight upstairs, played piano 8 o'c to 12, then wireless, lumped about till half 2 o'c.' On his days off work Power took refuge in the British Museum, transcribing music. In the summer of 1935 London's streets were full of bunting for George V's Silver Jubilee, an excuse for more music and more dancing. In late May, Edgar Hunt, who had been making a broadcast in Bristol and writing a 'Recorder Tutor' for Boosey and Hawkes, was working on a pageant at Tower Hill.

In June, when the Jubilee excitement was over, Sybil took some time off. Her friend from Grosvenor days, Sam Butler, was in London, worrying about a new job in South Africa; she gave him linocutting lessons, walked with him along the towpath in the sun and they feasted on asparagus. It was a brief lull. The tempo stepped up again ahead of the annual *Colour Prints* exhibition, coming round once again, in July. On the last possible day they cut the blocks, inked, printed and proofed Power's *Air Raid*, working until two or three in the morning and getting up again at six to deliver the prints so that they could be hung in time for the Private View. As well as their linocuts, both artists also had works in the monotypes section. 'Very tired', Sybil wrote after the show opened, before turning to her standard way of winding down – making raspberry jam. Then she could relax. At the end of the month she spent two days at the International Folk Dance Festival at the Albert Hall, 'enthralling'. The next day was a Saturday and since Cyril was not at work, they had a picnic in St James's Park and walked down to the river to see the dancers go into Lambeth Palace. Their afternoon ended at one of the countless self-service tea shops run by the Aerated Bread Company, which had become an alphabetic symbol of dusty, daily London life, a place where bus drivers ate bacon and eggs, shoppers ate crumpets, abandoned lovers wept into sugar bowls and writers grabbed a coffee and wrote in the corner for hours. But for Sybil it was bliss. She could stretch and relax, before going home to her favourite task. 'Great fun!' she said of the dancers. Then, 'On to Tate after and tea at an ABC afterwards. Feel better for it. Made Morello Jam in evening.'

———

At the end of July 1935 she went back to the Forest with Hal, setting up camp at Pitts Deep again, this time high on the gorse bank, safe from the tide. In the evening mist the sea looked like a sheet of glass, merging with the horizon and the sky. The water was warm and in the shallows, full of coloured shells, small fish played. Gulls, shanks and curlew called around them, 'a wonderful life'. From here they moved into the Forest, setting up tents in different places and giving them names: 'Birch Tree Camp' on Ober Heath near Brockenhurst, 'Viper Camp', near Highland Water where the woods meet the open heath.

In glorious weather, Cyril joined them, staying in a cottage near the site of Hal's old caravan. The Forest was new to him, and he spent the first day wandering through it alone, seeing a fox run across the ride and wild ponies on the common. On the heath, Sybil grabbed Cyril just as he was about to step on a large viper, to Hal's amusement: 'He is so scared of snakes I knew he would meet one as soon as he came here.' He was a city man, even when he played his pipe under the trees. When Hal went back to Bury, Sybil moved into Cyril's digs. For another week they explored the forest, rivers and creeks. Their final stop was the Rufus Stone, the place where Sybil's ancestor Sir Walter Tyrell was supposed to have shot William Rufus while hunting in the forest in 1100, his arrow, aimed at a stag, ricochetting off an oak tree, killing the king instantly.

A day later, on 13 September, tanned and easy, carrying full sketch-books, they took the train back to town. Next day: 'C back to work, S cleaned'. But from now on, driven by weariness of the art world and rumours of war, Sybil was impatient to move out of London.

29: CHANGE ALL AROUND

The Redfern exhibitions were changing. Linocuts were no longer the latest thing and sales were slowing. Rex Nan Kivell had already widened the range of the summer shows and after the gallery moved to Cork Street in 1935, he flung the net still wider, suggesting a rather desperate attempt to move stock. In 1936, cartoons by Daumier were followed by lithographs from Vuillard, Bonnard, Toulouse-Lautrec and Marie Laurencin, prints by Corot and Derain, etchings by Picasso, wood and line engravings by Eric Gill, colour woodcuts by Yoshijiro Urushibara, and many more. A Matisse print cost seven guineas – roughly the cost of a flight from Croydon airport to Paris – and a Picasso eight, while Toulouse-Lautrec reached a heady eighteen and Dürer's *Madonna with a Monkey* a sky-high £30 – but the linocuts and most of the other prints still cost between two and four guineas.

If linocuts were under pressure at the Redfern, Ward's Gallery, where Flight and his group were showing, would soon stop their linocut exhibitions altogether. Andrews and Power could hardly rely on their prints to keep them afloat. Andrews had small inherited funds in investments and government bonds, and Power had his regular job in the Architects' Department of the LCC, working first in the Hospital Division and later in the School Division. It was a steady income but County Hall was not a natural home for an old-style architect; as Andrews said, 'He belonged to the time when it was individual practice & he hated the big firms employing dozens of architects like so many office boys.' Their friend Tony Weatherhead made an affectionate sketch of Power bundled up against the cold, going off to work rather glumly.

One change in life at Brook Green in 1935 was that Andrews began to take pupils to add to her income. That autumn the American Ida Fischer arrived on her doorstep eager for lessons, having come to London with her sister Olga and her friend Risa Lowie, a teacher and poet. Now middle-aged, all three had been born in Vienna, moving to New York as children, and they brought a dash of colour to life at Brook Green. Power squired Risa Lowie round the city, showed her the sights and brought her back to tea, while 'Ida sent in tongue, wine & pickle & we finished the cakes from Thursday'. Another day, 'To Risa's for party in evening – self, CEP, Ida, Olga, & Mr Black – fine time'. On an impulse, Fischer had become determined to be an artist. A fine soprano singer, then a music teacher in the Bronx, she had seen the Grosvenor School linocuts at the Shanghai exhibition when she was in China on a sabbatical, and wrote to Andrews asking if she would teach her. At her first lesson, she was keen but unprepared, having, she said, never drawn or painted or had anything to do with graphic art. 'We struggled through the first day,' wrote Andrews:

> Since she knew nothing, it was hard even to begin. At last, on the second day, she put down her charcoal or whatever she was using and said: –
>
> 'I see, before I can make a good linocut print I must first learn to draw, learn to paint, learn to compose a picture, learn to understand colour and tone.'
>
> I said: – 'You must learn all these things'
>
> 'All right' she replied, 'teach me to paint.'
>
> This applies to anyone wanting to take up linocuts. Ignorance is no use – only knowledge and experience.

Fischer gained the knowledge and experience, and eventually gave up teaching and became an accomplished artist, whose abstracts and collages were bought by major museums.

Andrews charged 10s 6d a lesson, so a course of six lessons added up to a useful three guineas. In addition, Fischer commissioned some embroidery and Risa ordered a bookplate for her brother, Robert H. Lowie, a distinguished anthropologist and professor at Berkeley, known for his studies of the Crow tribe from the Great Plains. When Andrews finished the bookplate and sent it to New York, Risa responded with joy, writing to 'dearest Sybil' and sending all good wishes 'to Cyril too', saying how thrilled she was by the design. This now appears blatantly stereotypical but to Risa it was 'a truly fine interpretation of a high type of Indian . . . the feathers are so feathery . . . and the symbols, as if on a war blanket, stand out in distinctness yet in restraint.' It was also oddly prophetic, looking forward to Andrews' own interest in years to come in the tribal culture, costume and dance of British Columbia.

The Americans stayed in touch after they left, and Fischer in particular remained devoted to Andrews. While she was in London, she gave Andrews two tickets for the International Exhibition of Chinese Art at the Royal Academy, a stunning display of treasures from the imperial palace in Beijing, bronze and jade sculptures, ceramics and landscape scrolls. Ten years later, after Fischer paid another visit to China (where she sang the soprano solo in the *Messiah*), she sent Andrews a perfect set of Chinese cutting tools and brushes. Thanking her, Andrews wrote, 'I am aware so strongly of the hands which made these tools.' She felt nostalgic, she said, for the 'old China' of that exhibition, remembering 'lovely paper – lovely old silks & embroideries – bronzes – jade, joss sticks & incense – Chinese prints & paintings . . . I always hoped to visit China one day.'

At the same time, an equally astounding accumulation of riches was on display in the exhibition of Russian art at 1 Belgrave Square, filled with jewels, pictures and textiles, many smuggled out by White Russians before the Revolution. But both this and the Chinese exhibition had disturbing undertones, messages of the fragility of power: of the Russian aristocracy overtaken by the Revolution; of the

EX
LIBRIS
ROBERT H. LOWIE

government of China under Chiang Kai-shek, now threatened by the Japanese occupation and the rise of the Communist Party of China, currently regrouping under Mao Tse-tung. Regimes could topple, stability could disappear, freedoms could vanish.

For Andrews and Power, these two exhibitions were also links with another new contact, Baron George de Menasce. If Ida Fischer and Risa Lowie had given a dash of colour to London life, de Menasce, whose family were leaders of the Jewish community in Alexandria, brought a touch of true glamour. His father Felix, a financier and cotton trader, was one of the richest men in Egypt; his half-brother Jean de Menasce, a close friend of Cavafy, translated *The Waste Land* into French and was hailed by Eliot as 'my best translator'; his half-sister Claire Vincendon was known in Alexandria for her stage designs, costumes and reviews and her daughter Claude would become Lawrence Durrell's third wife. De Menasce himself was an avid collector, amassing what has been called the finest private collection of Chinese ceramics in the world, as well as acquiring Greek island tapestries, Roman and Syrian glass, Indian enamels, Turkish embroideries and gold snuff-boxes, Russian icons and Fabergé eggs. He was also a fine pianist, giving celebrated weekly recitals, and had heard of Andrews and Power through musical friends in Alexandria, Clement Barber, manager of the British Cotton Buying Commission, and his wife Eve, who organised madrigal singing, rather incongruously in that setting.

De Menasce, who was often in Paris and London, rang up without warning one Sunday in June 1936 and whisked Andrews and Power off for lobster salad and strawberries at Scott's in Mayfair. Towards the end of his stay, the Barbers came on leave from Alexandria and Eve Barber invested heavily in their linocuts, buying at least one impression of almost every print, and effectively acting as their agent in Egypt. De Menasce too scooped up a whole portfolio of linocuts, monotypes, drypoints and watercolours, including Cyril's painting of the sitting room in the Woolpit cottage. Without blinking, he paid over double the gallery price, another addition to Brook Green funds. Next spring he was back, taking them to more lunches and dinners and visiting the studio to watch them print. On Andrews' birthday in April 1937 he brought a friend to look through their prints, and took them all in his Daimler to dinner at Prunier's in St James Street, where two years earlier the Prince of Wales and Wallis Simpson used to stroll in for lunch. Andrews, however, was not one for rapture: 'Jolly good dinner' was all she wrote.

———

In 1936, as well as gasping at the treasures from China and Russia, Londoners encountered startling work from modern artists. Avant-garde art had begun to look different. In 1933 Paul Nash had founded the Unit One group, launched with a declaration of commitment to modernism, abstraction and Surrealism. Unit One, Nash said in his letter to *The Times*, 'may be said to stand for the expression of a truly contemporary spirit, for that thing which is recognized as peculiarly of to-day in painting, sculpture, and architecture'. The group held an exhibition in 1935, starting in Cork Street and then touring the country – their first and only show, before the group crumbled under inner tensions. The pioneering Seven and Five group (already transformed into the sleeker-looking '7&5') also changed course. Having purged all the figurative artists, Ben Nicholson followed Nash's lead by forming a strictly abstract group and organising a show, which included his own pure white reliefs, at the Zwemmer Gallery in Litchfield Street, off the Charing Cross Road, in October 1935. This too was a solitary venture, a first and last show.

Abstraction was here however, if not immediately welcomed. When Sydney John Woods put on a show of *Modern Pictures for Modern Rooms: Abstract Art in Contemporary Settings* at the small Duncan Miller Gallery in London in April 1936, he used words reminiscent of those of Claude Flight promoting the first linocuts: 'If you travel by car or tube or aeroplane, live in glass and concrete, move in a world where speed and space, light and precision are elements of importance, you expect an art arising out of this.' Not a single work sold. The first significant British exhibition of abstract art, *Abstract & Concrete*, opened in Oxford and travelled to Liverpool, Newcastle and Cambridge, before a London gallery, the Lefevre, dared to take the plunge, mounting the show in April and May 1936. As well as displaying work by young British artists, including Henry Moore's reclining figure and Barbara Hepworth's *Discs in Echelon*, the exhibition introduced new, continental movements: the Abstraction-Création group from Paris; the adherents of Concrete Art, intent on expressing abstract ideas in tangible form; the Constructivism of Naum Gabo and the austerity of the Dutch 'De Stijl' artists with their verticals and horizontals and primary colours, exemplified by Mondrian.

Then on 11 June 1936, something stunningly new happened at the New Burlington Galleries – the opening of the London International Surrealist Exhibition. Here works by leading continental artists – André Breton and Marcel Duchamp, Max Ernst and Giacometti, Klee, Picasso and Magritte, Dora Maar, Meret Oppenheim and Leonor Fini – were shown alongside those of British artists including Paul Nash and Eileen Agar, John Banting, Graham Sutherland and Sheila Legge. Two thousand people flocked to the opening, when Salvador Dalí gave a lecture. As he was wearing a full diving suit, this was totally inaudible and he almost suffocated, saved when his helmet was prised off with a billiard cue. In the catalogue Herbert Read warned:

Do not judge this movement kindly. It is not just another amusing stunt. It is defiant – the desperate act of men too profoundly convinced of the rottenness of our civilisation to want to save a shred of its respectability.

The philosophers, said Marx, have only *interpreted* the world in different ways; the point, however, is to *change* it. The artists too have only interpreted the world; the point, however, is to transform it.

The surreal was implicit in the linocuts of Andrews and Power, especially in Power's Tube stations and swings, where space dissolves and humans voyage to the depths or fly high, morphing into birds. And while they did not collect 'found objects' they sympathised with Paul Nash's response to the poetic quality of natural forms. Nash discussed this in articles in the *Architectural Review*, which Power took, and in essays like 'The Life of the Inanimate Object', published before his solo exhibition at the Redfern in May 1937, in *Country Life*, which they both read.

They made no comment on the anti-fascist concerns of the Surrealists. Sometimes, however, a small incident forced them to face the rise of fascism and the rolling out of violence across Europe. On Saturday 17 October 1936 they went to the New Burlington Galleries to see a show of French nineteenth-century painting. From there, in a jolting clash between old art and present conflicts, they went on 'to Felicia Browne's in Frith Street'. This was a memorial exhibition. That summer Browne – a committed communist, cheery and bespectacled with a pudding-basin haircut – had been driving through France and Spain with the photographer Edith Bone. They arrived in Spain just as war broke out and on 3 August Browne joined a communist militia. Three weeks later she was killed, while trying to dynamite a Nationalist munitions train, the first British volunteer to die in the Spanish Civil War. Her sketchbook was in her pocket.

Perhaps it was this atmosphere of tension, of the renewed threat to all they knew, and the loss of precious lives, that made both Power and Andrews turn back to religious themes for their prints. In the Redfern exhibition of 1937, Power showed a very different print to his exam rooms and concert halls, an archaic-looking figure of St

Cyril Power, *St Francis*, 1938

Francis. Plans for a new edition of his *Medieval Church Architecture*, which he was discussing with William Hanneford-Smith at Batsford, returned his attention to the Gothic, and his print had the feeling of a statue in a niche on an ancient facade – rather too fussy and complex to be successful as a linocut. Francis stands with arms outstretched and hands open, his face calm yet pensive. Behind him, Power left the buff tissue paper blank, making the saint float in light; above his rayed halo, the dove of the Holy Spirit shadows him with its wings. The moon and sun swim over his shoulders and birds flock to his sides. On his left, a peacock struts and on the right a wolf looks up – the Woolpit wolf perhaps. Between the tree roots, a toad creeps towards him. The central figure is embraced by borders of wings and curving lines of flight, and, at his feet, grass waving like the sea.

Andrews too returned to a religious theme in these years before the war in *The Prodigal Son*, although her finished linocut would not be shown until 1943. This is one of the most moving of her prints, and she always spoke of it with unusual tenderness. The two figures form an oval, embraced by curving shadows: 'You can see that the father forgives him,' she said, her fingers repeatedly tracing the curve on the print, 'the way he is touching his head. And there is the son, in all his humility.' In the parable in Luke's gospel, the father tells the resentful elder son who had stayed at home working in the fields, 'It is meet that we should make merry, and be glad: for this thy brother was dead, and is alive again; and was lost, and is found.' Most illustrations of this made Andrews impatient because they left out vital details, like the pigs. Her own print sweeps down to include them, running up the hill, a reminder of the son's time keeping swine in a foreign land, when hunger drove him to eat the pigs' food. Perhaps she thought of her own father Charles, near destitute, struggling in a land far from home, never to be reconciled with his own strict father. Perhaps, too, of the sons lost for ever in war.

IV: MOVING

Sybil Andrews, *Prodigal Son*, 1939

30: SEA AND FOREST

As the 1930s rolled on, the threat of war seemed to overhang everything. Disturbed by the mood of the times, many people, artists, musicians and writers among them, were leaving the capital. Yet for Andrews and Power the old routines continued. Their working calendar was still set by bursts of printing for exhibitions. Around these, life was solidly domestic, with Sybil marching Cyril off to buy a suit and sports jacket at Webb Miles and a mac from the Army and Navy, and looking after him, rather impatiently, when he was ill: 'C came home in high fever, put him to bed.' He went up to Hertford to see Dolly and to go to the wedding of his son Cyril ('Boisie') to Christina Peel in October 1936; their son John, Power's first grandchild, was born the following year. Every now and then his children appeared at Brook Green. When Toby turned up one Friday night, worried about the delivery of his thesis, due the following week, when he had to be at work at the bank in Hertford, Sybil dashed round with it to the university on his behalf. Kit came down on Saturdays; at Easter 1937 Cyril took Kit and Peggie to St Paul's and brought them back for supper.

Andrews' diary was still as full of Power's doings as her own, just as it had been fifteen years ago, alternating between the familiar 'C' and 'CEP' and 'JM', for Jest Master. They played music with Max and Stephanie Champion and Edgar Hunt. (In 1937 Stephanie and Edgar founded the Society of Recorder Players with Arnold Dolmetsch, and a year later Edgar married Elizabeth Voss, editor of *The Amateur Musician*.) They went together to friends' private views. They went to the cinema and to a rash of Shakespeare plays at the Old Vic and the open-air theatre in Regent's Park. In this familiar rhythm the seasons passed: fog blanketed the city at Christmas; snow, hail and sleet fell at Easter; on spring days they walked the towpath, on summer evenings they met at Waterloo after Cyril finished work at County Hall, took the train out of the city and walked on Box Hill in the sunset. Yet for both of them London life, which had been so exciting ten years ago, was beginning to feel humdrum. The excitement of speed echoed still louder, hollered out in the film *Night Mail* in 1936, with Auden's poetry and Britten's thrumming music, echoing the pounding of the train as it speeds from London to the Clyde,

> Towards the steam tugs yelping down a glade of cranes,
> Towards the fields of apparatus, the furnaces
> Set on the dark plain like gigantic chessmen.

But for Cyril and Sybil speed was losing its allure. They felt a need to slow down, to turn their backs on the city, to retreat into the country.

Holidays were different in 1936. They still went to Woolpit, walking and sketching and tackling the overgrown jasmine, but now that Cyril was working full-time the weeks of exploring village history were a thing of the past. Sometimes Sybil went alone, seeing her old aunts in Bury and walking in the moonlight to the Lady's Well. Hal was not there this summer – he was off to Scandinavia, sailing up the coast and hiking inland. Coming home in late August 1936 he wrote, '*Another* expedition ends leaving me brimful of new ideas of all kinds, and not at all wanting a settled existence for I don't know how long.' Not surprisingly he broke off his engagement to Norah – perhaps to her relief.

Any wanderlust that Sybil and Cyril felt had to be satisfied with short breaks. On Whitsun weekend their old friends Cuthbert Greig and Doris Holmes drove them down to Rhodes Minnis in the downs beyond Canterbury, where Cuthbert planned to build a house. They walked in the Elham valley and went down to Lympne, where Cyril had been posted during the war, then left at five thirty on Monday morning so that he could get to the office. In mid-August they were back again, surveying the plot for the house, which Cyril designed. (The following January he was up until two finishing the plans, with Sybil helping to colour them and eventually writing in relief, 'Finished Cuthbert's plans & took them along – thank goodness!') Then in late September 1936, a few weeks after their Whitsun trip, perhaps inspired by Paul Nash's new *Shell Guide* to the county, they went to Dorset, staying in Corfe Castle, exploring Worbarrow Bay and Flower's Barrow in a stormy sunset, and climbing the green terraces of Maiden Castle. At the time, Mortimer Wheeler was excavating the iron age cemetery, where the scattered white bones, glinting in the sunshine, appeared to Nash like 'nests of giant birds; the gleaming skulls like clutches of monstrous eggs'.

Dorset revived their interest in archaeology and history, and their mystical sense of the deep past: this year Andrews made a print that she called *Tumulus*, of a twisted, living tree emerging from a barrow, a prehistoric burial site. But their real escapes were still to Suffolk, to the quiet area south of Woodbridge between the rivers Deben and Alde. For a week in August 1936, and again the following year, they stayed in Shingle Street, an eerie and beautiful place where white coastguard houses stand out above the shore and waves grind on the pebbles of a six-mile beach. In this huge arc of sea and sky they bathed, sunbathed and walked on the dike, seeing the moon rise, sheltering under the lee of a boat when storms came. Some days they followed the coastal track to Bawdsey, getting sunburnt, watching the birds wheel in over the sea. On other days they went inland across the marshes, drawing willows by a stream and watching men cutting corn.

———

One day in their first holiday at Shingle Street Sybil went over to see a cottage near the church at the village of Shottisham. Much as she loved Woolpit, the cottage was small and she had been on the look-out for a larger home outside London ever since her house-hunting with Hal at Aldeburgh, not far up the coast. She had just enough money from bonds, and the value of the cottage, to let her hold on to this dream. It was also a gesture of independence. A home in the country would be hers alone, although Cyril would still be involved. She had become tired of London, she confessed, and now the dread of war gave her an added reason. She was struck by David Jones's *In Parenthesis*, published this year, 1937, mingling references to Arthurian myth and ancient Welsh poetry with the experience of infantrymen in the last war. 'Every newspaper was about what was going to come with Hitler and all that,' she said later, 'and I thought it was time I got out of London. That's why I found a place in the country.'

The chance came, not in Suffolk, but in the New Forest. In July 1937 she heard of a large auction of cottages and land from the estate of Pylewell Park, around the village of Norley Wood (or Norleywood) in Hampshire. The village was on the southern edge of the Forest, two miles inland from the Solent, and she had her eye on Lot 5, 'A Brick and Mud-Built Detached Thatched Cottage'. Hal went to see it and reported back, and she put in a bid. She went down at once, spending a blowy, sunny few days in Lymington, watching the boats, going to their old Castaway Camp, taking a bus to Norley Wood to see the house. While there, she looked at two more cob cottages, one of which, 'Fryers', was almost next door to Lot 5. She bought this too, from a Mrs Parsons. Back in London, in the hottest week of the year, she thought it over. On 6 August she wrote simply in her diary, 'Meditating'. Next day she was upbeat, 'Brainwave over Mrs Parsons' house. Have written to her offering £450.' She then rushed down again and took measurements, rashly agreeing 'to take the property somehow'. (Over the next year she and Cyril would clear and repair Fryers, showing people round and eventually selling it, with evident relief.)

By the end of the month she had decided on a name for Lot 5: 'Pypers' and then 'Pipers', easier for everyone to spell. She kept the sale catalogue all her life, writing in pencil, 'Became Pipers'. But although Cyril was already drawing up plans for its renovation and expansion, she still had to make sure of the money. In mid-September she found a buyer for the Woolpit cottage and also arranged to give the bank a charge on her £450 War Loan, in return for her overdraft. On 12 October the contract was finally signed and a month later she wrote, 'Formal possession of No 5 at last'. She and Hal spent a last weekend in Woolpit, 'then the stuff was packed', wrote Hal, '& taken down to her new property on edge of the Forest at Norley-wood.'

The village was a scatter of smallholdings, surrounded by farmland and heath with pockets of ancient forest, its thatched cob cottages interspersed with red-brick farms and houses. Deer grazed on the heath and Forest ponies ambled on the green. It was an easy walk down to the foreshore, where the mudflats and salt marshes were a haunt of shorebirds of every kind. The long, empty shore stretched between the Lymington River to the west and the Beaulieu River to the east, both full of fishing boats and yachts. A few miles further east the wide Southampton Water led inland to the port.

31: PIPERS

Power was always part of the New Forest plan. He would be there with her at weekends and holidays: it was his country retreat too. But it was the beginning of the end, although at first it did not seem so. While Andrews was caught up in a fever to leave London, Power was more deeply embedded than ever. In October 1937 he had taken on an extra job teaching evening classes in Putney, meaning that as well as his work at the LCC, he was committed not only to working on a new edition of *English Medieval Architecture* but to writing weekly Putney lectures (for which Sybil sorted out his lantern slides, as she had since the early Bury days, doubtless with a familiar mix of interest and impatience at her subordinate role). Yet busy as he was, he was excited about Pipers, working on the plans every weekend and sending them to Mr Figgins the builder.

Pipers stood – and still stands – on a shallow slope by a curving lane, a low building with a sitting room and kitchen downstairs and two bedrooms under the thatch with tiny windows at each end. Outside there was a storage shed, tool shed and pigsty, a well in the yard, and a large unkempt garden and paddock; and Sybil also had grazing rights on the common, as all New Forest commoners had for centuries. Cyril's scheme for the cottage's expansion was radical – they would knock down the outbuildings and build a separate two-storey house attached to the old one, which could be used as a studio. When it was finished a gallery would stretch across one end of the long sitting room, the 'great hall', with a small kitchen and bathroom at the other end. Above, the bedroom windows looked across fields and woods to the Solent. From here, Sybil said, she could see the Union Castle liners, heading out from Southampton

Pipers, with the original cottage on the left
Hal and Cyril gardening

on their way to Cape Town – thinking of Sam Butler sailing to South Africa.

In November, when Sybil finally gained formal possession of 'No 5' and the title deeds were in her hand, she bought Cyril a new pair of gum boots for the New Forest mud. A month later, their friend Tony Weatherhead drove them down one Sunday, braving fog and icy roads. They felt it was worth it even for a couple of hours. They spent Christmas together at Brook Green, walking across the park and along Piccadilly to St Martin-in-the-Fields, and at New Year they celebrated with their usual feast. While the building began in earnest in Norley Wood, they embarked on a January round of printing for the exhibition in Los Angeles, the hard work lightened for Sybil by her growing friendship with Edna Clarke Hall and by visits from George de Menasce and Sam Butler. De Menasce gave her, perhaps teasingly, a copy of Stefan Zweig's *Marie Antoinette: The Portrait of an Average Woman* (1932), a study of a woman's inner strength, while Sam took sheaves of prints back to South Africa, charging for framing and commission and sending cheery accounts of sales, one list headed 'sold . . . to son of millionaire'.

The Thames ice was so thick that they skated on the river in the evening, but they braved the ice and gales to go down and see how Figgins the builder was getting on at Norley Wood. Life was busy and sociable: Andrews took on new pupils and Power steered his Putney class round Westminster Abbey and Southwark Cathedral. They went to Tony Weatherhead's wedding, heard madrigals at the V&A and Bach's B Minor Mass at Westminster and saw John Gielgud's memorable *Three Sisters* at the Queen's Theatre, with Peggy Ashcroft as Irina. They also saw Disney's *Snow White*, sign of a new era – Mondrian, who moved to London this year, loved this film, signing himself 'Sleepy' on postcards home.

On 4 March, a lovely day, they walked down the towpath to see the swans on the Thames. But all the time, the news was threatening. Eight days later Sybil noted curtly, 'Germany invaded Austria.'

George de Menasce did not return that summer, as he usually did. After leaving London in February de Menasce had planned to stay for five weeks in Paris, seeing his fourteen-year-old son Pierre, who was at school in France. Fearing Europe was on the brink of war, he sent Pierre and his mother to America. In December 1938 he wrote to say how heartbroken he was to have his child so far away, 'and then all these sad events – and the persecutions of the poor German Jews – I really hadn't got the pluck to write.' Having heard of her house purchase and knowing that she planned to move soon, he hoped that in the Forest Sybil would still feel inspired, and that she would get more out of life away from the pea-soups of London. Sam Butler also approved of the planned move, writing from on board ship in a letter full of ellipses as if he didn't quite know what to say. Thanking her for helping him during the few days he had been in London, when he felt that he had got to know her as never before, he agreed that 'changes must take place within your lives':

> Your work must suffer if you remain in that environment . . . and somehow . . . I sense & feel the enthusiasm to have abated that at one time was almost overwhelming – overpowering . . .
>
> – The rent you pay of course staggers me . . . & with that pressure on your resources . . . how you work at all defeats me . . . and has always & always will defeat me . . . but then I haven't your courage.
>
> . . . Your work will change when you quit London . . . You frighten me not at all this time . . . But at other times . . . yes . . . almost always.
>
> . . . This time you were lovely . . . You have my gratitude always for your great help. Concentrate now on the new life . . . & it will sweep you up naturally & easily & you will find it transitional . . . & with it will come the refreshment you so richly deserve.
>
> Ever – with love –
> Sam.

Sybil could indeed seem frightening, with her feverish work ethic, her vehemence, her rapid, unpredictable passions for new projects and equally sudden reversals. But this time she was calm. The move to the New Forest was a considered, positive decision.

———

The building was hard work. The new additions were nearly finished, with inevitable hiccups: the septic tank was causing problems, the thatched roof had to be tackled, and Power needed to draw new versions of the tall chimney stacks. Soon, though, Andrews could imagine moving in. At the end of March, she wrote to her London landlord and he agreed that her tenancy could end at midsummer. Meanwhile they worked not on lino, but on watercolours and oils. Power's paintings, now lost, included one of 'Tenebrae', as well as what Sybil called 'a magnificent painting of the Irishman', others of a bargeman, 'tulips and wallflowers' and a portrait of Sybil herself.

At the end of April they went down to Norley Wood for a week, and the following Friday, after his week's work in London, she met him off the train again. They gardened all day, with Cyril sowing seeds and Sybil shifting planks. It was a glorious day, she wrote; 'nightingales in evening'. Next day she wrote a rather lovely listing of what it was like.

> Nightingales in the Dusk
> And at the turn of the Road
> > Another
> > And yet Another
> And as we dropped into Lymington
> > in the gathering darkness
> The moon rode clear.
> Mars & Venus in conjunction
> Blazed in the N.W. sky.

And from the saltings & mudflats
Came the cry of the shorebirds
    Curlews & Ringplover
Red Shank & Oyster Catcher
    And the mewing of gulls.
To me, a sound, a music
Almost more moving
Than the nightingales
The cry of shorebirds away
Over the lonely places
So pure, so wild & so lovely.

Later she typed this out, moving it to midsummer and calling it 'June Night'.

But if she was moving in June, and Cyril was still going to work in London, where would his new base be? At the last minute they faced this problem. The Hertford house felt big now that the children were leaving home. Power's son Cyril was already married, and this February Toby had become engaged to a young Frenchwoman, Lilian Muffant. They had met six years earlier when she went to teach and complete her research at Queen's University Belfast, and met again in 1937 when she moved to King's College, London; he brought her to tea at the studio that December. They would marry in July 1938, at Notre Dame de France, off Leicester Square, followed by a 'lively little party in a wine dive opposite the British Museum'. Sybil, who was fond of Toby, liked Lilian and was entertained the following year when they were expecting a baby. Dashing off a draft letter to a friend, she wrote, 'Toby's little wife is to bear an infant to their great delight. Toby must amuse the family by making enquiries as to if there was any record of triplets! It's good to find them wanting children, so many don't.' Catherine, Cyril's second grandchild, was born on 4 July 1939.

In the spring of 1938, however, knowing that Toby would soon be setting up home separately, Cyril needed to find a house for Dolly and her sister Eva, and for Kit, still at school, but soon to begin training as an architect, and Peggie, now twenty-three, commuting into town to work as a secretary for Cuthbert Greig at the Trade Protection Society. (In future years Toby's children were very fond of their aunt Peggie, remembering her as 'bright and cheerful, but horror of horrors, wore red lipstick'.)

In a single week in mid-May, after the evening of the nightingales in the dusk, all was settled. After Cyril talked to Eva one evening after work, Sybil took over, with typical speed. She consulted Stephanie Champion, settled on New Malden in Essex, where the Champions had lived, and early one morning she and Stephanie went to look at houses. Next day Cyril met Dolly, Peggie and Eva to talk things through, then Sybil rang the house agent, Dolly saw the house, Cyril went to Hertford to discuss it again, and finally he himself rang the agent and settled the tenancy. In the coming days, he and Sybil went to Malden, bought rugs and measured for curtains. Once again, Dolly seems to have met all these sudden decisions, the shunting around and interference from Sybil – even the choice of rugs and measuring for curtains – with a strange, easy acceptance. Finally, in the studio that week, Power and Andrews sorted out their music until late at night and, sadly, he took some of their instruments to Morleys to sell. On 20 June he moved, officially at least, to New Malden.

———

At 2.30 pm on Midsummer's Day, 24 June 1938, Sybil shut the door of the Brook Green studio for the last time. Cyril wrote 'Move to Norley Wood' in her diary very firmly, in ink, and saw her off at Waterloo. Figgins the builder met her at Lymington station.

It seemed dramatic but it was hardly a rupture. Next day Cyril was there, arriving by the 2.30 train, as soon as she had cleaned the house and settled in. A new routine developed. With Dolly in New Malden, Cyril spent the week in digs in London and came down to

Pipers on weekends and holidays, overseeing building, plastering and painting. As well as Sybil's furniture, they brought down many of his possessions, including the eight-foot table-top and trestles that they did their printing on, as well as more exotic things, like the inlaid Moorish stool, and the Nigerian stools and statues and embroidered marriage cloth bought at Wembley in 1924. The Nigerian door was sold to the Cranmore Ethnographical Museum in Chislehurst.

Determined to be part of Forest life, Sybil took riding lessons and by early August she was riding alone, on 'Sherry'. As the summer passed, they picked blackberries and tackled the garden, planting a holly hedge, clearing old grass from the borders and deciding on bulbs. A novice gardener, Cyril made lists headed 'Garden, September': 'make strawberry beds', 'collect seeds of annuals', 'plant Lilium Candidum', 'prepare ground for fruit trees', 'plant narcissi, & snowdrops', 'plant out wallflowers, primulas & forget me nots'.

By late September gardening and linocuts began to seem trivial. 'Bad newspapers', Sybil noted on 28 September, reading reports that Germany was holding to its claim to the Czech Sudetenland and threatened to invade on 1 October. In London, crowds prayed in Westminster Abbey, piled up sandbags, dug trenches in the parks as air-raid shelters and waited in line for gas masks. The day before the deadline, on 30 September, Neville Chamberlain met Hitler in Munich, with Mussolini and the French premier Edouard Daladier, and they accepted that the Sudetenland be yielded to Germany in return for no further claims. Thousands waited in the rain at Heston airport, as Chamberlain came down the steps from the plane, waving the paper that bore his personal non-aggression pact with Hitler. Later, addressing the crowd from an upper window in Downing Street, he spoke of bringing back peace with honour: 'Go home to your beds,' he said; 'I believe it is peace for our time.' In her diary Sybil drew a heavy pencil box round the date, adding one word, 'Peace'.

At Pipers in late 1938 they stubbornly went on gardening, shifting earth and planting fruit trees, tokens of faith in the future. The

November storms came, with rain 'like a waterfall', and then the first frost, silvering the trees. In the first days of snow, she was finishing paintings of 'Pitts Deep' and 'Frosty morning'. Then she turned to linocuts again, printing for the Los Angeles show of the Print Makers Society of California. They still had work to do on the house but by now it felt like home. Sybil stained and oiled the floors, put down rugs and made curtains, and bought a bike so that she could cycle into Lymington for supplies. Cyril was there at weekends, and after so many years they were used to sharing time and working together. In April she wrote a shaky note: 'I'm not going to find it very easy to see him go. If it is ever.' But she liked being alone in the Forest. She loved the house with the white hawthorn in the garden and the sparrows in the thatch. Looking back on this time at Pipers she wrote:

> I was lucky. I had the whole Forest to myself. There was not a soul about . . . never saw anyone, only Mr Keeping the woodcutter with his train of forest ponies. He was a huge man, a wrestler with the reputation of clearing out the bars when in drink . . . I expect he was surprised to see me pushing my bike laden with my painting gear. He would give me a wave. I have often thought there was a Keeping helping to bring in the body of William Rufus, after the 'glancing of an arrow' & there I was a descendant of that Walter Tyrrell who was accused of doing the deed just 800 years ago & I had another Keeping who helped me in the garden – so I always felt sure that I belonged to the New Forest.

———

Her solitude was broken in the spring of 1939 when Hal decided to give up his job at the museum, 'be shot of Bury for which I have little affinity now' and move to Pipers. He helped to shift earth to make a pond and walked in the Forest, but after a few weeks his urge to move took over. In early June he and Sybil spent a long day in London, 'purchasing Colonial hat etc. for my coming adventures' and meeting Cyril and their brother Geoff and at an Indian-Burmese restaurant. Then Hal was off, this time to the West Indies, taking tramp ships to Trinidad, Jamaica and British Guiana.

Without Hal, Andrews and Power kept on with their planting – silver birches, dogwood and rowans, and larkspur for blue shadows. When Cyril was in London Sybil sent him green beans and straw-berries, loading him with more when he caught the late Sunday train back to town.

32: WAR AGAIN

On 23 August 1939, the Nazi-Soviet Pact was signed, guaranteeing Russian neutrality if Germany became involved in war. A week later, German troops invaded Poland, and Britain and France issued an ultimatum. Plans for blackout and evacuation were put into action and people fled London. Ursula Fookes brought her elderly mother and aunt down to Pipers for a month and Sybil's sister Mike came from Ipswich. Shelters and first aid stations opened, gas masks were handed out, children from Southampton and Portsmouth were moved inland. On 2 September Sybil went into Lymington to buy blackout curtains. Finding there was none to be had, she hung up old blankets. Next day, her diary simply said 'War'.

Power was in St Albans with Dolly when war was declared but two days later he was back in Norley Wood. He tried to rejoin the Air Force as a camouflage specialist and was greatly put out to be told he was too old; on the form he had reduced his age by ten years (he was sixty-six in September 1939). Instead, he stayed on in London with the LCC. At Pipers, in this time of deep anxiety, he and Sybil walked on the shore, harvested their potatoes and got out the camera and 'shot snaps' of the house against the sky, as if determined to have a record of a peaceful life, to capture and hold safer memories. Cyril took many photos of Sybil over the next two years: in Katharine Hepburn-style slacks in the garden; reading in the porch in a long Liberty-print dress; in jodhpurs, pulling a roller over the new lawn. In October, when he put up wires for the climbing roses they counted eleven swallows gathering to fly south and went into Lymington to buy him a sou'wester to protect against the autumn storms. Sybil took a photo of him, drenched and grimly amused.

Cyril in his sou'wester

As the 'phony war' dragged on, he began to come down for a week each month as well as at weekends. Andrews was cutting her print of *Swans* – four birds, necks outstretched, their beating wings curving down and rising high, her most elegant and open print – and proofing a print of gypsies trudging up the hill against angular darts of cloud, their bodies bent under burdens of logs. Both these linocuts appeared that winter in a special Redfern exhibition. Another, however, had to be put aside. 'That print of mine I call "Wings", gulls following the plough,' she told Michael Parkin, 'was the one I was nearly arrested for while making the drawing of it back in 1939/40 by the Military Police.' In the country's nervous mood, even drawing, so near Southampton and the Solent, had begun to seem dangerous. Britain waited for the expected onslaught, a long uneasy pause. On 14 October the *Royal Oak* was torpedoed in Scapa Flow, killing more than eight hundred men and boys. By late October Poland was overwhelmed. A month later Russia invaded Finland. Andrews worried about Hal, who had been away all summer on his expedition to the West Indies. In December he got a place on a troop ship sailing in a convoy from British Guiana, landing safely in Liverpool, much to her relief. He was at Pipers over Christmas and New Year, a week that began with fog and ended with snow. In bright sun they skated on a nearby pond and hiked out into the Forest, Hal carrying the painting stool and easel slung over his shoulder and Sybil painting a watercolour 'sitting for three-quarters of an hour in several degrees of frost'.

Record cold temperatures brought ice floes on the river, and Hal noted, '100 degrees of frost in Finland, helping them in their tremendous struggle against the Russian hordes'. The snow continued until 21 February and four days later, somewhat unseasonably, 'British double summertime' began, allowing an extra hour of light for people to get home before the blackout. Hal joined the Home Guard, drilling and learning to use a Bren gun. From the start, he tried to join up, but, skinny and short-sighted, was consistently turned down: 'put in grade 4 and told I had best go on growing vegetables. Sure suits me!'

Sybil herself was edgy, thinking, although nothing came of this, of selling Pipers and moving to a smaller house. Anxiety levels rose. In mid-May the Whit bank holiday was cancelled after the German invasion of Belgium and Holland. At the end of the month came the evacuation from Dunkirk: Southampton was suddenly full of exhausted British and French troops. A few miles from Pipers, in the village of Dibden Purlieu, Richard Eurich painted his extraordinary *Withdrawal from Dunkirk*, which was used as the navy's Christmas card: soon he was an official war artist.

In mid-June, when the papers ran reports of German troops marching past the Arc de Triomphe and tanks rumbling down the Champs-Elysées, invasion fears grew. Roadblocks were prepared and new evacuation plans made. That summer thousands on the south coast watched the vapour trails across the sky from the Battle of Britain. By early September, the London Blitz was underway, the start of months when the air was acrid from smoke, when people walked on pavements of broken glass and the daytime seemed, as Elizabeth Bowen called it, only 'a pure and curious holiday from fear'.

Still working in Room 495, on the fourth floor of County Hall, Power became a surveyor for the Wandsworth Heavy Rescue squad, sent out to rescue people from bombed buildings. The team included council workers – plumbers and electricians and labourers – all trained in first aid, and as soon as the All Clear sounded they set out, with their steel helmets and oilskin capes, through streets littered with rubble and broken glass. Cyril's task was to work out how to make buildings where people might be trapped safe enough for the search to begin, ensuring electricity and gas were turned off and getting damaged walls shored up with timber props. Sometimes a bomb had come through the roof and upper floors before it exploded, blowing the walls out sideways so that the floors above collapsed like a pack of cards; survivors might be in the basement or cellar, or sheltering under the stairs. Working in the darkness with torches and hurricane lamps, the team would move deeper and deeper into the ruins. Nearly eight hundred bombs fell on Wandsworth between October 1940 and June 1941, and on 16 November six firemen died when Wandsworth Fire Station itself was bombed. When Cyril came down to Pipers in late October he was exhausted, sleeping like the dead, but leaping up again at the first sound of a bomb on the ports nearby.

Since early September, Sybil and Hal had been watching the flashes and hearing the roar of planes over Southampton attacking the Supermarine factory where Spitfires were built. There were moments of calm. 'Night watches cancelled. Went into garden & saw a hedgehog,' Hal wrote in mid-October. But it was only a brief pause. In late November sustained attacks on Southampton created a firestorm that could be seen from miles away, leaving hundreds dead and injured and thousands homeless. At Christmas the two siblings were on their own, but when Power came for a week at New Year they celebrated with presents, holly, mistletoe and crackers and had a brave but meagre wartime feast for Twelfth Night with all their pewter plates and jugs on the table. A week later the sky above Portsmouth, forty miles away, was red with fire.

Familiar landmarks in their lives were disappearing. Heatherleys was blown to rubble; the studio of Claude Flight and Edith Lawrence in Rodmarton Mews near Baker Street was utterly destroyed, with all their paintings and printing blocks; an incendiary reduced Brook Green studios to ruins; the Grosvenor School closed, never to reopen. In November 1940 a bomb hit the Cranmore Museum in Chislehurst; eventually its collections, including their precious Nigerian door, were sent to other museums. In the harsh winter, snow covered London's ruins like a shroud, cloaking shattered walls and furniture clinging to broken floors high in the air. The following year, on 10 May 1941, the Queen's Hall was hit by an incendiary. It would never be rebuilt. There were small reprieves. Edgar Hunt, sending Sybil some sheet music that Power had bought for her, told her that 'although all the furniture was destroyed and the viols broken to pieces, we have recovered all the music – some a little torn & battered – and all the recorders came out safely, including the Bressan and other old ones. So we have much to be thankful for.'

Over the next few years Power's sketchbooks were dotted with scenes from places he knew: old alleys and houses destroyed in Manningtree and gaps in the streets of Bury St Edmunds, as well as the destruction in London. Toby Power was in a reserved occupation in the bank and joined the Home Guard, and he and Lilian took in a London schoolgirl evacuee, Rita Pietnik. Power's middle son Cyril was in the RAF reserve and Kit joined the navy in January 1941, taking part in the Dieppe Raid, in the landings of 'Operation Torch' at Casablanca, Oran and Algiers in 1942 and then at Salerno, winning the Distinguished Service Cross for the North African landings. Hal, despite repeatedly failing medicals, finally got a job on a boat servicing anti-aircraft barrage balloons for ships at Southwick near Brighton in West Sussex, where the harbour and nearby chemical works and power station were heavily bombed. All of them, in different ways, were at risk.

Although she felt the force of devastation and death at home and abroad, and worried about Cyril in the London bombings, Sybil's only acknowledgement of personal danger – a very typical gesture – was taking shooting lessons, so that she would know how to use a gun. Her life followed its familiar course, walking, riding, gardening, painting, meeting Cyril off the train at weekends. Midweek letters, all now lost, flew back and forth between Norley Wood and London. One surviving envelope from this time, perhaps for her birthday, contained a huge paper star, elaborately folded from gold paper – she simply wrote on the envelope, 'Gold stars'. As the autumn chill set in in 1941 she lit fires in the hall and the studio and began, as always, to get ready for Christmas. When the holiday arrived and Cyril came down she iced the cake and decorated the tree while Hal put up holly: then it was 'music, cake, tree, feast at 8 o'clock'. On Boxing Day they planted bare-root roses sent by Cuthbert Greig. Then they painted each other's portraits, Cyril painting Hal, Sybil painting Cyril, Cyril painting Sybil 'in purple coat in snow'. It was determinedly, doggedly, normal.

33: THE YARD, AND WALTER

Just before Christmas 1941, wanting to join the war effort, and thinking back to the skills she had learned in her days as a welder in the First World War, Andrews had applied for a place on the training course in boat-building at Marchwood Park at Hythe, on the west bank of Southampton Water. Hubert Scott-Paine, whose British Power Boat Company made high-speed boats, had employed female workers during the previous war and was keen to do so again, buying the Georgian mansion of Marchwood Park and converting it into a residential centre and workshop to train women to build and repair boats for the Admiralty. In mid-February 1942, when Cyril left for London, Sybil set off on the bus, travelling the ten miles to Marchwood. Next morning, in her uniform of dungarees and beret, she went to her first lecture and 'made a beginning with saw and plane'. Most 'Marchwood girls', as she called them, were far younger than she was, some still teenagers, and there were netball matches and picnics as well as lectures. It was like going back to school, sitting in an echoing room at long desks covered with books and plans, and then moving to the workshop, learning riveting and turning and drilling under the eyes of white-coated instructors.

On 18 April, a day before her forty-fourth birthday, she gained her diploma in carpentry. A fortnight later, writing to Cyril and reading his latest letter, she scribbled a note, 'Nightingales in copse. Lovely day.' Cyril would be seventy this year, and the intensity of their earlier relationship had given way to a companionable ease and affection. He was now at Pipers most of the time and Sybil's diary was still full of notes on their work in the garden, their paintings and his visits to his family. But it was also full of boat-building, and the people from her work. When the Marchwood course was over she moved to work in the yards at Hythe, where they made the navy's vital 'little ships': motor torpedo boats (MTBs), motor gunboats – known as the 'Spitfires of the Sea' – and high-speed launches and air-sea rescue boats for the RAF.

The women lived during the week at Langdale House, a big manor house taken over by the Admiralty, but in the yards they worked alongside the men, divided into gangs, each member doing the same job on each boat that came her way. A former apprentice remembered the girls singing, making the workshop ring to songs of the day like 'Deep in the Heart of Texas', 'Moonlight Becomes You', 'That Old Black Magic' and, inevitably, Bing Crosby's 'White Christmas'. The yard was open day and night and the workers did sixty-hour weeks. Sybil's role in the gang was 'laying down decks'. By late June, when the strawberries were ripening at Pipers, she was a competent boat-builder, drilling and screwing battens, finishing the ammunition hatch, pleased to be told 'that I had done more than anyone else on the boat'. In the autumn she was given the top grade – 'skilled worker'.

'To me it was a wonderful experience,' she remembered, working side by side with the men, 'the life of the shipyard – the coming and going of vessels after night action – so much going on & yet not allowed to draw.' Frustrated, she asked if she could have permission to make notes of the boats being built for her to work on after the war, 'and to my astonishment I was given permission to make sketches.' She kept these typed permissions, addressed to 'Miss Andrews, Clock No. 34', carefully until she died. In the pocket of her overalls she carried a small sketchbook, making drawing after drawing, storing up the images of the yard. Two years before, Richard Eurich, whose house was only a mile or so away, had painted vivid, detailed scenes of these docks, with boats in the foreground and camouflaged sheds standing out against the sky. The sheds and the swirling grey skies above appear in the background of the paintings Sybil made after the war (PLATE 57). These form a brilliant, dynamic set. In one, the curving ribs of the growing hulls seem to swallow the men and girls working on them (PLATE 58); in another the finished craft is beached on the concrete dock like a stranded creature longing for the sea. The perspective shifts from the shop floor, with the blue hulls looming overhead, to views from above, looking down on the half-made decks like pools of gold under the lights, with girls drilling, polishing, nailing down the boards. She was one of the gang, seeing the work from within. Seven of her paintings, with Cyril Power's *Air Raid*, are now in the Royal Air Force Museum at Hendon. She too was a war artist, if an unofficial one.

Every now and then there was a scare and they were evacuated from the sheds into the station yard, but they were perpetually busy. Sybil's spirits were high. 'Wonderful search lights last night', she noted, or, on a night of raids, 'wonderful eclipse of the moon'. Exhilarated by the work, the constant rush and the undertone of danger, she was meeting new people and making new friends. Among them, in the summer of 1943, she met Walter Morgan.

Walter was four years older than Sybil, funny, craggily handsome, with thick fair hair and a tattoo of a dagger on his right arm. He had lost the left arm below the elbow during the First World War and now had a hook, which he used with astonishing skill both as a carpenter and as a cornet player. To Sybil his story was heroic. He was born in the Forest, the eldest of seven children of a market gardener, who died when he was eleven. His mother married again, another market gardener, and moved to Dorset with the children, and as soon as he could, at the age of sixteen, Walter enlisted in the Dorset Regiment. One of the first soldiers to land in France in August 1914, he fought in the retreat from Mons, on the Somme and at Passchendaele, until he was discharged with wounds in September 1917. Back home, he had worked as a carpenter and machinist. At the start of the war he was working at one of the oil refineries on Southampton Water, and his daughter Doris and her husband and small daughter had been living with him and his wife Winifred, whom he had married on leave in 1915; Winifred died of cancer in June 1942, a year before he met Sybil.

Walter's name first appeared in Sybil's diary in August 1943, making a new box for tools. In September and early October he was still 'Morgan'. Then things changed. She was always quick to move when she made a decision, and in wartime everything was speeded up. With characteristic rapidity, intensified by the wartime atmosphere, she took action. 'Take plunge', she wrote on Tuesday 12 October. Next day, 'I broke the news to JM – late.' There is no record of what she said – a significant and mysterious gap – but Cyril knew this was final. On a tune he had composed the previous September, 'Sandra's Self', from his 'Seven Pillars Suite', he wrote with a flourish, 'Dedicated to Sybil Andrews, by Cyril E. Power, October 13th, 1943.'

That week was busy in the yards, ending with her taking a finished boat out in rough weather, but Sybil's inner voyage was still rockier. She was thinking hard. 'What a merciful thing we are free,' she wrote on 27 October. Cyril was staying on at Pipers, but next day, when he went up to London, she wrote: '3 houses. Why wait. Sign a long contract.' On Tuesday 2 November she and Walter took their birth certificates into Lymington and next day they got the marriage licence. Walter wanted the wedding on the Saturday, three days ahead, so she simply asked for the day off and fixed the time. On the day, 6 November 1943, Walter rode up to Pipers on his bike about nine in the morning. They changed, dashed into Lymington and bought a ring, '& we were married at 12 o'clock sharp, & lunch at the Angel. Home by Taxi'.

Next day, they were back in the yard, 'news percolating'. Then she told her family. Her brother Geoff was delighted. 'Having now recovered from the shock', he congratulated her on being the first (in fact the only) one of the siblings to marry: 'I like the way you did it – tell no-body till it is over. I should act the same myself.' Her sister Mike, by contrast, declared that she was not surprised at all: 'It's exactly what I would have done if I'd been you.' Down on the

Walter

shore, Sybil photographed the rippling muscles of Walter's back as he looked out to sea; at Pipers she snapped him hammering in the yard. It was a whirlwind marriage, but a lasting one.

In the week after her wedding she took two days off, sorting out all Power's things. Then she sent them off, as fast as she could, to New Malden.

———

When Walter and Sybil had a few days' leave at the end of November they went to Stonehenge, a kind of honeymoon. Andrews sketched the stones in bold, fast strokes. 'I remember Stonehenge on a wild stormy afternoon of racing cloud and shafts of sunlight, on a grey, wild moor,' she wrote later. In her mind she longed to clear it of people, 'Reduce it to its dramatic, lonely position – & lean against one of those gigantic chucks of rock, with only the rushing clouds & the wind.'

Stonehenge was a sharp contrast to the present. While she and Walter settled at Pipers and worked at Hythe, the Forest changed around them, as it had since the start of the war. Conifers were cut for timber; defensive pillboxes were built; ammunition dumps were hidden in the glades; soldiers on their way to the ports slept in tents under the trees. Eight airfields had already been built on the heaths and in 1943 four temporary ones were laid down on farmers' fields, one at East Boldre, a couple of miles from Norley Wood. On Lepe beach beyond the Beaulieu river concrete slabs were laid to take the weight of tanks being loaded onto ships. In the first week of June 1944 an armada of ships filled the Solent, stretching from horizon to horizon, packed with men waiting for orders, and on the night of 5 June they sailed for Normandy. On the morning of D-Day hundreds of aircraft and gliders passed over Pipers, heading for France.

By the autumn, work was winding down in the yards, and 20 October 1944 was Sybil's last day there. She checked in her tools, got her pay and headed home in pouring rain. By the Norley Wood pillbox Walter was waiting.

V: PARTING

Cyril Power, *En grande tenue*, 1930

34: CYRIL

When Sybil and Walter Morgan took their taxi home from Lymington registry office, Cyril Power was sketching in St Albans Cathedral. Beneath his drawing, using her old nickname, he wrote, 'Sandra's wedding day. 4.30, 6 November '43'. His address on the front of his sketchbook was still 'Pipers', but next to it he wrote, 'The last Norley sketchbook'.

Four pages later he jotted down lines from Browning's 'By the Fireside'. The poem acknowledges Elizabeth Barrett Browning's role as guide: 'I follow wherever I am led,' but the lines that Power quoted were Browning's tribute to Italy, both a real and a psychological country.

> O woman-country, wooed not wed,
> Loved all the more by earth's male lands,
> Laid to their hearts instead.

This meant something different to him now. The sketchbook is dotted with such quotations. '*Varium et mutabile semper femina*', he wrote, from Virgil's *Aeneid*, Mercury's warning to Aeneas of woman's fickleness, and '*Latet anguis in herba*' – 'a snake hides in the grass' – from the Third Eclogue. One quote was from Bussy-Rabutin:

> *L'absence est à l'amour ce qu'est au feu le vent;*
> *Il éteint le petit, il allume le grand.*

> Absence is to love what wind is to fire;
> It puts out the small, it kindles the great.

Another, more painful still, quoted the famous lines of Catullus:

Odi et amo: quare id faciam, fortasse requiris.
Nescio, sed fieri sentio et excrucior.

I hate. I love. The cause thereof
I do not know, but feel 'tis so.
And I'm in agony.

———

Power swallowed his loss. But during his work in London he drew the ravaged city: the streets around the Bank of England and Cheapside; St Paul's at dusk during the blackout; bomb damage at Clapham Junction; Trafalgar Square with the equestrian statue of Charles I removed and its plinth boxed up for protection. He too boxed himself up. His address was now 24 Howard Road, New Malden, a bay-windowed house with a small garden. Amazing though it seems, Dolly, whom her sons described as a 'lovely, quiet woman', apparently accepted him back without a murmur. Her eldest granddaughter Catherine remembered her as short and plump, 'kind, softly spoken, but not expansive'. Catherine remembered too that nothing was ever said in the family about Power's long absence; she never even heard the name 'Sybil Andrews' until she was well into middle age.

They kept in touch. At the end of 1943 Cyril put together a book of music for Sybil to play on her recorder, full of the tunes that he had composed or arranged that summer and they had played together: 'Softly Robin', 'Pastourelle', 'The Lady's Lament' and many others. The following February, Sybil printed out a set of her linocuts for him, from the early *Concert Hall* and *Steeplechasing* to religious prints like *Golgotha*, *Pieta* and *Via Dolorosa* and recent Suffolk scenes such as *Michaelmas*, *Haysel* and *Market Day*. That April he

sent her a handmade and decorated Easter card. With it he enclosed
a separate card:

> In memory of
> many Happy Easters
> & especially Good
> Friday, 1920
>
> 'The sedge is withered
> from the lake
> and no birds sing.'
>
> To the Belle Dame
> Sans Merci
> Qui tiens ma Vie

A year later, in March 1945, when Sybil began working again on
the Stations of the Cross, she asked him about Russian icons and he
sent a list of references on a postcard, writing her name firmly 'Mrs
(Sybil Andrews) Morgan'. Later that day, in Zwemmer's bookshop
in Charing Cross Road, he found a book to send her and asked them
to set aside some prints and more books: 'If you don't want them I
shall have them myself.' He posted, too, the catalogue of the exhibition of Russian icons at the V&A: 'This is the one we saw together
in 1929.' It felt, briefly, as though they were still working as partners.

That was not to be.

———

Andrews, the skilled, brisk designer, could touch deep emotion in her
religious linocuts while her haulers and flower girls, show-jumpers
and speedway racers celebrated strength, determination, guts – a
leaping through life. Power's work was odder, more visionary, delving

deep into the city's anxiety and loneliness but finding moments, too, of gravity-defying exhilaration – sheer happiness – and questioning his own awe at the ageless fire-dance of death and desire. That too was past.

He made no more linocuts. He still kept his sketchbook in his pocket but he painted watercolours and oils, flower studies and landscapes, using the big front room at Howard Road as his studio. After the war, he took on work that looked back to his youth, when he had cycled across the country researching medieval churches and had been inspired by the early masons and craftsmen. Many church-es had been destroyed in the war and Power worked on their resto-ration, designing church furniture – carved reredos screens, pulpits and altar screens – with the ecclesiastical architect Romilly Craze (who had become drawn into this work when an engineer friend was asked to build a roof over the bombed Catholic cathedral in Southwark in 1945). Kit recalled how in 1948 his father designed panels for a hymn board, representing church seasons like Easter, Lent, Advent and Pentecost; a local sign-painter completed them and when Craze asked Power to submit his account, he said, 'Give my fee to the craftsman who painted them.' At the time his only income was his old age pension.

He worked hard to fit into New Malden, living with Dolly and Eva and Peggie, playing the organ in the parish church, teaching art history in the town. There was a comfort in retrieving the closeness of his early years with Dolly: she had put up with his fecklessness then, and she seems to have dealt with him almost as an errant child whom one is bound to support whatever they do. In this situation, he was the prodigal. She received him back, Toby said, 'with an air of normality'. He was pleased, but hesitant, about his grandfatherly role, appearing in family photos holding a baby beside a flowering pear tree and looking on as a family group have tea in a back garden. That family had now grown. Cyril (no longer 'Boisie') and Christina had John. Kit married Joy in 1945, and after the death of their baby

Christopher, Michael was born, and later Simon. By the end of the war Toby and Lilian, who had moved from Welwyn to Hertford, had four children, Catherine, Claire, Giles and Martin; their fifth, Lizzie, would be born in 1948. Power made charcoal sketches of them: Catherine with her teddy bear, and Claire as a baby, trying to roll over, a flurry of curves. He watched them more than they suspected, even their sibling rows: when Catherine, aged five, drew on Claire's arm in bed, and Claire bit her, he wrote a comic doggerel poem, 'O cannibal Claire', and recorded Claire's excuse – 'She writed – I bited' – with grandparently amusement.

In 1946, the first peacetime summer, he and Dolly went on holiday with the Hertford family to Quiberville, near Dieppe, where Power, Toby said, 'sketched and swam with gusto'. Catherine remembered it differently: 'CEP would spend his time sketching, apart from us, engrossed, certainly not playing French cricket with his grandchildren.' Two years later, when Lizzie was born and the older girls were in hospital with measles, he and Dolly stayed in Hertford to help with the family. But when the children came over to New Malden, Catherine felt that there was never much sign of him. 'The grandfather I remember was a man of few words, large and rather grumpy (I expect all old people seem that to children) but with a subversive twinkle.' He teased them, took them to feed the swans in the castle grounds, and in a 'Dolphin drawing competition', urged her to draw more boldly on the kitchen blackboard. She had one tender memory, of him saying goodnight and showing her how to fold her arms across her chest like an angel: that way, he said, 'you would go to Heaven if you died.' At the very end of his life, at Toby's request, he painted a fantasy coat of arms for Giles, surmounted by a small, alert dog.

He often stayed at Mistley, a place he continued to love. His sister Edna died in February 1947, but Yevonde and her daughter 'Vonnie' – divorced after an affair with a Polish officer in 1944 – stayed on in Mistley. During the war their sister-in-law Maud and

Cyril on the beach at Wrabness

her daughters Joyce and Beryl and their children had come to join them, and Cyril sketched and painted them all, writing silly poems incorporating their names. He drew the quay and the maltings and the farms. At Wrabness, five miles down the estuary, he sat on the beach sketching until dusk, looking out at the boats, with his back to the family on the beach. Increasingly, sketching and painting became ways of turning his back.

Kit later estimated that in 1950, Power worked on eighty-nine oil paintings, often using a palette knife, totally immersed. Some were flower studies but many were landscapes of places that he and Dolly went to on holiday, especially the Helford River and the coast around Falmouth in Cornwall, strong in shape, full of colour, warm in feeling. It was an enjoyable and fruitful time. A year later, on 20 May 1951, he died in New Malden, aged seventy-eight.

After his death Kit destroyed his father's linocut blocks, to prevent further impressions. Yet when interest in Power's work revived it was those linocuts, full of the patterns and colours of the 1930s, that people wanted. They liked his dizzying evocations of speed and modernity, and the darker tones of alienation in the modern city. They appreciated the grace and harmony in his studies of runners and dancers but also his understanding of the perilous allure of swinging high, off balance on the merry-go-round. He was a visionary and a craftsman. He could make water shimmer beneath the oars of *The Eight* and air hum beneath Blue Bird's wheels. He could show the panic of exam-taking students but also the vivacity of an orchestra, the music that kept his world alive.

In the late 1970s when the gallery owner Michael Parkin began to show the work of the Grosvenor School artists, Andrews sent him Power's prints as well as her own, making sure that the proceeds went to his family. Writing to Parkin, she made special mention of Power's *Air Raid*, with its planes rising and diving within back-to-back arcs of blue, their dark shapes trailing arrows of air, sky and blood, and smoke rising from a crashed aircraft, like a genie. In this print, speed, is both glorious and terrible, rushing towards us and away, like time. 'Air Raid is pure Power,' Andrews wrote, 'so typical of his cutting – I do not think anybody could cut that again to be convincing, it is so personal & individual & typically Power, his hand, and the paper he used which gave such lovely translucent colour is no longer to be had . . . . I would like to keep it if I may.'

35: SYBIL

Sybil was four thousand miles away when Cyril died in May 1951. She spent that day cleaning out the house, 'terrible stink', and working on a linocut of Pontius Pilate. From her studio she looked out not across fields to the Solent but over the waters of Desolation Sound to the lighthouse on Quadra Island, and the high peaks of the Rockies beyond. When she met Walter Morgan she was only half-way through her life. She had years of companionship and art ahead of her. After the war ended they stayed on at Pipers – Walter's daughter Doris brought his grandchildren Pearlie and Derek to play in the garden – but work was scarce, and times were hard. Hal joined them at Norley Wood, but on 1 September 1946, he wrote: 'my last day at Pipers, partly by reason of the others preparing to go to British Columbia, and partly through some friction I felt it incumbent on myself to get out.' He too was heading abroad, this time to work with the paleoanthropologists and archaeologists Louis and Mary Leakey in Kenya.

The Morgans had decided to emigrate to Canada, not to follow in her father's footsteps, but, Sybil said, because Walter had always been interested in British Columbia – the great sea, the fishing, the mountains. The month before Hal made his exit, she had found a Canadian sponsor, a friend of a friend who agreed that it was 'a splendid plan to tour Vancouver Island for a bit before settling down anywhere particular'. In the spring of 1947 Sybil sold Pipers. Before they left Walter built crates to hold all their possessions, including his machine tools and her studio equipment, his trumpet and cornet and accordion, an Indian tabla drum and her four Dolmetsch recorders, and their two bicycles. While they got new passports and went through the official hoops for immigration to Canada they stayed with Walter's family in Dorset, and climbed up to the mystical iron age fort on Badbury Rings. Finally they set sail from King George's Dock in London, on the Royal Mail ship *Loch Ryan*. It was the start of a slow six-week voyage, via Bermuda, Jamaica and Panama, passing through the canal in a violent storm before they sailed up to San Francisco, stopping for a day, and then on to Victoria, the capital of British Columbia. They arrived on 5 August 1948, unsure where to go: 'the only ones left on the dock, with our big consignment case, we felt, as did Abraham, who went out "not knowing whither he went".'

After hunting for a place to settle they picked Campbell River, then a small salmon-fishing port, around two hundred miles north of Victoria on the eastern shore of Vancouver Island. A couple of miles beyond the town, where the metalled roads ended, they bought a one-storey wooden house in Willow Point, 'at the head of the Gulf of Georgia – with the sea at my garden gate'. Their boundary was the high-tide line. When they arrived, there was much to do. When they found that the pipe from the stove went through the roof via an old Huntley and Palmer's biscuit tin, they set about building. Willow Point had a garage and a store, and a community hall for meetings, dances, weddings and amateur dramatics. Around it the scenery was wild, with high peaks and forests, where elk roamed and bears and cougars hid. It was beautiful but lonely, and at times Sybil found the contrast bleak. She was daunted by the vast emptiness, and in 'this land of interminable, monotonous Fir' she missed the varied trees of the New Forest. Winter snow and storms brought a strange beauty, she admitted, but her poem 'Black Rain' suggests her feelings:

> Black grey rocks where the eagle watches.
> Black green, blue & grey
> Granite rocks, octopus haunted
> Black carrion birds on a grey-black grey shore.
> Long ropes of olive, black-green kelp

> A sick wet smell of water & wet things.
> And rain
>
> > > Helpless
> > > Relentless
> > > Rain.
>
> The Ravens croak
> And the sea-mew calling.

The first five years in Canada were difficult, but although post-war unemployment was high it was a good place for a boat-builder. In 1948 Walter set up the Morgan Boat Company, supplementing this by working as a carpenter on building sites. Life improved when a pulp mill was built nearby in 1952, making paper from the fir and cedar that the large logging companies rejected. It was 'rotten timber scrap', as Sybil said in one poem, where 'uncouth men toil', but when Walter got a job working on the great band and radial saws, the mill at least gave them some sort of security.

From the start, she clung to her identity as an artist, printing and proofing her pre-war designs, though dismayed to find that several lino blocks had melted in the heat of the *Loch Ryan*'s hold. Until 1951 she worked largely on existing material, printing from her old blocks, apart from adding more prints to her Stations of the Cross. There is no account of her reaction to Power's death, but after 1951, as if released in some way, she turned at last to Canadian scenes, beginning with *Indian Dance*, showing the ritual wolf-dance of the local Nuu-chah-noolth (Nootka) men. Soon she was making linocuts of the great logging machines, the massive lorries carrying tree trunks up the steep hill and the loggers in the Esky Bar coffee shop on the corner across her street: 'They were so beautifully Canada. In all those plaid shirts.'

Local people remembered how Walter's work shed always had a boat in front of it to advertise his trade, until he retired from boat-building in 1964. A master wood-turner, he sold carved bowls and

Walter with his gun

candlesticks and made rocking horses for the Hudson's Bay Company to sell in Vancouver. Using his hook to hammer in nails, he made the white picket fence at the front of the house, to keep the dogs and rabbits in. For Sybil he made an easel, and linocut tools. He made easels, too, for her students. She had agreed to teach evening classes in the high school after people saw the oil paintings she was selling at the stationery store. A little later, when her monotypes were burnt in the fire at the Robertson Galleries in Ottawa in 1959, the insurance money allowed them to build a proper studio and the classes moved there: they continued for thirty years. She began by giving two-hour afternoon classes twice a week, with eight students sitting on wooden crates. The fee was two dollars a session – going up to five dollars in the 1980s.

The studio stretched across the back of the house, its long row of windows facing the garden and the sea. Her old dresser was here, with the pewter and china from Suffolk. A large plan-chest held her prints, sketches and drawings, and on the walls she hung her oil paintings and the painted recorder cases, a reminder of the Brook Green days. She went on teaching and painting and printing and made large woodcuts of the great Canadian trees, the blocks themselves works of art, beautifully carved. Her class found her patient but demanding. In *Artist's Kitchen*, the idiosyncratic manual that she wrote for her students in the mid-1980s, full of keen insights and vehement instructions, she insisted above all that they should learn to draw well, 'to know what to abstract, to recognise the essential and eliminate the non-essential and superficial . . . Work and Struggle to reach that higher rung.' 'Can you catch that?' she said, when asked about her approach to teaching. 'Can you get that sense of movement? So you draw and you draw and you draw. You have to learn to *see*, and that's the hardest thing, to teach people to see.' Learning and self-criticism should never end. The book's first epigraph was a note she had made when she was studying John Hassall's Correspondence Course in her teens, a saying carved over the entrance to an old Brussels studio: 'Let he who is Content with his work be discontent with his Content.'

She taught linocutting only rarely, to particular students. One was Gary Ratushniak, a local boy, to whom she became close: when her prints began to sell for large sums she funded his life and studies in England. Another was the artist Richard Calver, who remembered her talk of ways to capture light, mood and feeling. '"Grab it while it's white hot," she told her students. "Put it down violently, as violently as you can. Your violence will be used positively" – to create violently – what an amazing thing.' She had a strength and authority, Calver observed, which comes out in all her prints and pictures. There was no phoniness about her; she treated all the class equally, encouraged them to think their own thoughts, do their own drawings, passing on her energy, pouring on praise. Often they painted outside, in her wildflower meadow garden, or on trips to the islands, rainforests and to Hudson's Farm, the shoreline home of her friends Tom and Mavis Hudson. Walter played the trumpet with the Campbell River Concert Band and held film nights for friends and neighbours, while Sybil organised quartets and gave recorder lessons. Yet, as one student, herself an immigrant from England, said, 'She never got over it . . . the feeling of being a stranger.'

Although Sybil came to love Canada – 'I got to identify myself with the foresters, the fishermen and the Indians' – she stuck to her sense of being 'English', keeping her accent, scorning teabags, reading *Country Life* and *The Field,* and sending large donations to the National Trust. She and Walter never applied for Canadian citizenship because, she said, her 'heart was in England'. In the early years in Canada, in despair at the remoteness and bleakness of their life, she had formally joined the Christian Science church in Boston: she took the largely secular *Monitor* for its news reports (and taught herself French by ordering both the French and English versions of newsletters). But for book reviews, she read the *Times Literary Supplement.* She ordered books from Blackwell's in Oxford, following the writers and artists she admired. New books, like David Jones's *The Anathemata*, published in 1952, evoked old memories. Thinking back to the First World War, and the way that artists and writers had portrayed the conflict, she wrote, 'Armistice always sends me to *In Parenthesis* – David Jones carves with words as in granite, rock, bone, working all hard & sometimes a shower of splinters & shrapnel especially in *Anathemata* – how strange that when it comes to painting he often turns to a delicate medium like water colour.'

She kept her subscription to the *Transactions* of the Suffolk Archaeological Society, and returned again to Suffolk in her prints: to the ploughman in *Ploughing Pasture*, the turnips flying through the air in *Mangolds*, the great shire horses in *Day's End* and the gulls over the furrows in *Wings*. As time passed, she filled her scrapbooks with folk songs, and copied out poems by Tennyson, Masefield and T. S. Eliot, and long extracts from books. These ranged from Eric Gill's 1940 autobiography to the story of 'Grey Owl', the English conservationist Archie Belaney, who lived as a First Nations man among the tribes of Canada's wilderness. One of the books she copied from was *Lady Chatterley's Lover*, on the bestseller lists in Canada for months after the unexpurgated edition was published in 1959. Her choice of extracts was telling. They began with Connie Chatterley's despair at life with her disabled husband and her feeling 'as if thousands and thousands of little roots and threads of consciousness in him and her had grown together into a tangled mass, till they could crowd no more, and the plant was dying'. When she hires a nurse to look after him, she 'felt herself released, in another world, she felt she breathed differently'. Then the extracts moved to Connie's dismay at her husband's appeal that while he lives only for her, 'for you I am absolutely nothing'. What man, Connie thinks, 'would put this ghastly burden of life-responsibility upon a woman, and leave her there, in the void?' Against this passage, reading through her scrapbook, she drew two lines in red crayon. Perhaps that was what she had felt about Cyril in 1943, at the end of their time together.

The scrapbooks grew fat, interleaved with programmes of concerts and ballets, cards from the hotels where she and Cyril had stayed in St Malo and Rouen, drawings and plans and cuttings of articles, including one on Tom Smith, the craftsman who had thatched the new roof at Pipers years ago. Though far away, she looked back on that time as central to her life and her art. She held her bulging scrapbooks together with a strap from Cyril's LCC days. In the largest, 'Sybil's Delight', beneath carefully copied folk songs, she pasted the photos of her studios, of their musical instruments, of wall paintings at Woolpit, holidays in Sark and the New Forest, of Cyril gardening at Pipers, and Walter, hammering the packing cases in the yard.

36: ENDINGS

In the late 1950s an affectionate, humorous exchange of letters with her elderly aunt Mabel brought home to Sybil how hard her own father's departure for Canada had been for them half a century ago. Now she was the one far from her family, increasingly alone. After a brief spell in Kenya with the archaeologists Louis and Mary Leakey, as Warden of the Olorgesailie Prehistoric Site, then a post at Croydon museum, and ten years as curator of the museum in Saffron Walden (remembered as 'a gaunt gentleman in a long black cloak'), Hal retired to the New Forest. He died in Lymington in 1961, aged only fifty-nine. Her eldest brother Geoff died in 1966, and her sister Mike four years later; Joy kept her up to date with Bury news, until she too died, in 1979. Four years earlier, when Sybil finally finished her tapestry of the martyrdom of St Edmund, she sent it to be mounted at the Royal School of Needlework in London. Then she gave it to the cathedral in Bury St Edmunds.

Sybil Andrews' reputation had grown, nationally and internationally, over the years. Critics had begun to notice her work in 1948, after a show of forty linocuts at Vancouver Art Gallery, which then travelled across Canada. Three years later, after a solo exhibition in Victoria, she was elected to the Society of Canadian Painter-Etchers and Engravers: she would take part in most of their annual shows for the next twenty years. By the 1970s she was a respected Canadian artist. But she still sold few prints and they were living hand to mouth, as Walter had retired from the mill. The break came when the de Vooght Galleries in Vancouver organised a retrospective of her prints in 1978, with the Burnaby Art Gallery. A delighted Andrews, 'an amazing spry 80 year old, as fit and active as many half her age', took a group of her students to the opening – a rare trip to the city.

British gallery owners, too, began to appreciate the Grosvenor School artists. In November 1973 the Parkin Gallery in Motcomb Street, in London's smart Belgravia, held an exhibition of *Claude Flight and Edith Lawrence*. (Flight had died in 1955 and Lawrence died just a month before the show.) Keen to know more about the Grosvenor School, the ebullient Michael Parkin tracked Andrews down and she sent him prints by herself and by Power, which he included in the exhibition *Claude Flight and His Circle* in 1975. Five years later he gave her a show of her own, including her New Forest watercolours as well as her linocuts. Over the years he became a good friend, visiting her at Willow Point, and sending Fortnum and Mason hampers for Christmas, much to her delight. Suddenly, she was hard at work again. A large exhibition was mounted at the Glenbow Museum, Calgary in 1982, curated by Peter White, who worked tirelessly putting together a catalogue raisonné. More shows followed, and when Stephen Coppel, who would later write the influential *Linocuts of the Machine Age: Claude Flight and the Grosvenor School*, sent a catalogue from the Australian National Gallery in Canberra, she told him, 'Today I get busier and busier with exhibitions.' These included shows at the Mary Ryan Gallery in New York and the Redfern in London and a touring exhibition in Australia and New Zealand. 'I think it's funny when people talk about retiring – I haven't got time to retire. I haven't got time to die,' she said in a video for the Art Gallery of Greater Victoria in 1984. 'Too many exciting things to do in this world.'

Interest grew in Power's work too, and in the Grosvenor School as a whole. In the early 1980s, Gordon Samuel had discovered a few prints by Power, Claude Flight and Ethel Spowers lying forgotten in a drawer at the Redfern, and put on an exhibition. Toby Power dropped in to see this and in 1985, with the help of Toby and Kit, Samuel showed *British Linocuts of the 1920s and 1930s*. This

Sybil at her workbench, by Michael Parkin, 1985

included over a hundred Grosvenor School prints, including forty by Power. Many were new to critics, and as one reviewer declared, Power dominated the show: 'The sensation of physical participation is uncanny.' When Samuel sent Andrews the catalogue she was 'extra glad', she told him, to see that he had included prints from the individual blocks of Power's *The Eight*:

> . . . even to see one set of blocks together with the complete print is so exciting. Few people have the least idea as how a linocut print comes into being & are I find astonished and delighted to see the individual blocks which go to make up the whole, & those individual blocks are low-relief carvings in their own right & very beautiful, looking like old polished leather after many printings. They should be treasured & cared for carefully.

The Redfern put on a solo show of Power's work four years later. In 1990 a comprehensive exhibition at the British Museum, *Avant-Garde British Printmaking 1914–1960*, showing two generations of British and European artists working in a range of genres, placed Andrews and Power and their fellows at the Grosvenor School – Claude Flight and Lili Tschudi, Ethel Spowers, Eveline Syme and Dorrit Black, William Greengrass and Eileen Mayo – as a coherent group. The interest has continued ever since. In recent years fine catalogues of Andrews' and Power's linocuts have been published by Hana Leaper and Philip Vann respectively; in 2016 a new school in Bury was named the Sybil Andrews Academy; and appreciation of the whole group was sparked afresh by Dulwich Picture Gallery's *Cutting Edge: Modernist British Printmaking* in the summer of 2019 – a hundred years after Cyril Power and Sybil Andrews first met.

After Andrews' prints were shown in England in the 1970s old friends got in touch. Edgar Hunt wrote with memories of music at Brook Green. Hal's childhood friend, their second cousin Russell Plumpton, told her of changes in Bury. As she read these letters, and many others, memories came rushing back, edited with hindsight, crystallised into anecdote: of growing up in Bury, dances at the Angel, market day chaos, of Chinery's the bakers and Oliver's the grocers 'with that lovely smell of cheese, & fruit & good things', and a Christmas display of crackers upstairs 'which used to mean so much to we kids' – and the ironmongers itself, Andrews and Plumpton, where she had been born, with its smell of 'Parafin, oil and tools'.

Sometimes, however, the past jumped up and bit her. In April 1986, she wrote a rapid, vehement letter to Michael Parkin:

> It has come to my knowledge that there is a suggestion going round that Power and I were lovers. Would you please deny that absolutely and utterly – that was the assumption his wife made & acted upon almost before I really knew him & which has been the cause of all the trouble – it caused division when our families should have been friends – It hurt herself & the family most of all.

There was panic in her tone, as the past rushed suddenly into the present, as if she was being accused of adultery, and that this was a betrayal, now, of Walter. The rumours threatened their life together, invaded her privacy, rocked her sense of herself. Yet the suggestion was not so new. The Power family had always taken it for granted that they were lovers, and their friends had accepted them as a couple, without bother. If their relationship was platonic, it was intense and life-absorbing: the depth of their companionship was never in doubt.

In her shock Sybil was sweeping under a mental carpet all their years together, their joint work, their exhibitions and holidays, their music and medieval feasts. For years now she had been feted as an individual artist: she did not want to be thrust back into being one half of a collaboration. Asserting her independence, she turned not only on Dolly, who had put up patiently with years of separation, but harshly on Cyril himself. He was, she declared, one of the most insecure people she had known: 'In some way I gave him a sense of purpose & security which he lacked – & there was my studio when he could never afford a studio to work in.' On the faded carbon copy of this letter she scribbled, 'He followed *me*, not vice versa'. She pleaded in the same strenuous tones to Gordon Samuel: 'Power was a good friend but he had no studio of his own & never could afford one so he worked in my studio. The Truth is as simple as that.'

'Truth' is rarely so simple. But Sybil's distress was understandable. Less than a month before, Walter had fallen and had been taken into hospital. She had watched his decline since the previous summer. In the autumn she had cleared out the tools from his work shed, amused by the way every man who passed and saw the pile of chuck-outs 'made a bee-line & all found something "which might be useful" – 39 years of "might be useful" – unbelievable how the years have flown, busy years, full of activity'. Walter, who now slept most of the time, 'never saw his lathes go sailing off down the road, so did not grieve'. When he was in hospital Jean Looy, a younger neighbour whom Sybil had met on the beach, drove her to see him every day. Knowing her anxieties about the Power rumours, Jean has always loyally upheld her old friend's version.

Walter died on 16 August 1986, aged ninety-one. After his death Sybil lived as simply as ever. Neighbours helped out with deliveries and errands, and Jean Looy and her husband Dave looked after her – Jean called in every day, morning and evening, cooking for her, assisting with correspondence, cataloguing her art. Sybil's eyesight was fading but as demand grew she printed yet more linocuts, dismayed by the poor quality of the paper compared to her old Japanese tissue and gasping, at the age of ninety, at the continuing work: 'Sometimes I find it hard to face the printing bench!' By now almost all the editions of fifty were exhausted and she had only a few trial prints left. In 1988 she made her final linocut, *Six Waterpots of Stone*, Christ turning water into wine at the wedding in Cana, a feast of orange and brown, with the characteristic square-headed men lifting heavy water gourds and pouring the wine into round-bellied pots: life full to the brim.

She set aside her burst of fury at the talk of her relationship with Cyril. The portrait that she had painted of him in 1929, when he dropped into the office in Warwick Square and she made him sit for hours, still hung in the centre of her studio wall. She was pleased when his grandchildren got in touch after seeing their work in exhibitions. The first to write was Toby's youngest son, Martin, from Tasmania. In response Sybil posted him some gloves bought years ago at a little shop near the British Museum, and when he sent a photograph of a watercolour that he could not place, she told him it must be by Cyril, of the studio at Phoenix Place: 'I smile when I see the old gramophone with its horn – it takes me back through the years to see all the items in that picture.' Sending him Cyril's poem 'Our Ladye of Woolpit', she explained about the village and the well, just the sort of place his grandfather had liked. 'He was a very unusual man, so wide in his interests – history, prehistory, medieval history, archaeology, Architecture, Art, Music – A writer & a painter & a very fine musician. Any one of these would be enough for one person – but he had them all.'

Martin told her that Toby had long wanted to get in touch, but had held back, 'out of loyalty to his mother'. Toby died three years later, in May 1990, a year after his brother Cyril. When Toby's daughter Catherine wrote, sending news of her own daughters, Power's great-grandchildren, Sybil made a note of their names in a shaky hand, on a torn-off label. In late 1990 she wrote to Kit, after reading the Redfern catalogue to which he had contributed some biographical notes. Swiftly, and rather proudly, she said she wished that the catalogue had given more sense of Power's humour, colourful character and wide knowledge, explaining how they had shared the print books – his only writing about his work – but still insisting that he only used her studio, 'having no studio of his own where he could leave his work and subsequently a mess. He was a very untidy man.' She sent him a portrait of Power asleep in his chair, leaving Kit charmed and amused: 'I remember the suit he was wearing! (In fact it served *me* well for several years!)'

Writing to Kit and his wife Joy in December 1991, Sybil ended, 'Christmas blessings to both of you! I hope to see you in the near future.' But in April the next year severe cataracts and reduced mobility left her unable to look after herself and she moved into the Looys' house. On 1 April an exhibition of her Stations of the Cross opened in the gallery at Campbell River's Tidemark Theatre and she celebrated with friends and students. Her ninety-fourth birthday arrived, on 19 April. In early May the photographer Lincoln Clarkes came to take her portrait, with the journalist Robin Laurence. They looked through decades of her paintings, drawings and linocuts, and photographs of past days. 'I sensed Sybil was a little spent and started to plan a goodbye exit,' Clarkes writes. He watched as she sat back, 'looking out of the window at the long shadows and landscape. After a day of questions and conversation, I asked her curiously if she'd seen any owls near her cottage. She perked up as if I had switched on a light.' As she spoke vividly of owls she had known, 'it was beautiful to see that her heart was grounded in nature with art on her mind.'

Increasingly weak, in November, Sybil chose to go back to Wayside House, the Christian Science nursing home in Victoria where she had earlier spent a few weeks of respite care. She stayed there until the end, gradually slowing, but still curious and talkative and able to watch the birds in the garden. She died on the shortest day, the year's midnight, 21 December 1992.

'In my day, when I was a student,' Sybil had written in *Artist's Kitchen*, 'no one dreamt of becoming famous *before* the work was done. No one dreamt of it at all, there was too much to learn. Fame, if any, lay in the future anyway, *after* the work was done.' Since her death, the acclaim for her prints, and for Cyril's, has always continued. Today their linocuts hang in galleries across the world. Side by side.

Sybil Andrews by Lincoln Clarkes, 1992

ACKNOWLEDGEMENTS

Soon after I decided to write this book, I heard that Dulwich Picture Gallery were planning an exhibition, *Cutting Edge: Modernist British Printmaking*, featuring the lino-cutters of the Grosvenor School. Full of trepidation, convinced that there would now be no need for my book, I wrote to the curator of the show, Gordon Samuel. Instead of deterring me, Gordon was full of encouragement and has been unfailingly generous with his knowledge and time ever since. I am immensely grateful to him, and to Peter Osborne, and all at the Osborne Samuel Gallery, and I also greatly appreciate their kindness in providing so many images of the linocuts.

It has been a privilege to know the family of Cyril Power, all of whom have shown me watercolours, oils and other works that I could not have found elsewhere. I am especially grateful to Catherine Fox for her interest, her kind hospitality, and for permission to quote from archival material, including the memoir of her father Edward Roper Power (Toby). My thanks too to Giles Power, Claire Saunders, Lizzie Arrighi and Tessa Allingham, and to Michael Power for information about his father Edmund Berry Power (Kit), and for details of drawings and portraits.

With regard to Sybil Andrews, my first thanks go to Jean Looy for her continued concern and friendship, her sharing of copious material and her illuminating comments. In Bury St Edmunds, Andrew Gough, Edward Wortley and Sue Goode, all relatives of the Andrews family, have always been ready to meet and talk and provide information, and I have greatly appreciated their insights. My special thanks go to Shirley Chrispin with whom I spent a very enjoyable day reading the diary of Henry Andrews (Hal). I am grateful too, to Alex McWhirter of Moyse's Hall Museum, and to Laura Parker and Ben Ridgeon of Suffolk County Archives at West Stow. At the Glenbow Museum in Calgary, Doug Cass, the former Director of Library and Archives, looked after me with great kindness during my research there. I owe thanks too to Melanie Kjorlein, Chief Operating Officer, and am more than grateful to Daryl Betenia, Manager of Collections, for guiding me through the vast Sybil Andrews collection and providing illustrations. I would also like to thank the Glenbow for permission to reproduce the linocuts.

Hana Leaper, author of the catalogue of Sybil Andrews linocuts, kindly shared information about her 2019 exhibition in Calgary: she has been a joy to be in touch with, from the start of my research to her reading of the final text. I have also enjoyed my conversations with Philip Vann, author of the Cyril Power catalogue. Many other people have helped at different points, and I should like to thank the following: Philippa Bambach and Andrew Lambirth for information about Richard Eurich; Stephen Bartley, Archivist of Heatherley's School of Art; Lincoln Clarkes for his memories of photographing Sybil; Nigel Cochrane of the John Hassall archive; Stephen Coppel of the British Museum Department of Prints and Drawings; Rachel Dickson and Sarah Macdougal at the Ben Uri Gallery for information about Henry (Henryk) Glicenstein; Richard Gault of the Redfern Gallery; Alexandra Harris for her insights into 1930s historicism; Claude Heroys for fascinating details about his grandfather Boris Héroys; Janet Nicol for her knowledge of Sybil's life in Canada; Fern Seaboyer and Heather Hughson in Campbell River; Jane Norris on the Sark Art Group; Diana Parkin for photographs from Michael Parkin Fine Art; Gary Ratushniak; Chris Reeve for his early research into Sybil Andrews; Nat Williams in Canberra on the colourful Rex Nan Kivell; Dave Walker for sorting out the mysteries of Kensington mews, and Jane Weare for her mother's account of Portland House School.

I am extremely lucky to have Zoe Waldie as my agent, someone who manages to be both calm and exuberant at once. At Faber I have greatly enjoyed working with Alex Bowler, and it has been a huge pleasure to work once again on the production with the patient and skilful genius, Kate Ward. Thanks too to Eleanor Rees for her meticulous copy-editing, and to Anne Rieley for proofreading, Sarah Ereira for the index and Jonathan Pelham for designing the cover. In New York I am grateful to Melanie Jackson and to Jonathan Galassi and all the team at Farrar Straus. Extracts from T. S. Eliot's *The Waste Land*, *Four Quartets* and *Murder in the Cathedral* are reproduced with permission of Faber & Faber and Houghton Mifflin Harcourt Publishing Company.

Friends are always central to the making of a book. Vital early encouragement came from Lucy Hughes-Hallett and Dan Franklin (whose mother, Suzanne Cooper, was a student at the Grosvenor School). They in turn introduced me to Julian Francis, whose interest and wide knowledge have been invigorating, and whose book on Tom Chadwick, another Grosvenor student, is a thing of beauty and an inspiration. Alison Samuel always raises my flagging spirits, Carmen Callil has spurred me on, and talks with the perceptive John Barnard have made me think – thank you all. I want to give a special cheer, too, for my cousin David Crowther, who put me up, drove me around and shared his knowledge of Suffolk, as well as cooking a cracking shepherd's pie. Above all, my love and thanks to Hermione Lee, for talking, sharing, reading and being there.

Finally, without exaggeration, I owe everything to Steve Uglow, expert at tricky research, and the mainstay that keeps the ship sailing on.

PICTURE CREDITS

Unless specified, all works by Sybil Andrews are © Glenbow Museum, Calgary. Works by Cyril Power are from the Osborne Samuel Gallery, with thanks to the Estate of Cyril Power.

PLATE SECTIONS

West Suffolk Heritage Services 2, 4, 5, 41; Lizzie Arrighi 3; London Transport Museum 42, 44, 45, 47; Royal Air Force Museum, Hendon 57, 58

ILLUSTRATIONS IN TEXT

Private Collection, Campbell River 11, 17, 194, 318; Private Collection, Oxford 11, 78, 87, 150; Sybil Andrews fonds, Glenbow Museum Archives 20, 84, 238, 228, 242, 245, 260, 283, 293, 302; Cyril E. Power, *English Medieval Architecture* (1912) 37; West Suffolk Heritage Service 43, 92; Heatherley's School of Art 55; © The Estate of Claude Flight/Bridgeman Images 68, 186; Michael Parkin Fine Art 92, 113a, 325; British Museum, London, 135; Michael Power 312; © Lincoln Clarkes (1992) 331

PRINCIPAL EXHIBITIONS

Galleries are in London, unless otherwise stated.

1929–45

1929   *First Exhibition of British Lino-cuts*, Redfern, 4–27 July

1930   *British Linocuts*, Redfern, 23 July–23 August

1931   *Print Makers Society of California*, Los Angeles, March: also March 1934,
       1935, 1938
       British Lino-cuts, Shanghai Art Club, May
       British Lino-cuts, Redfern, July

1932   *Modern Colour Prints*, Redfern, 21 July–20 August
       Modern Colour Prints & Wood Engravings from the Redfern Gallery,
       Melbourne, 7–23 December

1933   *Sybil Andrews and C. E. P. Power*, Redfern, 5–28 January
       Colour Prints and Contemporary Oils, Redfern, 1 June–29 July

1934   *Colour Prints, also Paintings by R. O. Dunlop, Basil Jonzen, Richard
       Eurich*, Redfern, 12 July–4 August

1935   *Autumn Exhibition*, Walker Art Gallery, Liverpool
       Colour Prints, and Monotypes and Carvings by Elizabeth Spurr, Redfern,
       11 July–3 August
       Modern Colour Prints, National Gallery of Canada, Ottawa, 14 December
       1935–23 January 1936
       Two Hundred Years of British Graphic Art, British Council: Bucharest,
       Vienna, Prague, December 1935–June 1936

1936   *Colour Prints*, Redfern, 25 June–18 July

1937   *Linocuts from the Redfern Gallery*, Baillieu Allard Gallery, Melbourne,
       7–18 September

1938   *Summer Salon*, Redfern, 28 July–1 October

1939   *French and English Colour Prints*, Redfern, 29 November–30 December

1945   *Exhibition of Handcraft*, Gainsborough Galleries, Johannesburg, 22 May–
       2 June

CANADA, SYBIL ANDREWS, 1948–66

1948   Solo exhibition, Vancouver Art Gallery

1949–54 Society of Canadian Painter-Etchers and Engravers, Royal Ontario
         Museum, Toronto, annually, then 1959–60, 1962, 1964–5, 1969, 1981

REVIVAL, 1966–2020

1966   *'Off the Block', Modernist British Woodcuts, Wood Engravings and*
         Linocuts, Mercury Gallery, 7 February–9 March

1975   *British Printmakers 1850–1940,* P. & D. Colnaghi, 21 May–17 June
         Claude Flight and his Circle, Parkin Gallery, 19 November–6 December

1977–8 *Futuristi Inglesi: Claude Flight & la Sua Cerchia*: Genoa, Milan, Rome,
         Bologna, Brescia, Bolsano, Padua

1978   *The Movement of Flight,* Parkin Gallery, 27 September–21 October

1980   *Sybil Andrews, Paintings & Graphic Work,* Parkin Gallery, 22
         October–15 November

1982–3 *Sybil Andrews, Colour Linocuts,* Vancouver, Halifax, Toronto, Edmonton,
         Calgary, Saskatchewan, Victoria, January 1982–February 1983

1984   *Out of the Book and onto the Wall: The Relief Print,* National Gallery of
         Australia, Canberra, 20 February–13 May

1985   *British Linocuts of the 1920s and 1930s,* Redfern, 26 March–4 May

1988   *The Grosvenor School: British Linocuts Between the Wars,* Rhode
         Island, Cleveland, Santa Barbara, January–December

1989   *The Linocuts of Cyril Edward Power 1872–1951,* Redfern, December

1990   *Avant-Garde British Printmaking 1914–1960,* British Museum

1992–3 *Claude Flight and His Followers,* Australia: Canberra, Sydney,
         Melbourne; New Zealand: Wellington, Auckland, April 1992–July 1993

1999   *Modernity: Colour Linocuts of the 1920s and 1930s,* De La Warr
         Pavilion, Bexhill-on-Sea, 21 November 1999–16 January 2000

2008–9 *Rhythms of Modern Life: British Prints 1914–1939,* Museum of Fine
         Arts, Boston; Metropolitan Museum, New York; Wolfsonian, Florida,
         January 2008–February 2009
         Cyril Power Linocuts, Osborne Samuel, 27 November–24 December

2013   *The Cutting Edge of Modernity: Linocuts of the Grosvenor School,*
         Osborne Samuel, 11 April–11 May

2015   *Sybil Andrews,* Osborne Samuel, 22 October–14 November

2019   *Cutting Edge: Modernist British Printmaking,* Dulwich Picture Gallery,
         19 June–8 September
         Sybil Andrews, Glenbow, 19 October 2019–12 January 2020

SELECT BIBLIOGRAPHY

This list is limited to books directly concerned with the Grosvenor School. All other titles are identified fully on first mention in the notes for each chapter.

Books by the same author are identified in the notes with date of individual works. Exh. cat. is for Exhibition Catalogue.

Ackley	Clifford S. Ackley, *Rhythms of Modern Life: British Prints 1914–1939*, exh. cat. (2008)
AK	Sybil Andrews, *Artist's Kitchen* (1986)
Art/Art, RT	Video, *Sybil Andrews and the Art of the Linocut*, dir. Peter Horvath, Glenbow (1992); *Art*, RT: Research tape for video, interview by Patricia Ainslie (August 1991)
Carey	Frances Carey and Antony Griffiths, *Avant-Garde British Print-making 1914–1960*, exh. cat. (1990) with essay by Stephen Coppel
Coppel	*Linocuts of the Machine Age: Claude Flight and the Grosvenor School* (1995)
Cutting Edge	*Cutting Edge, Modernist British Printmaking*, exh. cat., ed. Gordon Samuel (2019)
Eurich	Judith C. Eurich, *Modern British Art: Vorticism and the Grosvenor School 1912–1935* (1992)
Flight *AC*	Claude Flight, *The Art & Craft of Lino Cutting and Printing* (1934)
Flight *LC*	Claude Flight, *Lino-cuts: A Handbook of Linoleum-cut Colour Printing* (1927)
C. Fox	Catherine Fox, *Boiled Eggs and Thimbles: A memoir of my early years, 1939–1957* (2016)
Leaper	Hana Leaper, *Sybil Andrews Linocuts: A Complete Catalogue* (2015)
Medieval	Cyril Power, *English Medieval Architecture*, 2 vols (1912); revised, 3 vols (1923)
Nicol	Janet Nicol, *On the Curve: The Life and Art of Sybil Andrews* (2019)
Parke-Taylor	Michael Parke-Taylor, *Confrontations of Form* (1990)
Reeve	Christopher Reeve, *Something to Splash About: Sybil Andrews in Suffolk* (1991)

Saler	Michael T. Saler, *The Avant-Garde in Interwar England: Medieval Modernism and the London Underground* (1995)
Samuel	*The Linocuts of Cyril Edward Power 1872–1951*, exh. cat., with essays by Gordon Samuel and Richard Gault (1989)
Samuel/Penny	*The Cutting Edge of Modernity: Linocuts of the Grosvenor School*, ed. Gordon Samuel and Nicola Penny (2013)
Urbanelli	Lora S. Urbanelli, *The Grosvenor School: British Linocuts Between the Wars*, exh. cat. (1988)
Vann	Philip Vann, *Cyril Power Linocuts: A Complete Catalogue* (2008)
White	Peter White, *Sybil Andrews: Colour Linocuts* (1982)

ABBREVIATIONS

'Aims'	SA and CEP, 'Aims of the Art of To-day', cyclostyled typescript, 1924, copies in Glenbow, Fox papers and Osborne Samuel
BH	SA's Baliol Holloway Scrapbook, Private Collection, Campbell River
BM	British Museum, London, Department of Prints and Drawings
BSEMS	Bury St Edmunds Museum Service, West Suffolk Archives
CEP	Cyril Edward Power
CF	Claude Flight
D	Sybil Andrews diary, 1922–49, Glenbow M8411-1 (1922–4), -2 (1925–9), -3 (1930–4), -4 (1935–9), -5 (1940–4)
Glenbow	Sybil Andrews fonds, Glenbow Museum, Calgary
HA	Henry Andrews; diary courtesy of Shirley Chrispin
IM	Iain Macnab
LCC	London County Council
Met	Leslie and Johanna Garfield Collection, Metropolitan Museum, New York
MP	Michael Parkin
OS	Osborne Samuel Gallery, London
Redfern	Redfern Gallery, London
RIBA	Royal Institute of British Architects
SA	Sybil Andrews
TP	Trial Proof
TS	'Tobie's Story', unpublished memoir, Edward Roper Power; Private Collection, Oxford
V&A	Victoria and Albert Museum, London

NOTES

Variations in spelling and slips of grammar in the original sources have been preserved in quotations.

BEGINNINGS

toothbrush. *The Star*, 4 July 1929.

1. WAR

swathed in bandages. SA to John Ashton, spring 1992, Glenbow M8411-99.

'It can seem very personal'. Joan Bowman, 'Powerful Works, Retiring Modestly', *North Island News*, Campbell River, 29 May 1992, quoted in Nicol, 25.

'A Perfect Day'. Sheet music, in possession of Sue Goode.

At six. Reeve, 4.

training exercise. *The Military History of the Brecks 1900–1949* (Report by the Breckland Society, 2016), 9–12. Over thirty thousand men took part: both sides had the latest equipment as well as seven aeroplanes and a single airship each.

'here were all these men'. SA to Shirley Chrispin, 6 April 1992, Glenbow M8411-115.

'the clip of the horses hooves'. SA to John Ashton, 1992, Glenbow M8411-99.

Dorothy Jarman. SA to Russell Plumpton, 6 April 1992, 25 August 1991, Glenbow M8411-115.

'dance music'. Rebecca West, *The Return of the Soldier* (1918), 49.

training camps. At West Stow and Ingham: the cyclists were from the 69th East Anglian Division.

'the most secret place'. See Roger Pugh, *The Most Secret Place on Earth* (2014).

nurse's uniform. Glenbow PA 3376.20. In 1915 the government launched the National Register of Women for War Work.

One incendiary. Gareth Jenkins and Chris Mycock, *Zeppelins over Bury: The Raids on Bury St Edmunds, 1915 and 1916* (1985). The LZ38 dropped three high-explosive bombs and fifty incendiaries.

funeral procession. Photographs: www.stedmundsburychronicle.co.uk/gallerywww1/gallerywww1page_04a and 04b.

testimonial. W. Sowells to SA, 25 January 1916, Glenbow M8411-18; she worked for Campbell & Sowells, Daventry.

'pitchforked into war'. Robin Laurence, 'The Essential Line of Sybil Andrews', *Interface 5*, No. 2 (February 1982), 71.

Robert Boby. Boby, Lloyd George Papers, Parliamentary Archives, Kew, LG/D/11/2/11; http://www.stedmundsburychronicle.co.uk/bobys/bobystory.

Miss E. C. Woodward. Photo, Glenbow PA 3376.59. According to the *Bulletin of the US Federal Board for Vocational Education*, 1917, No. 1, 14, 'This school has been efficiently maintained and is now recognized as a suitable training school for women welders. The students are trained mostly for aircraft work'.

'metal so welded'. Helen Fraser, *Women and War Work* (1918), Ch. 7. More than 800,000 women worked in munitions, but only five hundred as welders, mostly middle- and upper-class as they had to pay for the training. Women were not allowed to use heavy blowpipes, and had to fight for equal pay.

'Ten Little Welder Girls'. Glenbow, M8411-168. On the back SA noted, 'Transport and Carriage Co, Branch of Filton Aircraft, Bristol, 1918'.

'It frightened the life out of me'. *Art*, RT.

'There were five men'. SA to Michael Parke-Taylor, 12 February 1990, Parke-Taylor, 33.

photograph taken in Bristol. Glenbow PA 3376-28, signed by photographer, Gladys Methven Brownlee, 18 Charlotte Street, Bristol.

'I'm so sorry'. 'G' to SA, 17 August 1921, Glenbow M8411-86.

'architect's flying machine'. CEP sketchbook 16 (1909), OS.

Toby. TS. SA writes 'Toby' rather than 'Tobie', and I have followed this.

'No 8. Aircraft Acceptance Park'. Ian Philpott, *The Birth of the Royal Air Force*, (2013), 249–50.

'No sooner do we evolve' . 'Adventure in Archaeology', *Journal of the Antiquarian Association*, No. 3 (December 1930), 129–30. Private Collection, Oxford.

'steeped in history'. SA to MP, 23 November 1979, Glenbow M8411-64a.

'undone years'. Wilfred Owen, 'Strange Meeting', *The Poems of Wilfred Owen*, ed. Jon Stallworthy (1986). Deaths were higher among French and German troops.

Folkestone. *Kentish Gazette*, 24 May 2017.

Belcaire. The original architect was Sir Herbert Baker. See Alan Powers, *The Twentieth-century House in Britain: from the archives of Country Life* (2004).

CEP demobilisation. National Archives, Kew. WO 339/103939.

George and Alice Nunn, in Berril House. TS, 9–11.

Nunn sons' war record. Summary in TS, corrected from UK, Australian and Canadian census and war records.

2. SYBIL

'the centre of my life'. SA to Chris Reeve, 3 April 1991, Reeve, Introduction.

'Market day'. SA to Chris Reeve, 3 April 1991, Reeve, Introduction.

Ouida. 'Blue and Yellow, or how my Brother Fitz Stood for Cantitborough', *Bentley's Miscellany* 47 (1860), 304.

'a furnishing ironmonger'. 'Ironmongers on the same Bury site for 167 Years', *Suffolk Fair*, December 1979, 37.

Mayor of Bury. Funeral notice, *Bury Free Press*, 6 June 1914.

Charles Andrews' family. Charles Andrews, 1861–1922; Beatrice Martha née Trigg, 1868–1929; children: Geoffrey, 1894–1966; Joyce ('Joy'), 1895–1978; Sybil, 1898–1992; Margaret ('Mike'), 1902–70; Henry ('Hal'), 1904–61. Sybil was baptised in St Mary's Church on 17 May.

Babwell Friary. Founded in 1262: *Victoria County History: Suffolk*, Vol. 2, 124–5.

'one of the leading lights'. Steve J. Plunkett, 'The Suffolk Institute of Archaeology: Its Life, Times and Members', *Transactions of the Suffolk Institute of Archaeology* 39, Part 2 (1998), 174. He began by collecting stone tools from gravel and clay pits in the Brecklands, excavated tumuli and found pottery kilns on West Stow Heath. Many papers went to the Suffolk Institute.

'my childhood home'. Note on watercolour of Whiting Street, BSEMS 1992:46.

Lilian Burroughs. LR to SA, 5 May 1941, Glenbow M8411-86. Lilian (1885– 1955) was the first Ipswich and East Suffolk Joint Archivist, leading spirit in the Suffolk Record Office; daughter of Vincent Burrough Redstone, authority on Saxon charters and medieval records.

'rippling up and down the piano'. Robin Laurence, 'Remembering Sybil Andrews', *Canadian Art*, Summer 1995, 79.

great bed of fennel. *AK*, 209; also SA to Chris Reeve, 20 November 1990, Private Collection, Campbell River.

Ivy Lodge. SA to John Ashton, 19 December 1981, Glenbow M8411-99.

sedan chair: ten years later the chair took pride of place in Moyse's Hall.

'smell of Parafin' and 'Aunt Agnes'. SA to Russell Plumpton, 14 December 1990, 25 February 1991, Glenbow M8411-115.

a bevy of aunts. Andrews sisters: Annie, 1864–1944, m. Charles Nunn; Caroline ('Edith'), 1866–1938; Agnes, 1872–1958; Mabel, 1876–1967.

Pageant. *The Connoisseur*, 3rd Special Edition (1907), special souvenir edition for the pageant. For Parker's pageants, and their successors in the 1930s, see J. D. Esty, *A Shrinking Island: Modernism and National Culture in England* (2004), 54–62.

'a man of real courage'. SA to Russell Plumpton, 28 February 1982, Glenbow M8411-115, complaining about a statue of St Edmund that she thought 'looked like a schoolboy'.

half-hour film. Ronald James Bates, *The Bury St Edmunds Pageant, July 8–13, 1907*, East Anglian Film Archive, Cat. no. 527: also BFI Screen Online.

'paraded in fine clothes'. http://www.historicalpageants.ac.uk/featured-pageants/pageant-bury-st-edmunds-1907/ The website gives a detailed, illustrated account of pageant and context.

'Sybil *would* laugh'. Photograph, Glenbow, PA 3376-26.

'So I would have to flee'. Reeve, 5.

Her father's departure. Mabel Andrews to SA, 14 May 1957, Glenbow M8411-96.

'Did he ever show you?' Mabel Andrews to SA, 14 October 1966, Glenbow M8411-96.

'He was a rare one'. Mabel Andrews to SA, 8 April 1957, Glenbow M8411-96.

Maud and her family. Canadian census 1911, John Russell Edwards (b. 1865), Maud (b. 1869) and four children. Maud's mother Ann (née Vale) and Charles's mother Caroline were sisters. Maud trained as an opera singer before marrying.

'I suppose'. Charles Andrews to SA, 19 July 1917, Glenbow M8411-96.

'if I should be here another year'. Charles Andrews to Beatrice, 12 April 1922, and photo of grave, Glenbow M8411-96.

'We children'. SA to Peter White, 16 April 1980, White, 73.

'very kind and helpful'. SA to Chris Reeve, 20 November 1990, Private Collection, Campbell River. See also Chris Reeve, *Rose Mead: Artist of Bury St Edmunds, 1867–1946* (1989).

His advertisement. *The Bystander* 58 (24 April 2018), www.illustratedfirstworldwar.com/item/the-john-hassall-correspondence-art-school-ltd.

'The John Hassall Way'. John Hassall, Stratford Studios, Kensington (1917). See also V&A and John Hassall Collection, University of Essex.

'of hot milk'. Quoted in Graham McCann, *Do You Think That's Wise? The Life of John Le Mesurier* (2010).

'Drawing and painting'. Monica Dowsett to SA, October and December 1991, Glenbow M8411-99. Dowsett told Sybil that Le Mesurier had written of 'some kind, big girls who did up his boots for him. These must have been the Jacksons, Joan and Gabrielle, who are in the back of the picture. I never remember being kind to little boys.'

'getting all I could from it'. White, 73.

'I was one of five'. Robin Laurence, 'The Essential Line of Sybil Andrews', *Interface* 5, No. 2 (February 1982), 71.

'The refrain of this book'. *AK*, 208.

town directory. Nicol, 28.

3. CYRIL

to the market. TS, 10.

'snoozing by the fireside'. ibid., 11.

Power family history. CEP notebook 22, OS.

'Shipped slaves'. ibid.

his parents: Edward William Power (1849–May 1916); Amelia Poole Berry (1841–91).

Z. D. Berry. The firm made 'heavy kitchen equipment and swimming pool heating systems': it merged with Richard Crittall Ltd in 1967, later subsumed into Crown House Engineering, now part of the Laing O'Rourke Group. (See www. crownhouse.com.) Many of the seats remain on both sides of the river, between Westminster Bridge and Blackfriars Bridge. Photo, Private Collection, Oxford.

working plans. Vann, 17, says Power, but most sources say Vulliamy.

quick sketches. CEP sketchbooks 1–5 (1886, 1887, 1890), OS.

'Norman work'. CEP sketchbook 2, OS.

Southgate. 1890, CEP sketchbook 3 (1889), OS.

The Builder. St Cuthbert's, 18 July 1896, Walton-on Thames, 30 September 1899. Private Collection, Oxford.

St Cuthbert's. 'Churches and Chapels: Church of England', in *Survey of London: Volume 42, Kensington Square to Earl's Court*, ed. Hermione Hobhouse (1986), 368–86. Power claimed his plans had been prompted by 'one of the assistant clergy, with the approbation of the vicar, some 14 or 15 months ago' and presented at a meeting in the parish hall, 'presided over by the vicar'.

Soane Medallion. *The Times*, 6 February 1900.

raid on Dieppe. Vann, 18.

Ronald Knox. Knox was ordained in 1919.

'attracted by a rural church'. TS, 10.

followed him into his new faith. To mark the occasion she was given a copy of the Rev. J. B. McKinlay's *St Edmund: King and Martyr* (1893), inscribed on 18 July 1903.

'bijou rough-cast villa'. TS, 4.

'clutching his violin!' ibid., 5.

'seated on a box'. ibid., 6.

University College London. UCL prospectus 1907, 8, 9–10, Private Collection, Oxford. In 1907–8 the school also ran lectures by Edward Prior on English Medieval Architecture.

'Make the most of the materials'. CEP sketchbook 16 (1908–9), OS.

'to learn what is vital'. *AK*, 86.

Roger Fry's exhibitions. *Manet and the Post-Impressionists*, 1910; *The Second Post-Impressionist Exhibition*, 1912.

Marinetti. Interview in *Evening News*, 9 March 1912.

'a daring conception'. CEP, *English Medieval Architecture*, Vol. 2 (1912), 283. Published in three parts in 1912, revised in two volumes, 1923, and in a single volume, 1931.

'Though my mother'. TS, 2–3.

'a lot of opera'. ibid., 18.

'the angry throwing up'. ibid., 19.

Theatre Royal. *Bury Free Press*, Theatre Royal listings, 1919–21.

'free agricultural education'. Chadacre Agricultural Trust, www.chadacre-trust. org.uk/.

perfect patron. Commissions included Mount Tyndal, a house on the Kenwood estate in Hampstead, for C. H. Bland, Lord Iveagh's agent (TS, 21), and in 1920 the library extensions at Bradwell Manor near Mistley, Essex. Edmund Berry Power notes, 1989, Private Collection, Oxford.

Champness. Cyril's siblings: Edna Winnifred (1875–1947) m. Thomas Champness in 1899; Ralph Cecil (1876–1959) m. Maud Champness 1905, divorced 1918 [m. Rose Clifford 1919]; Yevonde (1879–1962) m. Leonard Champness 1905.

'trailed around'. TS, 14–15.

4. ANGEL HILL

'My window.' SA to Chris Reeve, 20 November 1990, Private Collection, Campbell River.

The Athenaeum. Reeve, 4. In 1991 this was in the St John's Street Gallery, Bury St Edmunds. Current whereabouts unknown.

Sybil's recollection. SA, ms. amendment to Reeve typescript, Private Collection, Campbell River.

related three times. The closest link was the marriage of Sybil's aunt, Annie Vale Andrews (1864–1944), to Charlie Hearn Nunn: she had four Nunn cousins.

thanked Sybil Andrews. *Bury Free Press*, 23 October 1920.

'dashing off before breakfast'. TS, 22.

Clausen's lectures. CEP sketchbook 12, OS. Wrongly placed as '1906', the date of Clausen's book, but the sketchbook address is Crescent House, Bury, so 1920–1.

'Sybil was born'. BSEMS 1992.9.665 and 666.

'On the spot'. BSEMS 1992.49.

shadows of the winter trees. CEP, *The Mount*, sold by Giles Power, see Dominic Winter Auctions, 17 July 2013.

Looms Lane. A pastel of this is at BSEMS 1992.9.662.

one of her watercolours. SA, 'Watchman's Lodge on Abbot's Bridge, Bury St Edmunds', BSEMS 1992.9.658.

violet shadows. SA, *Southgate Street* (1921), BSEMS 1992.9.659; *Greyfriars* (1919), BSEMS 1992.46; *Star Inn*, BSEMS 1992.9.660. CEP, *Star Inn*, Lizzie Arrighi; *Bury St Edmunds*, watercolour, sold Bonhams, 17 April 2012.

'lively discussion and argument'. TS, 2.

'Those to whom I am most indebted'. SA to Peter White, 16 April 1980, White, 73.

'born teacher . . . His book'. SA to MP, 20 July 1980, Glenbow M8411-64a.

Easter weekend. 2–4 April 1920. Noted on CEP Easter card, 1944. Private Collection, Campbell River.

'Behold me!' CEP sketchbook 38, OS.

Tom Jones. Bury Free Press, 3 December 1921.

'emphasising beauties'. *Bury Post*, 9 December 1921.

'Cyril to Chadacre . . .' etc. D, 9, 10 January 1922, Glenbow M8411-1.

'did excellent "eyes"'. D, 19 February 1992, Glenbow M8411-1.

church decoration. Commissions appear to have included St Chad's, Lichfield, Sacred Heart Church, Colne and churches in Birtley, near Newcastle, and Castle Eden near West Hartlepool. D, 1922, Glenbow M8411-1.

'splendidly executed diagrams'. *Bury Free Press*, 8 July 1922; CEP drawing, 'Restoration of the West Front of the Abbey of St Edmundsbury, *c*.1500', Private Collection, Oxford.

'most successful day'. D, 30 June 1922, Glenbow M8411-1.

5. THE MOVE

wrote from Canada. Charles Andrews to SA, 2 April 1922, Glenbow M8411-96.

that August he died. Sam Andrews, no relation, took the funeral service. Charles was buried in Woodlawn Cemetery, Saskatoon. Photo of gravestone, Glenbow PA 3376.

'saw EMU'. D, 7 May 1922, Glenbow M8411-1.

reference. Edith M. Underwood, 14 August 1922, Glenbow M8411-18.

'excellent I think'. D, 28 August 1922, Glenbow M8411-1.

'up to town'. D, 13 September 1922, Glenbow M8411-1.

'Such an interesting day'. D, 18 September 1922, Glenbow M8411-1. Heatherleys register: SA enrolled on 18 September 1922 for three months, giving her address as Crescent House. She started her next course in January 1923. CEP enrolled at the same time. (In the register his name is written 'Cecil Power'.) He came two days per week, SA attended daily. CEP's last day was 23 July 1923. SA returned in the autumn, coming in three days per week and attending a Composition class, until 12 November 1923. With thanks to Stephen Bartley, Archivist, Heatherley School of Art.

his father's 'defection'. TS, 22.

'anniversary feast'. D, 12 September 1922, Glenbow M8411-1.

'all eccentric'. Private correspondence, Bury St Edmunds.

6. HEATHERLEYS

'a Paris studio'. White, 73. In 1927 the school moved to larger premises, 11–13 George Street, off Baker Street.

'respectable girls'. Evelyn Waugh, *A Little Learning* (1964), 210–11.

'underbred houris'. *Diaries of Evelyn Waugh*, ed. Michael Davie (1984, 2010 edn), 180.

'a wonderful man'. *Art*, RT.

'He used to say'. White, 73.

'I didn't know'. *AK*, 123.

Treasure Island. D, 8 November 1922, Glenbow M8411-1.

'We had five minutes'. White, 73.

'Witness what happens'. *AK*, 40.

'He would lay a walking stick'. ibid., 42.

'Mr Massey very pleased'. D, 5 April, 18, 19 October 1923, Glenbow M8411-1.

'You can only learn by experiment', and succeeding quotes. https://heatherleys. wordpress.com/quotes/more-massey-quotes.

'My father always said'. *Arts Review*, 12 April 1985.

7. LONDON

'To Chelsea'. D, 27 January 1923, Glenbow M8411-1.

Dorothy Sayers. Francesca Wade, *Square Haunting: Five Women and London Between the Wars* (2019), 118.

'Buses swooped'. Virginia Woolf, *Mrs Dalloway* (1925, 1990 edition), 119.

Everyman. D, 15 April 1924, Glenbow M8411-1.

'I used to want to see'. SA interview with Harrill Bjornson, 'Bare Bones, Well Done', *Vancouver Sun*, 1 August 1992, quoted in Nicol, 34.

Hamlet, Merchant of Venice. D, 10, 26 June 1924, Glenbow M8411-1.

kept a scrapbook. SA, BH scrapbook, Private Collection, Campbell River. Holloway starred both at the Old Vic and in Stratford-on-Avon. SA also made many small drawings of actors and costumes, adding watercolour to indicate colour of robes.

Shoemaker's Holiday. CEP sketchbook 30 (1926), OS; BH to SA, n.d., post 1929, BH scrapbook, Private Collection, Campbell River.

'is a school'. *AK*, 34.

McKnight Kauffer. In *The Art of the Poster* (1924), McKnight Kauffer traced its history from ancient Chinese mosaics and Byzantine mosaics to the nineteenth-century influence of Japanese prints.

'On my first afternoon'. Evelyn Waugh, *Brideshead Revisited* (1945), Ch. 1.

Heal's. See the excellent history pages on their website: https://www.heals.com/heritage.

'an inherent distrust'. John Nash, *London Mercury*, December 1919, quoted in Andrew Lambirth, *John Nash: Artist and Countryman* (2020), 91.

'periodic explosion'. Seven and Five manifesto, 1920. Their object, they said, was 'merely to express what they feel in terms that shall be intelligible and not to demonstrate a theory nor to attack a tradition'. Artists in the mid-1920s included Ivon Hitchens, Evie Hone, Christopher Wood and Cedric Morris, David Jones, Frances Hodgkins, Henry Moore and Barbara Hepworth.

Futurists and speed. Paintings like Giacomo Balla's *Study of the Materiality of Light and Speed* (also 1913) expanded the Cubist use of abstracted blocks of colour, learned from Picasso and Braque, adding lines of motion and light.

'WE WANT'. 1914 Marinetti–Nevinson manifesto, quoted in Michael J. K. Walsh, *C. R. W. Nevinson: This Cult of Violence* (2002), 57.

'Time seems to pass so quickly'. Claude Flight, 'Dynamism and the Colour Print', *Original Colour Print Magazine* 2 (1925), 56, quoted in Coppel, 17.

Proms at the Queen's Hall. Prom 57, including Rimsky-Korsakov's *The Maid of Pskov*, and *Capriccio Espagnol*, Op. 34. Other pieces ranged from Purcell to Saint-Saëns, from Tchaikovsky to the premiere of Hubert Parry's *English Suite*: D, 17 October 1922, Glenbow M4811-1. www.bbc.co.uk/events/r2vg9r/by/date/1922/10.

Opera. D, 9, 16, 19, 30 October 1922. For the Royal Opera House and Beecham's new British National Opera, see Alexandra Wilson, *Opera in the Jazz Age: Cultural Politics in 1920s Britain* (2018).

Goossens. D, 22, 23 February 1923, Glenbow M8411-1. In November, SA and CEP heard Stravinsky's *Petrushka*, conducted by Goossens at the Queen's Hall.

'rhythm of the steppes'. T. S. Eliot, 'London Letter', *The Dial* 71 (October 1921), 452–5: see Ivan Hewett, 'The riot at the Rite', British Library, www.bl.uk/20th-century-literature/articles/the-riot-at-the-rite-the-premiere-of-the-rite-of-spring.

8. PHOENIX PLACE AND DRYPOINTS

'C did etchings'. D, 2 April 1923.

'Sandra'. Used by CEP re visit to Cromer, D, 18–28 July 1923, Glenbow M8411-1.

finished her spring course. D, 3 May 1923.

moved into her first proper studio. D, 17 May 1923.

many women artists. See Sacha Llewellyn, 'A One Man Show?' in *Fifty Works by Fifty British Women Artists 1900–1950*, exh. cat. (2018), 16.

'It was in a mews'. SA to Martin Roper Power, 17 February 1987, Glenbow M8411-132.

Phoenix Place. With thanks to Dave Walker, Local Studies director, Kensington and Chelsea Library, for solving this puzzle.

mending the road at night. Notting Hill Gate, 29 January 1923; Shops, greengrocers, 1924; Notting Hill Gate Tube, 1923. CEP sketchbooks 27, 28, 22, OS.

'picked up free copies'. Leaper, 32.

sketched the First Church. 'First Church of Xt Scientist, Sloane Square, Moonlight, Dec. 22. 1923', CEP sketchbook 27, OS.

drew the studio. CEP sketchbook 28, OS.

'Art and Artistic'. 'Aims', Introduction.

an apple. SA to Martin Power, 17 February 1987, Glenbow M8411-132.

bowl of dripping. *Art*, RT.

'found himself'. Aldous Huxley, *Antic Hay* (1923), Ch. 3.

'A theorist was H.G.M.' CEP sketchbook 28 (1924), OS.

'you would go to see'. Albert Garrett, *Wood Engravings and Drawings of Iain Macnab of Barachastlain* (1973), 1.

'devoid of tact'. ibid., 3.

wanted to be a sculptor. ibid., 33, and Herbert B. Grimsditch, 'Iain Macnab', *The Artist*, April 1937.

wood-engraving revival. This followed the founding of the Society of Wood Engravers in 1920, which drew artists such as Robert Gibbings, Gwen Raverat, Eric Gill, John and Paul Nash, David Jones, Eric Ravilious and Edward Bawden.

'much easier than drypoint'. IM to SA, 5 March 1928, Glenbow M8411-86.

commercial art printers. Printers are listed in drypoint print book ('Drypoint Aquatint Etching Print Book'), Glenbow M8411-137, as 'Wilsons' or 'Forster'; the main print-seller is 'Bells'. Some were published by Eyre and Spottiswood in 1928–9, notably *The Old Steelyard, Woodbridge, Cannon Street Railway Bridge, Pickle Herring Street, Queen's Gate, Trinity* and *Christ's College, Cambridge* (SA drypoint book 16, 18, 24, 37, 43, Glenbow M8411-137).

St Bartholomew. CEP, 'High Altar, St Bartholomew's Brighton', Private Collection, Oxford.

Oxford and Cambridge. Oxford D, 22 July; Cambridge 9, 11 August 1924; Oxford again 28 August; 'Finished Christ's Coll', 3 November 1924.

Canterbury. CEP, Norman Staircase, Canterbury, no. 138 of 166; Christchurch Gate, Canterbury, 20 February 1928, TP and no. 35 of 166, Private Collection, Oxford.

Lots Road Power Station. D, 22 November 1924; drawing, CEP sketchbook 26, OS.

Nevinson's bold lithographs. For example the London prints, *From an Office Window* (1918), *The Workers* (1919) and *Looking Down into Wall Street* (1919).

railway station. CEP, *The Railway Station*, drypoint, 1924.

The Viaduct. BM, 1987, 1107.22. Impressions of *The Viaduct* and *The Railway Station* were shown at the 1924 Autumn Exhibition, Walker Gallery, Liverpool. See also Bonhams catalogue, *The Grosvenor School and Avant-Garde British Printmaking*, 17 April 2012.

Cannon Street Railway Bridge. Bonhams, Prints and Multiples, 9 December 2014.

lorries in the cobbled yard. SA, *The Yard at Night*, drypoint book 35, Glenbow M8411-137. Power had digs in Battersea at the time.

'both framed prints sold'. D, 21 September 1924.

9. WEMBLEY

Olowe of Ise (*c*.1875–1939), see Alisa LaGamma, 'Naming rights – anonymity and attribution in African art', *Apollo*, 5 December 2020.

'many wonderful and strange things'. HA diary, Wembley visits, 7, 8–9 May, 9 June 1924.

'The Temple of Ceres'. CEP sketchbook 28, OS.

protests. Daniel Stephen, *The Empire of Progress: West Africans, Indians and Britons at the British Empire Exhibition, 1924–25* (2013); see also Ann Clendinning, 'On the British Empire Exhibition, 1924–5' in *BRANCH: Britain, Representation and Nineteenth-Century History*, August 2012.

Everything seemed packaged. Virginia Woolf, 'Thunder at Wembley', *The Nation*, June 1924.

Power's subjects. CEP Wembley prints: 'The Bhuli Gate, U-em-Bhili', 'The City of U-em-Bhili'.

Andrews was more down to earth. SA Wembley prints: 'The House of Bala Uem-Bhili', 'The Walled City', Glenbow, 194890.224, 156/157; SA drypoint book, 29–31, Glenbow M8411-137.

'The Temple of Isis', 'Topaz Mosque', 'Pilgrims'. Copies in Private Collection, Oxford.

Algeria. Brochure for 'The Polytechnic Tours to Algeria, 1923 and 24'. Private Collection, Oxford, Also University of Westminster Library, PTA/2/1/5.

collect some of the crafts. A list attached to a letter to the Cranmore Museum in 1937 (SA, White scrapbook, Glenbow M8411-187) notes the following: 'Doors "Yoruba from Oyo"; Mandigo loom from Sierra Leone in perfect condition & working order. With extra shuttles 7 specimens of dried yarn; Kola Bean box from Benin City, carved in wood in the form of a snake with a man issuing from its mouth; Very fine soup bowl and lid in black ware from Abeokuta; Two other food bowls, two lamps, all in black ware; Chief's staff from Munshi with brass handle; Three fine spears of different types; Rattle calabash.'

'The most important for me'. SA to Mary Ryan, 31 December 1986.

Lascaux cave. Garrett, 15. The cave was discovered in 1940.

10. 'THE ART OF TO-DAY'

'peering right through me'. Out-take from video interview with Nicholas Tuele for *The Women Artists of British Columbia: 100 Years*, produced by Verna Hall, Art Gallery of Greater Victoria, 1984. SA described the incident in the same words in video interviews with Jean Looy, 1990, for 'A Visit to Linocut Artist Sybil Andrews' (1992), edited by Hugh Smith, and Patricia Ainslie, 1991, *Art*, RT.

Jewish community. Translated minutes of National Yiddish Decorative Arts Society (later Ben Uri), April–November 1920 and 30 April 1921, Ben Uri Archive: With thanks to Rachel Dickson and Sarah MacDougall at the Ben Uri Gallery. Works bought included his sculpture *Messiah* and bronze of the Zionist leader Israel Zangwill. Glicenstein's work was used to illustrate an article on drypoint technique in the magazine *Drawing and Design* in 1922.

etched a portrait. In 1924, J. N. Duddington, director of the Whitechapel Gallery, gave a copy to the British Museum: 'The Laughing Girl', BM 1924,0712.204. SA gave the BM another impression in 1993.

'drawing from life'. SA interview with Jean Looy, 'A Visit to Linocut Artist Sybil Andrews' (1992), edited by Hugh Smith.

Holloway, whom he sketched. Signed and dated 24 June 1924, BH scrapbook.

three sketches of Power. D, 21 July 1924. Mentioned in their lists of possessions until 1943, but have now disappeared.

hammering out ideas. Notes in SA notebook, Glenbow M8411-175.

'What quality is shared'. Clive Bell, *Art* (1914), 8.

'dispense altogether'. Roger Fry, 'Essay in Aesthetics' (1909), reprinted in *Vision and Design* (1920), 25.

Kandinsky. Sybil Andrews books, Glenbow Library collection.

'unfinished meals'. 'Aims', 3–4.

Post-Impressionism. ibid., 12–13.

'the *Primitive*'. ibid., 14.

'an ugly age'. ibid., 15.

'may we take it'. Ralph Vaughan Williams, 'The Letter and the Spirit', *Music and Letters* 1, Issue 2 (March 1920), 87–93.

almost religious terms. Coppel, 50, describes this as 'quasi-religious language redolent of Catholic doctrine and the medieval philosophy of St Thomas Aquinas'.

'We are "out"'. 'Aims', 16.

Nevinson and Van Gogh. ibid., 20–1.

'stressed exaggeration'. ibid., 27.

'personal suppression of the non-essential'. *Bury Post*, 9 December 1921.

'shapes and rhythms'. White, 22.

'That certain arrangements'. Iain Macnab, *Figure Drawing* (1936), in Albert Garrett, *Wood Engravings and Drawings of Iain Macnab of Barachastlain* (1973), 72.

'FORM'. 'Aims', 16.

'RHYTHM' and 'DESIGN'. ibid., 28.

'WHAT DO YOU MEAN'. *AK*, 32.

11. THE GROSVENOR SCHOOL

Hal's twenty-first birthday. HA diary, 14 May 1925.

Stour Lodge. BH scrapbook; CEP sketchbook 1929, 'Stour Lodge visits'.

sketched the men at work. 'Mistley quay', 28 August 1925, 'Sunset 7.30 pm'; 'Mistley shipyard', CEP sketchbook 28, OS.

'a too vigorous pull'. Herbert B. Grimsditch, 'Iain Macnab', *The Artist*, April 1937.

'Have possession'. IM to SA, 10 October 1925, Glenbow M8411-86.

'I hasten to reassure you'. IM to CEP, 26 October 1925, Glenbow M8411-86.

'a still-life room'. Eveline Syme reminiscences in Chris Deutscher and Roger Butler, *A Survey of Australian Relief Prints, 1900–1950* (1978), 75–6.

33 Warwick Square was the address. CEP sketchbooks 30, 31, 34 (1926–7), OS. Also on electoral register 1926–7, living with Iain Macnab and Hugo MacLean.

'Sybil Andrews, Secretary'. SA, 5 December 1925, BH scrapbook.

'entirely responsible'. IM, Reference for SA, 13 January 1928, Glenbow M8411-18.

'to encourage students'. 1935 Prospectus, in A. C. R. Carter, *The Year's Art* (1935).

'from 10–1'. Ethel Spowers, 'The Grosvenor School of Modern Art', *The Recorder*, April 1932, quoted in Coppel, 13.

tender nude study. CEP sketchbook 30 (1926), OS. (SA writes 'modelled all day' in her diary, 30 January 1927. But she probably means modelling the bust of Baliol Holloway, whom she had seen the previous day.)

'Students are requested'. Grosvenor School Prospectus, 1927, Glenbow.

Malet, Christopherson, Morgan. Quoted in Julian Francis, *Tom Chadwick* (2013). See also Katy Deepwell, *Women Artists between the Wars* (2010), 57, and Albert Garrett, *Wood Engravings and Drawings of Iain Macnab of Barachastlain* (1973), 97, 98.

'Opera district & shops'. CEP sketchbook 28, OS.

Bruges and Ghent. D, 30 April–9 May 1928.

Pickle Herring Street. Sketch dated 26 February 1926, CEP sketchbook 30, OS.

drypoint, *Pickle Herring Street*. Dated 1928, SA drypoint print book, 24, Glenbow M8411-137.

Frank Rutter. *Sunday Times*, 10 April 1927.

12. THE ARRIVAL OF FLIGHT

magazines. *Colour* 1 (July–August 1925) and 2 (March 1926); *Artwork* 1 (May–August 1925) and 2 (January 1926). *Ray* 1 (1926), edited by Seven and Five member Sidney Hunt, reproduced his abstract watercolour *Trawler at Sea* (1925).

after the war. Flight was a captain in the Royal Army Service Corps, in charge of obtaining horses for troops, receiving the Ordre du Mérite Agricole from the French government.

German Expressionist. See Philip Vann, 'Pulsating Rhythms: The Radical Achievement of Claude Flight and his Printmaking Pupils', in *Cutting Edge*, 38, for Kirchner and Münter. Kandinsky's linocuts included *The Mirror*, *Women in the Woods* and *Moonlit Night*.

Olga Rozanova. Illustrations to 'Zaum' poetry in *Zaumnaia gniga* (*Transrational Book*) (1915). See Coppel, 14, and Nina Guriana, *Olga Rozanova and the Early Russian Avant-Garde, 1910–1918* (2012), 58–65.

Gaudier-Brzeska. Flight included *Wrestlers* with two Brodzky prints in the first linocut exhibition in 1929.

British Institute of Industrial Art. S. B. Malvern, 'Inventing "Child Art": Franz Cižek and Modernism', *British Journal of Aesthetics* 35, No. 3 (July 1995), 262.

Paris Omnibus. cf. Gino Severini in 1913 defending the London Futurist show: 'Motor-omnibuses passing and re-passing in the crowded streets, covered with letters, red, green, white are far more beautiful than the canvases of Leonardo or Titian.' Gino Severini, 'Get Inside the Picture: Futurism as the Artist Sees It', *Daily Express*, 11 April 1913, in Ackley, 15.

'This metaphysical business': 'The Premier and the Cobbler', *Colour* 1 (April 1926), 3–4, in Saler, 76.

'In England'. CF, 'Mr Flight Explains Himself', *Arts & Crafts Magazine* 1, No. 4 (July 1928), 12, 182–5.

'People live in smaller rooms'. CF, 'The Modern Colour Print', *Arts and Crafts Quarterly* 1, No. 2 (April 1925), 7; Coppel, 20.

'plain, light-coloured modern wall'. James Laver, 'Modern Paintings and Their Place in Modern Rooms', *Good Housekeeping* 94 (May 1932), in Saler, 83.

return to craft. See Jay A. Clarke in 'Linocuts between the Wars', in *Machine Age Modernism: Prints from the Daniel Cowin Collection* (2015).

'his daily beer'. Flight *LC*, 4.

'Claude Flight did good work'. SA to Stephen Coppel, 26 June 1984; Coppel, 54.

'He is a small man'. Dorrit Black, 'London Letter', *Undergrowth: A Magazine of Art and Ideals*, January–February 1928; Coppel, 13.

'Sometimes in his classes'. Eveline Syme, 'Claude Flight and His Teaching', *The Recorder* (Arts and Crafts Society of Victoria), No. 3, September 1929, 3; Tracey Lock, 'Relaxing the Line: The Linocuts of the Australian Artists Dorrit Black, Eveline Syme and Ethel Spowers', in *Cutting Edge*, 69.

'with one or more of the curves'. CF to Dorrit Black, 14 February 1928; *Cutting Edge*, 70.

'futurist'. S. C. Kaines Smith, 'Painters of England', Medici Society, 1934, quoted in *Claude Flight and Edith Lawrence*, exh. cat. (1973).

precise drawings. SA notebook, Glenbow M4411-171, and drawings, Glenbow 993.121, 441, 579, 583.

'Form alone'. Wassily Kandinsky, *Concerning the Spiritual in Art*, ed. Michael Sadleir (1910, 1947 edition), 66.

Naum Gabo. Philip Vann, 'Pulsating Rhythms', in *Cutting Edge*, 47, describes Gabo's *Standing Wave* (1919) in relation to the Grosvenor School.

Bill Kermode. D, 25 March 1924.

Japanese colour woodcuts. Coppel, 15.

'printed on linoleum'. ibid.

'linocutting'. D, 12 February 1923.

'that was Macbeth'. *Art*, RT. SA, 'The Chieftain', Glenbow 1922,990.224; CEP, 'Roman Centurion', Bonhams, *The Grosvenor School and Avant-Garde British Printmaking*, 17 April 2012, wrongly dated *c*.1929.

grand auction. Sales brochure, 'Woolpit, 18 Freehold Houses', 18 May 1926. With thanks to Andrew Gough.

Elmer's Mill. The mill collapsed in 1963. Mills Archive Trust website, and photographs in the Muggeridge Collection, University of Kent.

13. HAY LANE AND BROOK GREEN

'as a result of a request'. TS, 31.

'able to finance the family'. ibid., 22.

Ursula Fookes. D, 15 January, 12 March, 9 July 1927.

Sam Butler. He also went with Andrews to see Holloway in *Othello* and *The Comedy of Errors*. D, 16 March–6 April 1927.

'Moved to B Green'. D, 8 October 1927.

Her studio. *AK*, 210.

rapid sketches. CEP sketchbook 32 (1927–8), OS.

'How are you both?' BH to SA and CEP, 29 October 1928, from New York. BH
  scrapbook, Private Collection, Campbell River.

Ghent and Bruges. D, 30 April–9 May 1928.

'the spot he most preferred'. SA to Roland and Cathy Hudson, n.d., Glenbow
  M8411-109.

'a wonderful easy position'. Video interview with Jean Looy, 'A Visit to Linocut
  Artist Sybil Andrews' (1992), edited by Hugh Smith. Painting, Glenbow
  990.220.61.

earnest list. In Address book 2, Glenbow M8411-26. SA's list included C.
  H. Douglas, *Social Credit* and *Economic Democracy* (both 3s 6d); C. M.
  Hattersley, *This Age of Plenty*; Maurice Colbourne, *Economic Nationalism*; and
  A. L. Gibson's pamphlet *What is this Social Credit?* (6d). Social Credit proposed
  a kind of economic engineering, national distribution of money/credit to raise
  earnings and purchasing power in line with prices.

Birket Satterthwaite. Electoral Register, 1928–36; see 'The Versatile Work of a
  Young English Artist', *The Sphere*, 28 August 1928.

Leon Underwood. Born in Shepherd's Bush in 1890, studied at the Royal College,
  and after the war with Tonks at the Slade. For the school see Jane Hill, *The
  Sculpture of Gertrude Hermes* (2011), 9–14.

'Art alone'. Leon Underwood, *Art for Heaven's Sake: Notes on a Philosophy of
  Art* (1934), 2–3.

Chelsea. SA to Gary Ratushniak, 16 July 1985, M8411-34. Classes, D, 21 January
  1930, 'Began general's class, 10/6'; 18 March, 'last day general's class'.

'an exotic, eccentric'. Claude Heroys, correspondence, 16 April 2020.

Héroys family. 'Thumbnail Interviews with the Great: General Heroys de
  Monigot', *The Sphere*, 21 August 1926.

'unconstrained Bohemian character'. Boris Vladimorovich Héroys, 'The Story of
  My Artist Life' (1935), in *Izmailovskaya Starina*, a journal of émigré officers in
  Paris, 1937. Translated by Dorothy Barkworth, edited and corrected by Claude
  Heroys. In London he was head of Special Military Supply for White Russian
  forces, 1918–20.

'instead of a Field Marshal's baton'. ibid.

enrolled at Chelsea. *Westminster Gazette*, 19 January 1927.

left his Russian wife. Héroys married Sophie von Hilchen in 1904, before the
  Russo-Japanese war. By 1925 Sophie was in Bath, with their two teenage
  children, Helene and Vladimir: *Wiltshire Times*, 19 September 1925; *Western
  Daily Press*, 25 September 1925 and in 'Bath Visitors' book for succeeding
  years. Dorothy Barkworth was the daughter of a Dorset landowner, barrister
  and magistrate. See Foreword by Lieutenant General Alexander Héroys to John
  Elverson, *To Serve the Russian Empire: The Autobiography of Boris Héroys*

(2018), and Jonathan Smele, *Historical Dictionary of the Russian Civil Wars, 1916–1926* (as 'Gerua').

'It was he'. SA to Peter White, 16 April 1980, White, 73.

'Draw a *bold* line'. Claude Heroys, correspondence, 16 April 2020.

Edna Clarke Hall. See Carolyn Trant, *Voyaging Out: British Women Artists from Suffrage to the Sixties* (2019), 56–60. Also Alison Thomas, 'Edna Clarke Hall (1879–1979)', *ODNB*, and Anna Thomasson, 'Edna Clarke Hall's Watercolours', *Tate Etc.*, No. 43 (1 July 2018). Her husband felt a career in art was unsuitable for a respectable wife and a mother.

'the most imaginative'. *The Times*, 9 February 1926, in *ODNB*.

'Such splendid drawings'. White, 73.

'break away'. SA to MP, 13 January 1980, Glenbow M8411-64a.

14. COLOUR

'so I had already been thinking'. White, 73.

'Just up my street'. *Art*, RT.

'that builds up block by block'. Flight *LC*.

colour wheels and charts. Colour wheel, loose, in notebook, Glenbow M8411-175, 'Little treatise on colour', notebook M8411-175, notes for *AK*, M8411-80.

Sometimes they used both. Rachel Mustalish, 'Materials and Techniques of the Grosvenor School Artists', Ackley, 201. For technique generally I am indebted to Mustalish's essay, Ackley, 189–203.

'We would have breakfast'. Kit Power, typescript memoir, Private Collection, Oxford.

Low Water, Limehouse. SA, Drypoint book, 35, Glenbow M8411-13.

Limehouse. See Leaper, 23–4, Cat 2, 47.

another experimental linocut. *Untitled* (1926): only one print survives. See Leaper, 46.

'Shadow pattern'. CEP sketchbook 30, OS.

'a tremendous sight'. Interview by Patricia Ainslie, August 1991, *Art*, RT.

'some fascinating young female'. Leslie Ayre, *The Wit of Music* (1966), 65.

'I had been watching'. SA, in Robin Laurence, *Interface 5*, No. 2 (February 1982), 73.

'We only paid sixpence'. TS, 33.

Bernard Miles. Bernard Miles to SA, 14 October 1975, BH scrapbook, Private Collection, Campbell River.

'Sadler's Wells, before rebuilding 1929'. CEP sketchbook 38 (1929), OS.

'Open spaces are not voids'. Nicol, 96.

15. THE FIRST SHOW

planning this for over a year. CF to Dorrit Black, 14 February 1928, in *Cutting Edge*, 70.

Nan Kivell. John R. Thompson, 'Rex de Charembac Nan Kivell (1898–1977)', *Australian National Dictionary of Biography* (2000).

wrote a flyer. 1929, Glenbow M8411-71.

two earlier prints. *Festa* and *Expulsion* (1914): both in Brodzky's portfolio published in New York in 1920.

Dominion Artists Club. Vann, 49.

oriental Tao. ibid., 27.

'People are pouring in'. CF to Dorrit Black, 7 July 1929, 'Claude Flight and His Australian Pupils', *Print Quarterly* 2, No. 4 (1985). See Leaper, 22–3; Coppel, 273–4.

'Works of Art on Linoleum'. *Star*, 4 July 1929.

'quite distinguished little works of art'. *Apollo*, August 1929.

'the difficulty of using a natural scene'. ibid.

'illuminating and intimate study'. *Sunday Times*, 14 July 1929; other favourable reviews included *Christian Science Monitor*, 22 July 1929, and *The Spectator*, 13 July 1929.

The *Star* agreed. *Star*, 4 July 1929.

In October. CF to Dorrit Black, 16 October 1929, Coppel, 19.

'as societies always get stuck'. CF to Dorrit Black, 17 October 1929, Coppel, 20.

on the shows went. The tours were as follows: USA 1929 (various cities), 1934 (Brooklyn Museum); China (Shanghai) 1931; Australia (Melbourne) 1932 and 1937; Canada (Ottawa) 1935–6.

16. WOOLPIT

'Sat up all night'. D, 1 August 1929.

'Mother is laying'. ibid.

'very peacefully'. HA diary, 7 August 1929, also D, 1–7 August.

'There were church murals'. Alexandra Harris, *Romantic Moderns: English Writers, Artists and the Imagination from Virginia Woolf to John Piper* (2010), 10. Harris also talks about pageants, Beaton, Piper and Vaughan Williams.

John Betjeman. Betjeman to Lionel Perry, 29 March 1932, Revd J. M. Thompson, 1 January 1935, Jack Beddington, 14 January 1935. John Betjeman, *Letters*, Vol. 1: *1926 to 1951*, ed. Candida Lycett Green (2006), 102, 147, 148.

'my real riches'. HA diary, 30 April 1929.

'START OF A NEW LIFE'. ibid., 10 July 1929.

Geoff took his share. HA diary, 28 August 1929. Geoff appears to have had financial problems; Beatrice left his share in trust, to be administered by Sybil and Joy.

'The last of 117 Northgate Street'. HA diary, 28 August 1929.

'Cottage very effective'. ibid., 5 October 1929.

Sybil stayed with him. 'To Puckpitts', D, 29 August 1930; 'to Brockenhurst', 31 October–4 November 1930.

Hal stayed in Woolpit. HA diary, 28 February 1931.

small watercolour. CEP, '"Up" Woolpit', Private Collection, Oxford.

'poor, lost cottage'. SA to MP, 10 November 1986, Glenbow M8411-64a.

brick-making sites. See Information 126, *British Brick Society* (April 2014), 16–21. They closed in 1939, for fear the fire of kilns might be seen by enemy bombers. An attempt to open one in 1946 failed when a spring flooded the pit: Elizabeth and Edward Cockayne, 'Woolpit history', www.woolpit.org/information-2/a-short-history/.

'its old name'. Woolpit postcard, scrapbook, Glenbow M8411-167.

the warrior Ulfketel. 'Woolpit history', www.woolpit.org/information-2/a-short-history/.

Hal recorded. HA note, in possession of Andrew Gough.

'Dame Elizabeth Andrews'. SA handwritten genealogical chart, Private Collection, Campbell River. Anna Maria's mother was Anne Browse; Edmund Tyrell (1744–99) of Gipping Hall was a sheriff for 1774 (*Ipswich Journal*, 20 November 1773).

Gipping. HA diary, July 1931. Earlier he recorded a trip with a friend to Witnesham Hall near Woodbridge, 'House once lived in by Tyrells!', HA diary, 2 February 1929.

Coat of arms. Tyrell family, Glenbow 995.013.391.

Loose notes and British Museum Reading Room card, 18 May 1934, in scrapbook, Glenbow M8411-167.

'St Thomas More'. C. Fox, 37, and conversation. More was sanctified in 1935.

slowed drastically. The slowdown came after Winston Churchill, Conservative chancellor of the Exchequer, restored sterling to the gold standard at pre-war rates: this made exports more expensive, and industries responded by cutting wages.

Rabelais, Froissart. Marked 'self' in present list, memo at end of D, 1930.

tapestry. In 1975, Andrews gave the tapestry to the cathedral in Bury St Edmunds: on view in the Chapel of St Edmunds. Hal was working on similar tapestries in the winter of 1929, of the killing of Rufus in the forest, and the martyrdom of St Edmund. HA diary, 29 December 1929, 3 February 1930.

porcupine. Interview in *Vancouver Sun*, 1 August 1992, Nicol, 118.

'Just darning'. Kathleen Niwa, MA thesis, University of Victoria, 1986, quoted in Nicol, 123.

'Adventures in Archaeology'. *Journal of the Antiquarian Association*, No. 3 (December 1930). Private Collection, Oxford.

'The Pyx Veil or Sindon at Hessett', ibid.

'we often grabbed'. SA to Gordon Samuel, 16 March 1985, Glenbow M8411-72.

'How sad'. 'The Pyx Veil', 127.

pencilled diagrams. CEP sketchbooks, Private Collection, Oxford, and OS; SA notebook, Glenbow 8411-170.

'Humph'. 'The Pyx Veil', 127.

17. UNDERGROUND

'printed 36 prints'. D, 13 March 1930.

Kew. CEP sketchbook 41, OS.

Brittany. ibid. Many sketches in coloured pencil, some across two pages.

their work in the exhibitions. Redfern shows: 1930: SA, *Steeplechasing, The Winch, Wet Race Meeting, Pas Seul, The Bathers*; CEP, *The Merry-go-round, Lifts, Whence & Whither?, The Eight, Giant Racer, The Runners, En grande tenue*. 1931: SA, *Golgotha, The Water Jump, The Gale, The New Cable, In Full Cry, Pieta, Hyde Park*; CEP, *Hockey, Southampton–Havre, Revolution, Fire Dance, Monseigneur St Thomas*. 1932: SA, *Joseph and Nicodemus, Pieta, Timber Jim, The Captive*; CEP, *Tube Station, Samson and the Lion, Skaters, Speed Trial*.

Ashfield. Albert Stanley, Baron Ashfield, Managing Director then Chairman of Underground Electric Railways Company 1907–33, Chairman of London Passenger Transport Board (LPTB) 1933–47.

Frank Pick. Commercial Manager of UERL 1912–33, CEO of LPTB 1933–40. See Christian Barman, *The Man Who Built London Transport* (1979).

'Gothic workshop'. 'The Temple of the Winds', *Architectural Review* 117 (November 1929), 13–14. For 55 Broadway, see David Ashworth, *London Underground: A Cultural Geography* (2013), 79–81.

Marinetti's vision. *Marinetti, Selected Writings*, ed. R. W. Flint (1972), 91, quoted in David Welsh, *Underground Writing: The London Tube from George Gissing to Virginia Woolf* (2010), 144.

light and shadow. Sketches, 'Pattern & rhythm, Albert Hall Mansions', August 1928 (CEP sketchbook 32); St Pancras gasworks, 1928 (CEP sketchbook 28); W. C. Seat; mantelpiece, 1929 (CEP sketchbook 37); Tube escalator (CEP sketchbook 35); shadow patterns (CEP sketchbook 32), OS.

Charing Cross station. CEP sketchbook 34 (1928), OS.

'he wanted the drawing'. SA to MP, 14 June 1983, Glenbow M8411-64a.

'the man who went up the escalator the wrong way'. CEP sketchbook 33 (1927), OS.

swooning effect. Samantha Rippner (Ackley, 94) suggests the curved ceiling and perspective may have been influenced by the hooped ceilings in Van Gogh's drawing *Corridor in the Asylum*, shown at the Leicester Galleries in 1923–4 and 1926–7.

'edges of man'. 'Escalator', print book 1, Glenbow M8411-138.

wax crayon sketch. Coppel, 53; Studies I, II, III and 'Homo mechaniens', Wolfsonian-Florida International University.

'Please keep moving'. Ashfield pamphlet, quoted in Stephen Halliday, *Underground to Everywhere: London's Underground Railway in the Life of the Capital* (2013).

'One contributory cause'. ibid.

'Puppet!' Dated 'about 1932', copied out in CEP notebook 49, OS.

18. ACTION

'The Victorians'. *Art*; Nicol, 50.

'the curve of the movement'. Out-takes from video interview with Nicholas Tuele for *The Women Artists of British Columbia: 100 Years*, Art Gallery of Greater Victoria, 1984.

'See how the rope is held'. *Art*, RT.

'emotion on the face'. S. Mertens, 'Splash with Art', *Vancouver Sun*, 16 January 1982.

'*heave* ho'. Interview with Patricia Ainslie, August 1991, *Art*, RT.

Taking her sketchbook. SA described the scene and the costumes in the video interview with Jean Looy, 1990.

'keep lower part'. 'The Gale', SA print book 1, Glenbow M8411-138.

'Almost every period'. *AK*, 19.

'I draw the jump'. Interview with Nicholas Tuele for *The Women Artists of British Columbia*.

otter hunt. HA diary, 14 September 1932.

'Focus Point'. *AK*, 203.

19. IN THE BODY

They lean to each side. In technical terms, the 'drive' position, after the 'catch' when oar meets water, followed by the 'release' when the oar is lifted out, and the 'recovery' position (in Power's sketches) when the blade is pushed back above the water towards the bow.

'Fairly heavy'. 'The Eight', print book 1, Glenbow M8411-138. For preparatory studies see Redfern catalogue 1985, and Vann, 62.

'C printed 6 eights'. D, 29 April 1933.

'pulsating arrangement of lines'. 'Aims', 28.

women running. *The Relay Race* and *The Runners* (both *c*.1930).

Lili Tschudi. See Coppel, 59.

list of possible subjects. Back pages of print book 1, Glenbow M8411-138.

Bror Meyer. See diagrams in *Skating with Bror Meyer*, 1921, Internet Archive archive.org/details/skatingwithbrorm01meye.

Ice Club. *Ottawa Citizen*, 12 February 1927; British Ice Skating NGB, www.iceskating.org.uk/about-ice-skating.

Prints of skaters. Including prints by Edith Lawrence and Ursula Fookes, 1929, and Eveline Syme, 1931.

'Note: the Red'. 'Skaters', print book 1, Glenbow M8411-138.

'the machine age'. Ida Buergel Goodwin, in *Idun*, July 1914, quoted in Richard Emerson, *Rhythm & Colour: Hélène Vanel, Loïs Hutton & Margaret Morris* (2018), 33.

'I look at dancing'. ibid., 43.

deep V of the dark green. 'Divertissement', print book 1, Glenbow M8411-138.

'Rays and shadows'. 'Folk Dance', print book 1, Glenbow M8411-138.

20. FALLING OR FLYING

'impression of Modern Lift Speed'. *The Builder*, 10 January 1930. Hammond and Champness had made lifts since 1905: in 1932 they were taken over by Pollard & Co., but ran as a separate company under the old name.

cut the red bars. Proofs and print from Johanna and Leslie Garfield Collection, in Rachel Mustalish, Ackley, 194, Fig. 16.

Wembley funfair. See Josephine Kane, *The Architecture of Pleasure: British Amusement Parks 1900–1939* (2016).

'with more fervour than skill'. www.hampsteadheath.net/heathfairs. This site also has photographs of the swing boats and merry-go-round.

swing-ride. CEP sketchbook 32, OS.

British Pathé film. *Hampstead Heath Fairground*, available on YouTube, https://youtu.be/DlXCtq_QoNo.

'a new beauty'. Marinetti, 1909, quoted in Coppel, 18.

'Bentley Boys'. Brooklands Museum, Bentley 4½ litre 'Le Mans', https://www.brooklandsmuseum.com/explore/our-collection/cars/4-litre-le-mans-bentley.

'I thought we were all driving'. Evelyn Waugh, *Vile Bodies* (1930); Coppel, 18.

21. 'OUR LADYE'

'hard at linos all week'. D, 14 March 1932.

watercolour sketch. n.d., Private Collection, Oxford. Similar watercolours are held at Glenbow.

Kibbo Kift. See Annebella Pollen, *The Kindred of the Kibbo Kift: Intellectual Barbarians* (2015).

'a new garment'. HA diary, July 1932.

'effected a considerable emancipation'. ibid., October 1932.

'very busy'. ibid., July 1932.

'a pond shaped like a *phallic symbol*!' ibid., 22 October 1932.

'Our-Ladye's well'. D, 30 July 1932.

'in one corner'. SA to MP, 10 November 1986, M8411-64a. Parkin had just sent her a copy of Power's poem about the spring.

'In the moonlight'. SA to MP, 10 November 1986, M8411-64a.

'The trackway runs twisting'. CEP sketchbook 42 (1932), OS.

'Samhane'. SA scrapbook, Glenbow M8411-167.

'C doing a great deal of painting'. HA diary, 22 October 1932.

'herd boys'. Also reference to chalk, pastel and watercolour, SA to MP, 10 November 1986, Glenbow M8411-64a.

Colin Clout. An Everyman figure in Skelton's 'Colyn Clout' (1521), a satire against Wolsey; a singing and piping shepherd in six Spenser poems, including the eclogue 'Colin Clout's Come Home Again' (1595), *Faerie Queene* (1596) and *Shepherd's Calendar* (1579).

'Sandra'. CEP sketchbooks 32, 35, 47, OS.

'Herde-gromes Consort'. Photographs, SA scrapbook, Glenbow M8411-167.

'And pypes made of grene corne'. Chaucer, *The House of Fame*, *c*.1380, lines 1223–6.

tackled the wall painting again. D, 23 September 1933.

could swear fluently. HA to SA from Jerusalem, 10 July 1933, Glenbow M8411-96. Henry Andrews wrote a detailed account of his travels and his time at Moyse's Hall as 'Life of the Wandering Foot', unpublished typescript, Private Collection, Bury St Edmunds.

new job as curator. D, 27 April 1933: the job was agreed then, but he did not begin until 2 October 1933.

'great sound of pipes'. D, 18 September, 6–7 October 1933.

'for his good wit and humour'. SA to Kit Power, 12 December 1990, Glenbow M8411-132.

'We have had great times'. HA diary, October 1933.

Boxing Day. HA diary, 1 January 1934; 'Feast of Saint Stephen'. Menu, loose, and 'Boar's Head Carol', both SA scrapbook, Glenbow M8411-167. On the menu Cyril's son Toby, who may not have turned up, is listed as 'The Chaplain'.

22. FORMS OF FAITH

'What is God?' Mary Baker Eddy, *Science and Health* (1875, 3rd edition 1917).

'a transfiguring spirituality'. David Allan Mellor, 'A Spectral Modernity', in *Paul Nash*, exh. cat. (2017), 26; Stanley Spencer, television interview (Tate Archive), quoted in www.stanleyspencer.co.uk/cookres.htm.

'a sculpture'. Barbara Hepworth, quoted in Lucy Kent, 'An Act of Praise: Religion in the Art of Barbara Hepworth' in *Barbara Hepworth*, exh. cat. (2015); see also Kent's *Spirituality and British Modernism: Christian Science Influence in the Work of Ben Nicholson, Winifred Nicholson and Barbara Hepworth* (2012), and article on Ben Nicholson, *Burlington Magazine*, July 2015.

'all that is made'. Gill Clark, *Evelyn Dunbar: War and Country* (2006), 163.

brief memoir. Winifred Nicholson, 'Kit', Tate Archive; quoted in Sebastian Faulks, *The Fatal Englishman: Three Lives* (2010), 48.

'*innermost* consciousness'. *AK*, 180.

'cannot be confined'. ibid., 63.

'Before you can BE'. ibid., 75.

'she was a curious mix'. Jean Looy to author, 2 March 2021.

'hold the emotional side'. *Art*, RT.

'by far the most memorable'. Coppel, 56. 'Golgotha', print book 1, note, no. 23 'to Miss Lilli [*sic*] Tschudi, in exchange for two of hers'; no. 24 'to Flight for Broadway show'.

'Stond wel Moder'. The pencilled line is on the copy in the British Museum, 1993,0228.22.

'Go, bear him in thine arms'. *King John*, Act IV, Scene 3. Print book 1, Glenbow M8411-138. Another circled note on the page reads 'Baliol Holloway King John Shakespeare'.

23. SAINTS AND MATRIARCHS

'my print'. 'Monseigneur St Thomas', print book 1, Glenbow M8411-138.

'I had a great deal to do with'. SA to MP, 20 September 1978, Glenbow M8411-64a.

'Peace'. T. S. Eliot, *Murder in the Cathedral* (1935; 2013 edition), 48.

'if I touch them'. ibid., 82.

Orthodox saints. CEP sketchbook 37, passim, OS.

Josef Strzygowski's *Origin of Christian Church Art*. Trans. by O. M. Dalton and H. J. Braunholtz (1923). This early work has no trace of the later Aryan bias.

'O sages'. W. B. Yeats, 'Sailing to Byzantium', in *The Tower* (1928).

'O You, who are in Life'. Corneilla-de-Conflent, CEP sketchbook 3, OS.

'Far sight'. From Immanuel H. Fichte, *Psychologie* (1864), quoted in Ludwig Goldschieder, *El Greco* (1938). Power adds a note: 'verify the exactitude or correctness of this translation'. CEP sketchbook 35, OS.

'a tendency'. Evelyn Sharp, 'Sex Equality', *Daily Herald*, 5 September 1922.

Power's list. CEP sketchbook 3, OS.

love poetry of the ancient Egyptians. Note on Max Müller, 'Die Liebespoesie der alten Agypter' (1899) and *Egyptological Researches*, Vol. 1 (1906), Vol. 2 (1910), CEP sketchbook 35, OS.

'has influenced our generation'. T. S. Eliot, Notes to *The Waste Land*, *Collected Poems 1909–1962* (1966), 80.

series of books on myth. CEP sketchbook 42 (1932); Jain figure, CEP sketchbook 35 (1929); Peruvian symbol, CEP sketchbook 42 (1932), copied from Cyril G. E. Bunt, 'Symbolism in Peruvian Art', *Art in America and Elsewhere*, Vol. 12 (1924); also Religious notebook, Glenbow M8411.

'rent him'. Samson story, Judges 14, King James version.

24. 'OUR SHOW'

every surface was covered. Ten photographs of Brook Green Studios, mid-1930s, Glenbow PD-315-vol. 1.

'No true enthusiast'. F. Hindle, 'Exhibition of Lino-cuts Examples of New Trend in Modern Art on Show at Shanghai Art Club', *North China Daily News*, 2 May 1931. Full review, Glenbow M8411.31.

'perhaps . . . most daring'. ibid.

three years to pay. D, 11 April 1934.

Ward Gallery. Coppel, 57.

'End justified by means'. Note at end of D, 1931; also 4 November 1931, 'Saw Nan Kivell re Flight'.

'joyful news'. D, 6, 12 September 1932.

'Rex's honour'. SA to MP, 20 September 1978, Glenbow M8411-64a.

signed the agreement. D, 24 October 1932.

'unhampered by any tradition'. Cutting from *East Anglian Daily Times*, 17 January 1933, Glenbow M8411-31.

catalogue. *Sybil Andrews and Cyril E. Power* (January 1933), 2.

Monotypes had seen spurts. Others who experimented briefly with lino included

Pissarro, Mary Cassatt and Toulouse-Lautrec, and later Picasso, Chagall, Miró and Matisse. See John Ross, Claire Romano and Tim Ross, *The Complete Printmaker* (revised edition, 2009); *The Painterly Print: Monotypes from the Seventeenth to the Twentieth Century*, exh. cat. (1980).

more Redfern artists. Several were included in an exhibition in 1935: Redfern catalogue 1935, *Colour Prints, and Monotypes and Carvings by Elizabeth Spurr.*

'it was in the air'. See 'Post-war Lithography and Monotypes', in Carey, 148–77; G. Samuel, 'The Monotype 1900–1950', *British Printmaking* (1993), 287–93.

'most characteristic'. Redfern catalogue, *Sybil Andrews and Cyril E. Power*, 2.

'6 Tube stations'. D, 7 August 1932; drypoints, D, 14, 15 August 1932.

'started monotypes'. D, 16 August 1932.

brick fields. SA, *Woolpit Brick Works* (1925), monotype, BSEMS. For the Woolpit brick fields see Information 126, *British Brick Society* (April 2014), 16–21.

portraits. CEP, 'Sybil Painting', BSEMS; SA, 'The Artist', Private Collections, East Anglia and Oxford.

'looking for subjects'. D, 5 November 1932.

hasty titles. D, 4 November 1932: the lists continue 6 November to 3 December.

'cold boiled mud'. D, 5, 28 November 1932.

'CEP Fête'. D, 17 December 1932.

'Festivity'. D, 8 January 1933.

'two artistic "languages"'. *The Times*, 11 January 1933.

'I once observed'. *Apollo*, February 1933, Glenbow M8411.

the case ever since. Gordon Samuel to author, 2019.

'They call it a print'. Signed 'written after our monotype exhibition at the Redfern gallery', CEP notebook 40, OS.

shopping list. D, 3 February 1934.

'144 all told'. D, 20 April 1933.

Then they started. D, 16 April–26 May 1933.

'two artists'. Cutting, 'Contemporary Colour Prints', by Ywain, 11 June 1933, source unknown, Glenbow M8411-131.

More and more sales. D, 4–10 June 1933.

'Did not go'. D, 1 June 1933.

25. THE SPORTING LIFE

Some were well known. See Oliver Green, *Underground Art: London Transport Posters, 1908 to the Present* (1990); David Bownes and Oliver Green (eds), *London Transport Posters: A Century of Art and Design* (2011).

'There is room'. Frank Pick, notes for talk 'Underground Posters', 1927, in Oliver
    Green, 'Appearance Values: Frank Pick and the Art of London Transport', in
    Bownes and Green (eds), *London Transport Posters*, 56.

'The English tradition'. Frank Pick at the first CAI meeting, 30 January 1934,
    Saler, 123.

'modern Medici'. N. Pevsner, *Architectural Review* 92 (1942), quoted by Green, in
    Bownes and Green (eds), *London Transport Posters*, 40.

'but an impulse'. *The Listener* 25, 1 (1 June 1932), Saler, 127.

The Seven Niches. The design is reproduced in Vann, 78.

'Andrew Power mess up'. SA to MP, 28 April 1986; also SA to Gary Ratushniak,
    September 1985, Glenbow M8411-64a.

'a beauty'. SA to Carol Collier (for Curator Oliver Green), London Transport
    Museum, Glenbow M8411-59.

most women artists. See the excellent survey in Carolyn Trant, *Voyaging Out:
    British Women Artists from Suffrage to the Sixties* (2019).

digging out some posters. SA to MP, April 1989, Glenbow M8411-64a.

Dora Batty and Heather Perry. See Emmanuelle Dirix, 'Fashioning the Tube:
    Women and Transport Posters in the 1920s and 30s', in Bownes and Green
    (eds), *London Transport Posters*, 131–46.

'Delilah's' posters. Michael Parkin Gallery, *Printmakers of the 20s and 30s and
    Adolfine Ryland*, 1987. Card from Delilah, 'To Cyril and Sybil', Glenbow
    M8411-86.

never saw the light of day. Designs for the Richmond Horse Show, Royal
    Tournament at Olympia, Lord Mayor's Show and alternative design for Epsom
    in the Glenbow collection, 995.013.

'finished poster'. And poster work: D, 19 March–8 April 1933.

'Proof from Undergrd'. D, 20 April 1933.

'tearing my hair out'. SA to Carol Collier, October 1985, Glenbow M8411-59.

different colours: SA, list of posters sent to MP, April 1980, Glenbow M8411-64a.

'Bounding Basque'. Notes on this inspiration, and that for *Hockey*, came from
    Power's sons Toby and Kit.

Bunny Austin. SA to MP, November 1986, Glenbow M8411-64a.

'a wonderful dancer'. *Art*, RT.

poster for the Aldershot Tattoo. Finished on 15 March 1934, D. The entry also
    mentions '3 Greyhound Posters', and on 5 March 'for Trooping of the Colour',
    unfulfilled.

Empire Pool at Wembley. Description of opening, *Guardian*, 26 July 1934. SA
    began her design on 28 October/1 November 1934 and finished it on 13
    December.

'ice hockey panel'. D, 7 December 1934.

'Cricket poster'. SA to MP, 4 March 1985, Glenbow M8411-64a. D, 13 April 1934, 'C took amended cricket poster back again'.

'seeing these boys'. Out-take from video of interview with Nicholas Tuele for *The Women Artists of British Columbia: 100 Years* (1984).

'Find the lines'. *AK*, 56.

Tattenham Corner. SA print book 2, 13, Glenbow M8411-139.

'greed, rapacity'. Mike Huggins, *Horseracing and the British, 1919–39* (2003), 15, 5, 34–8.

26. PIPES AND VIOLS

'Heaven!'. Dolmetsch Concert programme, March 1933, loose insert, SA scrapbook, Glenbow M8411-167. Performers included Arnold Dolmetsch, his third wife Mabel, daughters Cécile and Nathalie, and sons Rudolph and Carl. They went back to Dolmetsch London concerts in 1934 and 1936.

'The feebleness and mechanility'. T. H. Yorke Trotter, *Music and Mind* (1924), 221, quoted in Alexandra Mary Williams, *The Dodo Was Really a Phoenix: The Renaissance and Revival of the Recorder in England 1879–1941*, PhD Thesis, University of Melbourne (2005), 114.

'a body of English song'. Peter Warlock [Philip Heseltine], *The English Ayre* (1926), 9.

Ulysses. Warlock, *English Ayre*, 9.

Joyce himself admired. Richard Ellmann, *James Joyce* (1959, 1983 edition), 52.

'the singing in any period'. *AK*, 30.

Vaughan Williams. He discussed 'National music' in lectures at Bryn Mawr, October and November 1932: 'If the roots of your art are firmly planted in your own soil and that soil has anything to give you, you may still gain the whole world and not lose your own soul.' Reprinted in *National Music*, 1934, quoted in Alexandra Harris, *Romantic Moderns* (2010), 163.

'She is German'. Dora Carrington to Lytton Strachey, June 1929, *Carrington's Letters*, ed. Anne Chisholm (2017), 359–60.

'*good*'. On the programme for 'All England Festival of English Folk Dance and Song', Albert Hall, 10 January 1931. With thanks to Sue Goode.

'Westron Wynde' and other song titles. SA scrapbook, Glenbow M8411-167.

'the cult of the village pump'. 'Folk-Song and Folk-Dance: From Oxfordshire Byways to the Albert Hall', *Country Life*, 6 January 1934, in SA, Green scrapbook, Glenbow M8411-187.

Diana Poulton. See Thea Abbott, *Diana Poulton: The Lady with the Lute* (2013).

striking players at Haslemere. Edgar Hunt, 'Edgar Remembers' (1999), 40.

Memoir deposited in the Centre for the History of Music in Britain, the Empire and the Commonwealth (now Music Department), University of Bristol. See also Richard Taruskin, 'The Pastness of the Present and the Presence of the Past', in Nicholas Kenyon (ed.), *Authenticity and Early Music* (1988), 152.

'All I have learnt of drawing'. White, 74.

'In the still air'. SA scrapbook, Glenbow M8411-167, with loose file-card containing Power's quotation.

'a "recorder"'. Ezra Pound, 'Arnold Dolmetsch' in *Pavannes and Divisions* (1918), 143.

'Here was an instrument'. Miles Tomalin, 'Early Days', *Recorder & Music*, 4/8 December 1973, 271–4, quoted in Williams, *The Dodo*, 96. Tomalin's father, head of the Jaeger firm, was a patron of Dolmetsch, and in the early 1920s Miles worked as Dolmetsch's teaching assistant at Bedales.

daringly splashed out. List of 'Sybil's Dolmetsch recorders', Green scrapbook, Glenbow M8411-187.

Spanish Civil War. There is a photo of Tomalin playing the recorder in XV BDE Anti-tank brigade, in the Spanish Civil War, 1938.

Ebor Marionettes. Douglas Hayward Archive and British Puppet and Model Theatre Guild Archives, http://www.iandenny.co.uk/page45k.htm. Doris died in 1954 and John married artist Rhoda Dawson, who had worked with them as a puppeteer and scenery maker.

Within a week. D, 17–29 July 1933.

'got my first recorder'. SA scrapbook, Glenbow M8411-167; group photograph, Sue Goode.

'S copying lute MS'. D, 22, 26 January 1934.

'No lute'. D, 11 January 1934.

Hans Jordan. ibid.

ivory flute. Hunt, 'Edgar Remembers'; Williams, *The Dodo*, 100.

'we could probably have some music'. Edgar Hunt to CEP, SA scrapbook, Glenbow M8411-167.

pasted a photograph. SA scrapbook, Glenbow M8411-167, with letter from Hunt to CEP, 9 July 1934.

drew his hands. D, 23 January 1935. Hunt's first two books, both 1935, were *A Practical Method for the Recorder*, with Robert Donington, and *A Concise Tutor for Descant, Treble and Tenor Recorders: For Use in Schools*. See obituary, 'Edgar Hunt (1909–2006)', Hélène de la Rue, *Galpin Society Journal* 59 (May 2006), 288–91. The school recorder movement was supported by the Inspector of Schools, Cyril Winn, and promoted by nationwide concerts.

Brook Green Consort. First meeting, Sunday 4 November 1934, D.

consort of viols: the prescribed range was bass, tenor and treble: the Hans Jordan viola da gamba (bass), the viola d'amore (tenor), the Henry Jaye (treble).

'It's certain that we'll'. CEP poem, sketchbook (exercise book) 49, OS.

covers for their recorders. Sketches, Green scrapbook, Glenbow M8411-187, finished cases PA 997.39. The Museum also has the finished covers. For the Woolpit 'Herde-gromes Consort', she made a different set.

'In the winter'. Medora Heather [Alannah Medora Heather Bent], *Errislannan: Scenes from a Painter's Life* (2002), Ch. 19.

cittern. D, 4 November 1934, 17 January 1935.

building a collection. When this was insured on 30 March 1936 it was valued at £200 (over £14,000 in 2020). Allied Assurance Company, policy HC 614502, Household effects, 356, Etching press £44, Paintings and prints £200, instruments £200: total amount £795 11s 6d.

In one photograph. Instrument collection, double-page spread of photographs. SA scrapbook, Glenbow M8411-167.

began collecting books. Canon Francis Galpin, *Old English Instruments of Music: Their History and Character*; Robert Donington, *Work and Ideas of Arnold Dolmetsch: the Renaissance of Early Music* (both 1932). Sue Goode correspondence with author, July 2020. The books contain pencilled comments, press cuttings and letters.

'all such instructions'. Simpson quote in SA scrapbook, Glenbow M8411-167. This also contains a loose file-card with Power's quotation of Bonar's hymn.

'when I play on the viol'. Both viol poems, CEP sketchbook (exercise book) 49, OS.

27. 'PEOPLE AND FREEDOM'

'as well as exhausting'. Kit Power, typescript, Private Collection, Oxford.

'People and Freedom Group'. TS, 36, 38.

exam room at Conduit Street. CEP sketchbook 34, OS.

28. OUT OF LONDON

'King Edward VIII abdicated the throne'. D, 11 December 1936.

coronation. D, 11 May 1937.

the rosy ideal of the village. See Alexandra Harris, *Romantic Moderns* (2010).

'the conversation rises'. T. S. Eliot, *East Coker* (1940), in *Four Quartets* (1943, 2001 edn).

'On a summer midnight'. ibid.

'transparent golden ochre'. SA print book 2 (1935–9), 10, Glenbow M8411-139.

'Day's End'. SA to Catherine Ryan, 2 April 1989, Glenbow M8411-60.

'get the horses dark'. SA print book 2, 23, Glenbow M8411-139.

Michaelmas. SA to Mary and Catherine Ryan, 31 January 1990, Glenbow
 M8411-60.

Norah. HA diary, 4 February, 18 March, 2 April 1934.

'Meet Hal'. D, 17, 18 July 1934.

took the train. HA diary, 18 July 1934.

'I look and feel medieval'. ibid., 20 July 1934.

Dame of Sark. Feudalism was not abolished on Sark until 2008.

artists then joined in. Others included Guy Malet, who came to live on the island,
 and Peter Barker-Mill, creator of lithographs of natural forms, and his future
 wife Elsa Masters (taking his middle name, as Elsa Vaudrey). See Mel Gooding
 and Lucy Inglis, *Elsa Vaudrey* (2018).

Andrews and Power works for Sark. *Guernsey Press*, 1 September 1934, with
 thanks to Jane Norwich for information about the Sark Art Group and details
 of the participants in these exhibitions.

Ala Story (Emilie Anna Maria Heyszl von Heyszenau), later director of the
 American British Art Center, New York and the Santa Barbara Museum of Art.
 See Gill Hedley, 'Three Female Gallerists Who Changed the Course of British
 Art', *RA Magazine*, Autumn 2016.

'Ala mucked everything'. D, 25 August 1934.

postcard to Edgar Hunt. D, 28 August 1934.

'So sorry to hear'. Edgar Hunt to CEP and SA, August 1934, SA scrapbook,
 Glenbow M8411-167.

'lovely day'. D, 10–16 August 1934.

'interesting talk'. Medora Heather [Alannah Medora Heather Bent], *Errislannan:
 Scenes from a Painter's Life* (2002), Ch. 19.

'A roving'. SA scrapbook, 350–63, Glenbow M8411-167.

In the cold February of 1935. Power monotypes, D, 18 February 1935; New
 Forest watercolours, 31 January, 7, 12, 14, 16 February 1935.

'awful banging'. D, 23 November 1934.

'Hell's delight'. D, 12 April 1935.

Colour Prints exhibition. 1935. Linocuts: CEP, *Air Raid*, *Concerto*; SA,
 Michaelmas, *Storm*, *Via Dolorosa*, *Speedway*. Monotype section: CEP,
 Terminus; SA, *Pickle Herring Street*, *Mud*.

'Very tired'. D, 15 July 1935.

'enthralling'. D, 18, 19 July 1935.

'Great fun!' D, 20 July 1935.

camp at Pitts Deep. HA diary, 24–26 July 1935.

'He is so scared'. ibid., 7 August 1935.

'C back to work'. D, 14 September 1935.

29. CHANGE ALL AROUND

In 1936. Redfern catalogue, *Colour Prints*, June–July 1936. Power's linocuts were *Air Raid* and *Trio*; Andrews' *The Giant Cable*, *Flower Girls*, *Tumulus*, *Market Day* and *Haysel*. They also showed monotypes: Andrews' *Ebb Tide, Limehouse* and Power's *Wet Day, Rouen Quay*.

Hospital Division. Kit Power, typescript, Private Collection, Oxford.

'individual practice'. SA to MP, 21 June 1983, Glenbow M8411-64a.

'Ida sent in tongue'. D, 23 November 1935.

'To Risa's'. D, 30 November 1935.

'We struggled'. *AK*, 124. Known for collages and relief mosaics, Ida E. Fischer also studied in Vienna and Nuremberg: her works are in collections at MoMA and the Frick in New York and in galleries in San Francisco, Santa Barbara and Pittsburgh.

'a truly fine interpretation'. Risa Lowie to SA, 6 June 1936, Glenbow M8411-86.

'old China'. SA to Ida Fischer, 25 January 1949, Glenbow M8411-104.

de Menasce. See Michael Haag, *Alexandria: City of Memory* (2004) and *Vintage Alexandria* (2008). George de Menasce gave many Greek island and Ottoman embroideries to the Fitzwilliam Museum, Cambridge in the 1940s; his collection of Chinese porcelain and works of art was sold by Spinks in 1971–2. His wife was the American heiress Elinor Kaske and their son Pierre was born in 1924, but Elinor returned to the US. He was allegedly the model for the Coptic banker Nessim Hosnani in Lawrence Durrell's *Alexandria Quartet*, and his concerts during the Second World War were a cover for illicit operations, particularly smuggling Jewish refugees into Israel.

Scott's in Mayfair. D, 28 June 1936.

Eve Barber. SA print book 2, M84111-139: purchases, 37, 38 and 1943. Several, returned in a terrible state after the war, are marked 'destroyed'.

'Jolly good dinner'. D, 19 April 1937. De Menasce was in London 2 March–2 May 1937.

'a truly contemporary spirit'. Paul Nash, letter to *The Times*, 12 June 1933.

'If you travel'. S. J. Woods, 'Why Abstract?', Decoration, January 1936, quoted by Frances Spalding, 'The Association between Ben Nicholson and John Piper', *Burlington Magazine*, October 2007.

Abstract & Concrete. Organised by Nicolete Gray and Helen Sutherland.

'Do not judge this movement kindly'. Herbert Read, Catalogue for International Surrealist Exhibition, 11 June–4 July 1936, Introduction, 13.

French nineteenth-century painting. D, 17 October 1936. The French exhibition was put on by the Anglo-French Art and Travel Society; the Felicia Browne exhibition was organised by her artist friend Nan Youngman.

Power showed. Redfern catalogue, 'Summer Salon', August 1937. Other work here was by Macnab, Eurich and Clarke Hall, and also by Christopher Wood (who had died in 1930), Stanley Spencer, Paul and John Nash, Epstein, Gill, David Jones, Ravilious and Clare Leighton.

'the father forgives him'. *Art*, RT. Additional material, video interview with Jean Looy, 1990.

'It is meet'. Luke 15, v. 32.

30. SEA AND FOREST

'C came home'. D, 20 October 1936.

wedding of his son. D, 3 October 1936.

thesis. D, 20 June 1936.

Easter. D, 10 April 1937.

'rash of Shakespeare plays'. These included *Romeo and Juliet*, *Henry VIII* (with Baliol Holloway), and *As You Like It*, *Midsummer Night's Dream* and Milton's *Comus* in Regent's Park.

'Night Mail'. W. H. Auden, written for the documentary produced by the General Post Office, premiere in Cambridge Arts Theatre, 4 February 1936.

'*Another* expedition'. HA diary, 17 July–21 August 1936.

Rhodes Minnis. D, 29 May–2 June 1936.

'Cuthbert's plans'. D, 6, 19, 20 January 1937.

Dorset. D, 19–27 September 1936, sketches Glenbow M8411-176.

'nests of giant birds'. Paul Nash, *Architectural Review*, November 1936, 208; Sarah Fill, 'Paul Nash, Surrealism and Prehistoric Dorset' in *Paul Nash*, exh. cat. (2016).

Shingle Street. The atmosphere of this 'sandbanked strand', where sea-mews shriek and grey seals roll, is beautifully evoked by Blake Morrison: 'The sea out front, the marsh out back,/Just one road in and one road out', in 'The Ballad of Shingle Street', in *Shingle Street* (2015).

Bawdsey and Shottisham. CEP list of places, 'Hollesley Holiday 1936', sketchbook 45, OS; D, 4–10 August 1936, 3–11 July 1937.

'Every newspaper'. *Art*.

auction of cottages. Sale catalogue notes '25 Country Cottages, 3 Small holdings and 40 residential building sites. Wednesday 21 July 1937, at the Hall, South Baddesley'. The Pylewell estate dated from the twelfth century: sale followed its inheritance by William Ingham Whitaker III in 1936.

days in Lymington. D, 21 July–5 August 1937. SA stayed at the Bugle Inn in the High Street.

'Meditating'. D, 5–7 August 1937. A handwritten note records '1937 Bought Fryers'. Deed of sale, 27 September 1937.

eventually selling it. D, 3, 4 November 1938, records Fryers sold 'to Mr & Mrs Blair'.

arranged to give the bank. D, 15, 16 September 1937.

'Formal possession'. D, 12 November 1937; the title deeds, dated 6 November, arrived the following Tuesday.

'stuff was packed'. HA diary, 16 October 1937.

31. PIPERS

sending plans. D, 28, 29 September 1936. SA New Forest sketchbook and oils of Pipers are in Glenbow 993.121.

Union Castle liners. SA to Kit Power, 5 March 1991, Glenbow M8411-132.

fog and icy roads. D, 19 December 1937.

Sam took sheaves. Sam Butler to SA and CEP, 17 February 1938, Glenbow M8411-86. He also arranged for the inclusion of their prints in a craft exhibition at the Gainsborough gallery in Cape Town in 1945.

new pupils. D, January–February 1938.

de Menasce had planned. D, 21 February 1938.

'all these sad events'. De Menasce to SA, 16 December 1938, Glenbow M8411-86.

'changes must take place'. Sam Butler to SA, February 1938, Glenbow M8411-66.

Power's paintings. D, 15, 18, 23–30 April 1938.

'nightingales in evening'. D, 8 May 1938.

'Nightingales in the Dusk'. 9 May 1938, notebook, 1937–9, Glenbow M8411.

Later she typed. MS dated 10 May 1938, typed version Glenbow M8411-168.

'lively little party'. TS, 40, Private Collection, Oxford. They moved to a rented house in Welwyn Garden City. Lilian had first come to Britain doing research on Katherine Mansfield for her Paris doctorate. Toby & 'Mlle Muffant' came to tea at the studio, D, 7 December 1937.

'Toby's little wife'. Pencilled draft of letter, probably to Sam Butler, SA notebook, Glenbow M8411-176.

'bright and cheerful'. C. Fox, 71.

a single week in mid-May. D, 12–19 May 1938.

many of Power's possessions. Listed in CEP sketchbook 47, headed 'Goods at Pipers provided by CEP for joint use', OS. Another page has lists of SA's furniture and possessions (including Nigerian swords, helmet and drums), and Hal's dresser, chest of drawers, bed, and chairs.

Nigerian door. Sale of door, Cranmore, Glenbow M8411-86. The museum at Cranmore Place was destroyed by bombing, and the collection built up by the founder Harry Geoffrey Beasley was sent to other museums, principally the BM.

'Sherry'. D, 9 August 1938.

'Garden, September'. SA scrapbook, loose, Glenbow M8411-167.

'Go home to your beds'. Robert Self, *Neville Chamberlain: A Biography* (2017), 40.

finishing paintings. D, 24, 27 November, 2 December 1938. Linocuts printed included impressions of Andrews' *Timber Jim*, *Tillers* and *Via Dolorosa* and Power's *Concerto* and *Tube Station*.

Power was there. At Pipers, Easter, Whitsun, a week in July and another in August, and many weekends: D, 1938, passim.

'I'm not going to find it very easy'. Memo at foot of page, D, 22 April 1939.

'I was lucky'. SA, draft letter to Gary Ratushniak, 9 August 1985, Glenbow M8411-134.

'be shot of Bury'. HA diary, March 1939.

32. WAR AGAIN

blankets. D, 2 September 1939.

'War'. D, 3 September 1939: she went to church with Mike.

rejoin the Air Force. Kit Power, typescript notes, 1941, Michael Power.

photos. SA scrapbook, Glenbow M8411-167.

sou'wester. Note at foot of page, D, 14 October 1939.

proofing a print. *Gypsies*, 1939. There was a Roma camp near to Pipers and Power listed many Romany words.

'Wings'. SA to MP, 23 November 1980, Glenbow M8411-64a. She cut it in 1940, and later found two proofs inside a *Daily Telegraph*, 13 February 1946, but some blocks were lost, perhaps among those melted in the hold on the voyage to Canada: she cut it again in 1979.

Sybil painting. HA diary, 13 January 1940.

'put in grade 4'. ibid., January 1941.

Withdrawal from Dunkirk (1939). Painted using photographs and his knowledge of the port. The painting was the cover for the exhibition *Britain at War* at MoMA, New York, 1941. See Andrew Lambirth, *The Art of Richard Eurich* (2020).

'a pure and curious holiday'. Elizabeth Bowen, *The Heat of the Day* (1949), Ch. 5.

Sometimes a bomb. David Feeberry, writing about his father Bert, BBC Archive, *WW2 People's War*, Article A3198477.

Nearly eight hundred bombs. Wandsworth, in 'Mapping the WW2 bomb census', bombsight.org.

six firemen. Plaque on Wandsworth Fire Station, West Hill, London SW18.

he was exhausted. D, 30 November 1940. Andrews photographed him with his ARP (Air Raid Precautions) armband, scrapbook, Glenbow M8411-167, and painted a portrait of him in his helmet.

roar of planes. HA diary, June 1940.

'Night watches cancelled'. ibid., 14 October 1940.

holly, mistletoe. ibid., January 1941.

Portsmouth. On 10 January 1941, with the rest of Britain under thick cloud, this was the only clear target: 153 bombers dropped forty thousand incendiaries and high-explosive bombs. Eurich went down next day, using his drawings of the wreckage for *Night Raid on Portsmouth Docks* (1941).

'all the furniture'. Edgar Hunt to SA, n.d., Sue Goode.

Manningtree. CEP sketchbook 35, OS.

Rita Pietnik. TS, 45.

Kit joined the navy. Short article by Edmund Berry Power, 'A Wartime Memory of a Life in the RNVR', with thanks to Mike Power.

barrage balloons. HA diary, November 1942.

'Gold stars'. Glenbow M8411-129.

'music, cake, tree'. D, 25 December 1941.

portraits. D, 27–29 December 1941.

33. THE YARD, AND WALTER

Marchwood. See film, 'The Marchwood Park Training Centre and Power Boats', Bfi.org, made for Hubert Paine-Scott, a keen amateur film-maker. Also British Power Boat Company videos on the 'Southampton on Video' YouTube channel, including memories of 'Stan', an apprentice there 1942–5.

'made a beginning'. D, 19–20 February 1942. The Admiralty bought the Georgian mansion and converted it into a residential training centre and workshops. Now the Priory Hospital.

gained her diploma. Diploma 16 April 1942, with notebooks from her training classes, payslips and rough notes, Glenbow M8411-189, 191.

'Nightingales'. D, 2 May 1942.

'done more than anyone else'. D, 27 June 1942.

'skilled worker'. D, 8 January 1943.

'wonderful experience'. SA autobiographical notes for Chris Reeve 3, Glenbow M8411-16.

'Miss Andrews, Clock No. 34'. Bristol Power Boat Company permissions, from S. N. Barker, Managing Director, 24 February and 27 March 1943, Glenbow M8411-188.

Eurich. *The British Power Boat Company* and *A Motor Boat of the British Power Boat Company* (both 1941), National Maritime Museum, Greenwich.

paintings Sybil made after the war. Now in the Royal Air Force Museum at Hendon. See correspondence in Parkin catalogue file, Glenbow M8411-64a.

'Wonderful search lights'. D, 27 August 1943; eclipse, 15 August 1943.

Walter Morgan. Walter William James Morgan, b. 7 December 1894, Fordingbridge, Hampshire. After his father's death his mother moved to Wimborne with the seven children, still as a market gardener. Walter joined the Dorsetshire Regiment on 5 December 1912.

'Take plunge'. D, 12, 15, 16 October 1943.

'Sandra's Self'. Private Collection, Campbell River.

'What a merciful thing'. D, 27 October 1943; '3 houses', 28 October.

'& we were married'. D, 6 November 1943.

'Having now recovered'. Geoff Andrews to SA, 17 November 1943, Glenbow M8411-96.

'It's exactly what I would have done'. Margaret ('Mike') Andrews to SA, 18 November 1943, Glenbow M8411-96.

Stonehenge. SA sketchpad, Glenbow M8411-173.

'I remember Stonehenge'. SA draft letter to Gary Ratushniak, 12 June 1985, Glenbow M8411-133.

night of 5 June. 73,114 men and 9,188 vehicles sailed on ships from Southampton, Portsmouth and the Solent. Over the next month 650,519 men and 137,249 vehicles were transported, while 34,222 prisoners and 53,423 wounded soldiers came back to the UK through the Solent. www. maritimearchaeologytrust.org/embarkation-hards.

34. CYRIL

'Sandra's wedding day'. CEP sketchbook 47, OS.

'O woman-country'. ibid.

quotations. ibid.

'kind, softly spoken'. C. Fox, 39.

book of music. 'Lilian's Book of Tunes for the recorders, collected by CEP', MS, Private Collection, Oxford.

set of her linocuts. Print books 1 and 2, Glenbow, M8411-138, 139. She sometimes sent two or three prints, with two dates of printing, 1 February to 16 May 1944.

Easter card. Courtesy of Jean Looy.

Russian icons. CEP card and letter re Zwemmer's, 12 March 1945, Glenbow M8411-172.

'the one we saw together'. V&A catalogue, Glenbow M8411-172.

'Give my fee'. Kit Power typescript, 1989, Private Collection, Oxford.

'sketched and swam'. TS, 63.

'CEP would spend his time sketching'. C. Fox, 4.

'The grandfather I remember'; 'go to Heaven'. C. Fox, 39, 71.

Mistley. Until her death in 1947 Edna lived in Tendring with her daughter Joan, while Yevonde (d. 1962) was a poultry farmer at Lynwood House, Mistley. Maud Power (née Champness) lived first with Edna and then with Yevonde. The latter household included Maud's daughters Joyce de Kock, Beryl Paramor and Diana Power.

Wrabness. His comic poem 'Whapsody at Wrabness' incorporates the names Paramor, Greenwood and Champness, with sketches of the family, Mistley and Wrabness beach. CEP sketchbook 51, OS.

'Air Raid is pure Power'. SA to MP, 8 April 1979, Glenbow M8411-64a.

35. SYBIL

years of companionship and art. For SA's Canadian years and much of the local detail in this chapter, I am indebted to Janet Nicol.

'last day at Pipers'. HA diary, 1 September 1946.

all their possessions. List of 'Personal possessions'; passport (issued 26 May 1944), change of address registered 14 May 1947, Glenbow M8411-20, 21.

official hoops. Immigration board, Sackville House, Piccadilly. File no. 19-36873, 5 May 1947; sponsorship, Mrs W. A. Innes, PO Box 245, Mission City, BC. Midland Bank transfer of £1,250; Madge E. H. Innes to SA, 15 August 1946: all Glenbow M8411-22.

Badbury Rings. Walter Morgan's mother and stepfather were living in Wimborne, a couple of miles from the Rings, but in 1947 they stayed with family members at a farm near Blandford. SA sketchpad, dated 8 October 1944, also 10 June 1947, Glenbow M8411-176.

'the only ones left'. AK, 211. Loch Ryan bill of lading, 27 August 1947, lists 2 kit bags, 2 tin trunks, 1 tea chest, 1 trunk, tool box, coal box, bikes & trailers. Household goods: dresser £15, table £5, 2 stools £1, drawing table £5, armchair £5. They lost some goods when the baggage room was broken into; a letter from a friend at Thomas Cook, 15 August 1947, says they were covered by insurance. SA also took her air rifle (not regarded as a weapon, so no customs declaration was required). Permit 9.4.47. All in Glenbow M8411-22.

'at the head of the Gulf of Georgia'. SA autobiographical notes, Glenbow M8411-16; also AK, 211.

Willow Point. Nicol, 70–2.

vast emptiness. SA to MP, 24 July 1980; 'this land', SA to MP, 24 May 1983. Glenbow 8411-64a.

'Black Rain'. Handwritten early version, dated December 1947, Private Collection, Campbell River. A different version appears in typescript, and SA recites a variant in Art, RT.

first five years. SA to MP, 1 April 1989, Glenbow M8411-64a.

melted. The prints were *Straphangers*, *Theatre*, *Sculls* and *Hyde Park*.

Stations of the Cross. Three prints from the series were included in a show of modern religious art in Buenos Aires in 1954.

Canadian scenes. *Indian Dance* (1951, exhibited 1952); *Logging Team*, *Hauling*, *Coffee Bar* (all 1952).

'so beautifully Canada'. *The Art of Sybil Andrews*, video by Nicholas Tuele, Art Gallery of Greater Victoria (1991).

woodcuts of the great Canadian trees. *BC Rain Forest* (c.1970), *Western Red Cedar* (c.1977), *Douglas Fir* (1982).

'to know what to abstract'. *AK*, 4–5.

'Can you catch that?' Richard Calver, in *Art*, RT.

'Let he who is Content': *AK* epigraphs.

Gary Ratushniak. See correspondence and substantial financial payments, Glenbow M8411-133, 134.

Richard Calver. Nicol, 128, and *Art*, RT.

'She never got over it'. Nicol, 175.

'I got to identify myself'. 'Patterns of Life', *The Spectator*, 27 April 1991; Nicol, 76.

Christian Science. Certificate of membership of First Church of Christ Scientist, Boston, 2 November 1951, Glenbow M8411-23.

'heart was in England'. Jean Looy to author, 18 March 2021.

taught herself French. Jean Looy to author, 3 March 2021.

'Armistice'. SA to MP, 23 November 1979, Glenbow M8411-64a.

Suffolk in her prints. Rural prints made after the war in Canada include *Ploughing Pasture* (1955) and *Mangolds* (1956). The shire horses reappear in *Day's End* (1961) and the fields in *Plough* (1961) and *Wings* (1979, originally cut in England in 1946, but some blocks melted on voyage in 1947).

she copied from. D. H. Lawrence, *Lady Chatterley's Lover* (unexpurgated edition 1959), Chs 8 and 9; copied into SA scrapbook, 108, Glenbow M8411-167.

36. ENDINGS

Mabel. Mabel Andrews to SA, 18 April, 14 May 1957, 14 October 1966, Glenbow M8411-96.

'a gaunt gentleman'. Len Pole, 'A History of Saffron Walden Museum', *Saffron Walden History* No. 28 (1985). HA to SA, 9 December 1950, 4 January 1953, Glenbow M8411-96. With thanks to Edward Wortley for information about Kenya and Croydon.

Lymington. Sybil's address book has the entry: 'Henry Andrews & Margaret Andrews, "Pewters", 6 Cannon St, Lymington, Hants'. Glenbow M8411-27.

Critics. *Vancouver Sun*, 17 November 1948; *Campbell River Courier*, 24 November 1948. The travelling exhibition was organised by the Allied Arts Centre.

The break came. Nicol, 118.

'an amazing spry 80 year old'. ibid. Andrew Scott, *Vancouver Sun*, 29 June 1978

Michael Parkin. *Claude Flight and his Circle* (19 November–6 December 1975), with fifteen prints by Andrews and six by Power (other artists included Eileen Mayo, Lili Tschudi and William Greengrass). SA wrote to him in 1977, suggesting he might like to see her prints. He replied, offering either to buy them, or to sell them on commission of 35 per cent, and asked her for information about CEP. MP to SA, 7 October 1977. He also included her work in *Print Makers of the 20s and 30s, and Adolphine Ryland* (1978).

a show of her own. *Sybil Andrews, Paintings and Graphic Works* (22 October–15 November 1980). He had also included her prints in the exhibition *The Movement of Flight: Claude Flight, His Circle and His Pupils* (27 September–21 October 1978).

'Today I get busier and busier'. SA to Stephen Coppel, 26 June 1984. Coppel also curated *Claude Flight and His Followers: the Colour Linocut Movement between the Wars*, touring public galleries in Australia and New Zealand (1992–3).

Exhibitions. Mary Ryan Gallery, New York (1982); Redfern (1985), touring exhibition, Australia and New Zealand (1992). Curators such as Peter White, Mary Ryan, Stephen Coppel at the National Gallery of Australia, Canberra and later at the British Museum, and Gordon Samuel at the Redfern were vital in building the reputation of Andrews and Power. In 1992, Mary Ryan arranged for fifty-six prints to be shipped as a gift from SA to the British Museum. MR to SA, 10 October 1992, M8411-61. For significant shows see 'Exhibitions', p. 337.

'I haven't got time to retire'. Video interview with Nicholas Tuele, *The Women Artists of British Columbia: 100 Years* (1984). Tuele also made the short film *The Art of Sybil Andrews*, Art Gallery of Greater Victoria (1991).

'The sensation'. *Arts Review*, 12 April 1985.

'even to see'. SA to Gordon Samuel, 16 March 1985, Glenbow M8411-72.

solo show. Gordon Samuel, *The Linocuts of Cyril Edward Power 1872–1951* (1989).

exhibition at the British Museum. Frances Carey and Antony Griffiths, *Avant-Garde British Printmaking 1914–1960* (1990).

catalogues. Philip Vann, *Cyril Power Linocuts* (2013); Hana Leaper, *Sybil Andrews Linocuts* (2015). Leaper's catalogue of the Glenbow Sybil Andrews exhibition in 2019 was postponed because of Covid-19. In Bury St Edmunds the new secondary school, Sybil Andrews Academy, opened in 2016, while in Campbell River the cottage, studio and workshop have been restored.

Edgar Hunt. EH to SA, 21 October 1980; SA to EH, 16 November 1980. Included in Parkin catalogue file, Glenbow M8411-64.

dances. SA to Russell Plumpton, 8 December 1989; market day, shops, 'lovely smell of cheese', 28 February 1982; 'Parafin', 14 December 1990; Glenbow M8411-115. The ten-year correspondence was continued by Russell's daughter, Shirley Chrispin. Additional memories are in correspondence with John and Josephine Ashton, 1991–2, Glenbow M8411-99, and former pupils Phillippa Buckton and Monica Dowsett, 1991, Glenbow M8411-96.

'Would you please deny'. SA to MP, 3 April 1986, Glenbow M8411-64a.

'Power was a good friend'. SA to Gordon Samuel, 8 April 1986, Glenbow M8411-72.

'made a bee-line'. SA to Mary Ryan, 25 October 1986, Glenbow M8411-60.

'sometimes I find it hard'. SA to MP, 21 November 1988, Glenbow M8411-64a.

'I smile'. SA to Martin Power, 17 February 1987, Glenbow M8411-132.

'out of loyalty'. Martin Power to SA, 8 March 1987, Glenbow M8411-132.

Catherine wrote. Catherine Fox to SA, 8 December 1990, Glenbow M8411-132.

'having no studio of his own'. SA to Kit Power, 2 December 1990; Kit Power to SA, 10 January 1991, Glenbow M8411-132.

'I remember the suit'. Kit Power to SA, 7 August 1992, Glenbow M8411-132.

'Christmas blessings'. SA to Kit Power, 11 December 1991, Glenbow M8411-132. Kit and Joy were in Vancouver in 1992, but Sybil eventually cancelled their planned visit.

'I sensed Sybil was a little spent'. Lincoln Clarkes to the author, 1 March 2021. The visit was on 6 May 1992, for an article in the Vancouver magazine, *The Georgia Strait*.

'In my day'. *AK* prelims. This irresistible statement, also quoted by Hana Leaper and Janet Nicol, now appears on the sign at the entrance to the Sybil Andrews and Walter Morgan Cottage in Willow Point, Campbell River, British Columbia.

INDEX

302; visiting Pipers, 292; work in
Ipswich, 149

Andrews, Sybil: family background, 16,
18, 151–2, 190, 195, 264; birth, 18;
childhood, 5, 16, 18–25; reading, 71, 94,
146–7, 153, 320–1; wartime experiences,
5–7; father's departure, 22–4, 26, 323;
first studio, 27, 40, 41; meeting Cyril,
41; joint exhibition with Cyril, 46–7;
father's death, 51; move from Bury to
London, 51–2; at Heatherley School
of Art, 54–8, 70; life in London, 61;
theatre going, 63–4, 138, 157, 220, 277,
284; scrapbooks, 2, 64, 155, 195, 233,
234, 240, 260, 321–2; admired artists,
65; nickname ('Sandra'), 70, 195, 302,
307; print making, 74; etching, 74, 76,
131; drypoints, 76, 91, 110, 131, 215,
262; 'Benin door', 83, 84, 89, 289,
296; learning from Glicenstein, 91,
93; holidays in France and Belgium,
106–7; first linocuts, 69, 119, 131–3,
135; abstract work, 135, 137, 200;
wood-engraving, 124; mother's death,
146–8 opera and ballet going, 69, 157,
178–9, 220, 225, 322; cinema going,
157, 277, 284; holiday in Brittany
(1930), 158; jam-making, 193, 220,
225, 263; monotypes, 212–18; holiday
in Folkestone, 220; holiday in Sark,
257–60, 261; photography, 260, 292,
304; camping in New Forest, 263–4;
holidays (1936–7), 278–80; house-
hunting, 280; move to New Forest,
285–6, 288–9; riding lessons, 289;
gardening, 289; shooting lessons, 297;
wartime life, 297–8; meeting Walter
Morgan, 301–2; marriage to Walter, 302,
307; sends Cyril's things to New Malden,
304; emigration to Canada, 315–16;
Cyril's death, 315, 317; reputation,
323–4, 330; Walter's death, 328; old age,
330; death, 330

APPEARANCE: childhood, 17, 20; Cyril's
photographs, 292; dress, 62, 220, 246,
262; eyes, 52; hair, 52, 124, 246; hats,
70, 91, 92, 220, 262; on holiday in
Sark, 259, 261; The Laughing Girl, 92,

93; ninety-fourth birthday, 330, 331;
portrait in The Trio, 246; rapid walk,
52; at twenty-four, 52; at twenty-two, 9,
10; at work (1985), 325

CHARACTER: dealing with emotional
pain, 9; energetic enthusiasm, 240;
feverish work ethic, 286; sociable, 58;
vehemence and passions, 286

DIARY: 'anniversary feast', 53;
appointments, 2; Cyril making entries
in, 47, 70, 256, 288; entries about Cyril,
47–8, 188, 195, 277; entries about
Walter, 302; gardening, painting and
war work, 299–300; house purchases,
280; 'linocutting', 119, 133; newspaper
advertisements, 193; 'Peace' (Munich
agreement), 289; politics absent from,
252; printing and shopping, 219;
shared with Cyril, 70, 256–7, 259,
262; tracking down a holy well, 190;
Underground posters, 224; view of
Flight, 212; 'War', 292

EDUCATION: Thetford Grammar School,
7; Women's Welding School, Notting
Hill, 8; John Hassall's Correspondence
School, 25–6, 319; Heatherley School of
Art, 54–8, 70, 72; life classes with Boris
Héroys, 126–7; training course in boat-
building, 299

EMPLOYMENT: office work, 7; welding
(war work), 5, 8–9, 25; teaching,
26–7, 51, 265–7, 284; Grosvenor
School secretary, 100, 101–2, 122–4;
boat-building (war work), 300–1, 304;
teaching in Canada, 319–20

EXHIBITIONS: joint exhibition with Cyril
(Bury, 1921), 46–7; Autumn Exhibition
(Walker Art Gallery, Liverpool, 1924),
80; Royal Society of British Artists
(1925), 140; First Exhibition of British
Linocuts (Redfern, 1929), 1, 140–5,
146; British Linocuts (Redfern, 1930),
145; Print Makers Society of California
(Los Angeles, 1931, 1934, 1935, 1938),
211, 262, 284, 290; British Lino-cuts
(Shanghai, 1931), 145, 211; British
Lino-cuts (Redfern, 1931), 200; Modern
Colour Prints (Redfern, 1932), 188, 201,

212; *Modern Colour Prints* (Melbourne, 1932), 145; *Sybil Andrews and C. E. P. Power* (Redfern, 1933), 212, 216–19; *Colour Prints and Contemporary Oils* (Redfern 1933), 219–20, 221, 224, 237; *Colour Prints and Contemporary Oils* (Redfern, 1934), 256; *Colour Prints* (Redfern, 1935), 263; *Modern Colour Prints* (Ottawa, 1935–36), 145; *Two Hundred Years of British Graphic Art* (Bucharest, Vienna, Prague, 1935–36), 145; *French and English Colour Prints* (Redfern, 1939), 294; solo exhibition (Vancouver, 1948), 323; *Society of Canadian Painter-Etchers and Engravers* (1949–54), 323; *Claude Flight and His Circle* (Parkin Gallery, 1975), 324; *Sybil Andrews, Paintings and Graphic Work* (Parkin Gallery, 1980), 324; *British Linocuts of the 1920s and 1930s* (Redfern, 1985), 324, 326; *Avant-Garde British Printmaking 1914–1960* (British Museum, 1990), 326; exhibition of her Stations of the Cross (Tidemark Theatre, Campbell River, 1992), 330; *Cutting Edge: Modernist British Printmaking* (Dulwich Picture Gallery, 2019), 326

FINANCES: choice of career, 26; rent paid by mother, 70; going hungry, 72, 74; living on savings, 72; money from mother, 72; need to earn money, 74, 77; sales of prints, 79, 82, 88, 211, 212, 215, 218, 220, 265, 269–70, 323; purchases at Wembley exhibition, 83, 89, 289; Brook Green studio tenancy, 123, 262, 285, 286; legacy from mother, 147–8; buying Woolpit cottage, 147–9; London Underground posters (as Andrew Power), 222–3, 224, 262; purchase of recorders, 237; purchase of Great Bass viol, 237; shopping, 262; inherited funds, 265, 280; income from teaching, 265–7; buying Pipers cottage (Lot 5), 280–1; buying and selling Fryers cottage, 280–1; selling Woolpit cottage, 281; sale of Pipers, 315; in Canada, 323

FRIENDSHIPS: Baliol Holloway ('Ba'), 64; Bickerdikes ('Dot' and 'Bicks'), 238–9;

Brook Green Consort, 240–1; Cuthbert Greig and Doris Holmes, 124–5; Edgar Hunt, 239–40; Edna Clarke Hall, 284; Fookes family, 122; Hodsons (Alec and Margaret), 239; Looys (Jean and Dave), 328; Michael Parkin, 324; Sam Butler, 122

HEALTH: Christian Science, 9, 197, 330; eyesight, 328, 330; illness (1923), 70; pneumonia, 9; reduced mobility, 330

HOMES AND STUDIOS: Guildhall Street, Bury, 5, 42; Northgate Street, Bury, 5, 7, 19, 148, 211; studio at Crescent House (Bury), 41, 46, 52; flat in Bernard Street, London, 51; studio at Phoenix Place, 70–2, **84**, 101; rooms at 34 Warwick Square, 101; Brook Green studio, 123, 125–6, 188, 211, **227**, 256–7, 260, 262, 265–6, 285–6, 288; Woolpit cottage, 147–53, **150**, 157, 188–95, **194**, 212, 216, 252, 260, 278, 280; house-hunting, 193, 280; sale of Woolpit cottage, 281; Pipers cottage, Norley Wood, 280–1, 282, **283**, 284, 286, 288–90, 292, 294–6, 299–300, 302, 304; move to New Forest, 285–6, 288–9; sale of Pipers, 315; Willow Point, Campbell River, Vancouver Island, 316

LINOCUTS: *The Bathers*, 173; bookplate for Robert H. Lowie, 267, **268**; *Bringing In the Boat*, 1, 176, **Plate 27**; 'carving', 90; catalogue of, 326; 'The Chieftain', 119; *Concert Hall*, 137, 142, 308, **Plate 11**; *Day's End*, 254, 321, **Plate 54**; *Deposition* (*The Darkest Hour*), 201, **Plate 36**; *Fall of the Leaf*, 253–4, **255**, 256; *Flower Girls*, 168, 170, 180, **Plate 23**; *The Gale*, 170, 258; *The Giant Cable*, 168, **Plate 17**; *Golgotha*, 200–1, 211, 308, **Plate 35**; gypsies, 294; *Haulers*, 142, 144, 167–8, **169**, 258; *Haysel*, 256, 308, **Plate 53**; *In Full Cry*, 171, **Plate 24**; *Indian Dance*, 317; *Joseph and Nicodemus*, **202**, 203, 205; *Limehouse*, 132, **135**; *Mangolds*, 321; *Market Day*, 16, 308, **Plate 6**; *Michaelmas*, 254, 256, 308; *Mother and Son*, 201; *Mowers*, 256; *Oranges*, 142,